W9-AVM-953

THE BROKEN AMERICAN MALE

Also by Rabbi Shmuley Boteach

THE BROKEN
AMERICAN MALE

AND HOW TO FIX HIM

·

Rabbi Shmuley Boteach

ST. MARTIN'S GRIFFIN ❈ NEW YORK

This is a work of nonfiction, but I have changed names and personal characteristics of some people to protect their privacy.

THE BROKEN AMERICAN MALE. Copyright © 2008 by Rabbi Shmuley Boteach. All rights reserved. Printed in the United States of America. For information, address St. Martin's Press, 175 Fifth Avenue, New York, N.Y. 10010.

www.stmartins.com

The Library of Congress has catalogued the hardcover edition as follows:

Boteach, Shmuley.
    The broken American male : and how to fix him / Shmuley Boteach.—1st ed.
        p.cm.
    ISBN-13: 978-0-312-37924-7
    ISBN-10: 0-312-37924-2
    1. Men—United States. 2. Men—United States—Psychology. 3. Masculinity—United States. 4. Man-woman relationships—United States. 5. Success—United States. I. Title.

    HQ1090.3.B677 2008
    155.3'320973—dc22

                                                                2007038864

ISBN-13: 978-0-312-54150-7 (pbk.)
ISBN-10: 0-312-54150-3 (pbk.)

First St. Martin's Griffin Edition: April 2009

10   9   8   7   6   5   4   3   2   1

To my father, Yoav Boteach,
who taught me that broken things can be fixed,
and broken men can be healed

Contents

Contents

THE BROKEN
AMERICAN MALE

1.

I Am a Broken American Male

A T THE heart of modern American living is a paradox that no one can quite figure out. On the one hand, America is the richest, most prosperous country in the history of the world. Its standard of living has no parallel and no precedent. America has given us comforts and opportunities that are the envy of the world. On the other hand, our country is becoming more and more depressed. All this treasure has not brought us contentment.

Our country is full of people who aren't happy: men who feel like failures, women who feel they're not good enough. Joy in America seems elusive, and few seem satisfied with their lives. This is curious. We have more choices than anyone who has lived before us. We are better educated, with more college degrees than any generation that has preceded us.

So why on earth are we so miserable?

And I don't merely ask this question about others. I ask it about myself as well. I'm not, thank G-d, a depressed man, but I could be a lot happier. I often wonder what percentage of the time I'm happy. I'd be lucky if it's 60 percent—at most. And this percentage is much higher than it used to be.

Like you, I often feel dissatisfied with my life, as though something's passing me by, as though I'm missing something. I feel like I'm not maximizing my potential, like I'm not being everything I could be.

I often find myself thinking about a conversation my mother used to have with my father long ago. I was a little boy, growing up in Los Angeles. My parents were not happy together. There was a tense atmosphere at home. My father would come home pretty late, just before we kids went to bed. Invariably, he did not come home with a giant smile on his face. He came home looking a little sullen, a little defeated. Part of this was attributable to his having worked very hard. We did not have a lot of money and my father's life, as an immigrant who came to the United States barely speaking English, was never easy. But exhaustion alone could not explain his unhappiness. Something was bugging him, and my mother sensed it. She understood that no matter what he had, he wasn't satisfied with it. He always seemed focused on what he *didn't* have. Something was eating away at him. I remember her repeatedly coaxing my father to find more fulfillment in his blessings. "Yoav, you have five healthy children. You have a wife who loves you. You have a beautiful family. Why isn't that enough?" But it wasn't enough. It was never enough. Not enough to make him happy, not enough to make him feel good about himself, and certainly not enough to make him feel successful.

Their conversation plays in my mind repeatedly, on an endless loop. It haunts me because I wonder why I have in many ways become like my father. I, thank G-d, have eight beautiful children and a wife who loves me and is extremely devoted to me. Why isn't that enough? What's eating away at me? Why can't I find real joy and fulfillment from my blessings? What is missing in my life? Why do I feel like a failure?

Men today seem so darn angry. Turn on the radio and listen to the endless conversations taking place on conservative and liberal talk stations. While they speak from different ends of the political spectrum, the one thing they have in common is anger. Each side endlessly identifies the enemy within that bothers them. Talk radio is an overwhelmingly masculine medium. Listen to the men who call up and join the radio hosts to vent about their favorite bogeyman of the day. They seem really bothered by things happening in this country. Most of all, they seem bothered by life.

As I was completing the manuscript for this book, the story broke of the horrific massacre at Virginia Tech in which twenty-seven innocent students and five faculty members were slaughtered in cold blood. The murderer, Seung-Hui Cho, sent NBC News a now infamous multimedia manifesto in which he raged against the world and the fellow students he sought to punish. There have been far too many mass shootings in America by angry and deranged people (and the killers are nearly always men rather than women). Two things immediately came to mind as I reviewed Cho's deranged ramblings: first, the evil choices this murderer made in venting his anger at people who didn't cause it, and second, the highly unhealthy culture in which this young man was immersed and how it seemed to exacerbate the anger already inside him.

Cho's rage is not an isolated incident. True, not every college student pulls out a gun and starts blowing away his classmates. But that does not mean death is not on their minds. American students, a group you might think would be filled with verve and life, have depression and suicide rates that are scarcely believable. *The New York Times* recently reported that "suicide is the second leading cause of death for college students. Almost one in 10 college students has made a suicide plan. Nearly half of all students report having felt so depressed that they could not function in the previous year" (April 25, 2007). And if that's what's happening to students who have yet to live much of their lives, just imagine the impact on those of us whom life has already disappointed.

It is the men today who are especially broken. From our earliest years we men are conditioned to perform in order to become successes. We are never allowed just to be. Whether it's performing on the sports field, striving to be popular among the girls in class, or earning money to impress a boss or our peers, we have scant opportunity to simply be human. Men today are angry because, as psychologist Warren Farrell points out, they are not allowed to be human beings but instead are conditioned to be human doings. The result is that they rarely form deep, intimate relationships where their souls can be nurtured. Stripped of their humanity, a lot of men are becoming very angry.

> **Men today are angry because, as psychologist Warren Farrell points out, they are not allowed to be human beings but instead are conditioned to be human doings.**

They feel unloved, disenfranchised, alienated, and rejected. They don't have a place to call home. They are frustrated at the injustice of being judged for their grades, or by the kind of girl that will talk to them at a party, or by the kind of job they can get after they graduate.

The rage builds up to fever pitch until it explodes. And we are witnessing more and more horrific explosions. Anger in men is on a continuum and nearly all men today are somewhat angry, Cho being very much more than most. But he is scarcely alone. Whether it's the young gunmen at Columbine who exploded due to feeling bullied and marginalized at school, or the explosion of violence at a day-trading company because the gunman felt ripped off, or the increasingly frequent eruptions on university campuses, the anger of the broken American male is becoming deadly. And it must be addressed.

We have to begin to nurture our men. From their earliest years, we have to put less emphasis on success and more emphasis on emotion. We have to make our boys feel valuable whether or not they are great athletes and whether or not they get into a great university. We have to make husbands and fathers feel special even if they can't buy the big house or take us on the exotic vacation. We have to find criteria other than the *Forbes* 400 to identify success.

Only by directly addressing the disenfranchisement of the broken American male can we hope to avoid unspeakable tragedies like the one that occurred at Virginia Tech.

In this book I hope to address why so many American men today are broken, and how, in their brokenness, they are damaging their wives, harming their children, and ruining their families. If we heal America's men, America can have happier and more intact families. And perhaps in the process I will also heal myself.

IT WAS the holiday season, 2006, and *The New York Times* saw fit to run a series of page-one stories about the huge bonuses being brought home by Wall Street investment bankers. The numbers were staggering. To give you an idea of the flavor of the articles, the second story in the series was titled "Wall St. Bonuses: So Much Money, Too Few Ferraris." The *Times* listed one trader after another who was either taking home a fifty-million-dollar bonus or buying a twenty-million-dollar apartment in Manhattan. As I read, I started to get depressed. That old feeling of personal failure began to gnaw away at me.

To be sure, I had seen stories about rich people before, and the *Forbes* list of the four hundred richest Americans. Lists like these always made me feel a bit worthless. I wasn't reading about someone else's success but about my own failure. After all, the winners were on the list. Losers like me weren't. But this time it was a lot worse. I had just turned forty the month before, in November; I had entered middle life, and most of the people I was reading about were either my age or even younger. And this wasn't a list of just a few hundred superrich people. Rather, this was a whole class of individuals, investment bankers, in their thirties and forties—hundreds of them, thousands of them—who were taking home cash bonuses averaging about a million dollars apiece. And living in the New York area, I knew a lot of these people. They were my friends and acquaintances. I read on, feeling tinier and tinier as I did.

I examined the reasons for my feelings of insignificance and could identify them all too well. I had been through this hundreds of times before. It wasn't that I had eight children whom I struggled to support, because G-d had always been kind to me and, while my wife and I were never rich, we were usually able to maintain a comfortable middle-class and, later, upper-middle-class lifestyle. Less so was it the feeling that these men could afford luxuries and opulence that were beyond my reach, because, aside from being blessed with a beautiful home, I have never much been into luxury or opulence. Rather, it was the feeling that these men had made it and I had not. They had made the right choices in life, going into fields where the money was, where success was, whereas I had become a rabbi, lecturer, and writer where, for the most part, the money wasn't.

Like many of you, I work pretty hard. I am primarily motivated by a religious calling to spread values, morality, and ethics. But I am also motivated by a desire to provide my family with a good and comfortable life, as well as to achieve recognition for my work. But clearly, based on the moving of the bar to impossible standards, I had not achieved much at all.

I knew that my feelings of insignificance were unjustified. I am blessed to host a national TV show and have written many books. I am invited to lecture around the world. Most important, I have a wonderful and loving family. So why, when I read those articles, did I feel like a failure? In a really good year, I can make a few hundred thousand dollars, which by any standard should be considered enough. But compared to these bonus billionaires, I was nothing. A big zero. I didn't even rate. If I got a really good book advance of, say, eighty thousand dollars, that's what these guys blew on a weekend of gambling. And on a single trade in their hedge funds, they could make ten times that in an instant. By the single standard of success that had become entrenched in American culture—how much money you have and how much money you make—I was just another loser. No matter that in my life I had saved hundreds of marriages and rescued a great many children from destructive choices. No matter that in the course of eleven years as rabbi at Oxford University in England I had reintroduced thousands of Jewish students to their ancient heritage and had helped tens of thousands to better commit themselves to a life of values. And no matter that I was an involved father who truly loved his children and actively raised them. No, none of that mattered. The only thing that mattered in America was money and success. And they were synonymous. I could no longer appreciate myself because I had bought the great American lie that life

is about the endless pursuit of wealth. If I didn't have the cash, then I hadn't lived. I could not take pride in my achievements because they were too modest. Sure, I was a counselor on TV. But

> **I could no longer appreciate myself because I had bought the great American lie that life is about the endless pursuit of wealth. If I didn't have the cash, then I hadn't lived. I could not take pride in my achievements because they were too modest.**

I wasn't Dr. Phil. His TV show dwarfed my own. I was a personality in the media, but I wasn't Oprah. Her name recognition obliterated mine. Relative to all the truly successful people, I was a failure.

To be sure, I had struggled with low self-esteem throughout my life. My parents divorced when I was a boy and I grew up with my father living thousands of miles away and with a single mother who worked her guts out just to make ends meet. Children of divorce wrestle with issues of self-esteem more than most. That lack of self-esteem propelled me in my boyhood to spend way too much time trying to prove myself to others. After my parents split up and my mother moved us to Miami from Los Angeles, I would give presents to the cool kids in my class to try to get them to like me. I would invite them to my home in the hope that they would reciprocate. But I always thought that this was mostly an adverse effect of my turbulent childhood, because I was not given the security of a peaceful two-parent home and therefore internalized a lot of insecurity. I always thought that as I got older, the feelings of worthlessness would slowly diminish. They did, but not by much. As I grew older, I did become conscious of the fact that my unhappy childhood was only one factor that led to feeling like I was inconsequential. After all, I knew way too many people—men especially—who were exactly like me. And many had had happy childhoods with involved parents who rarely fought. No, there was something more, something else that was affecting me. Whatever it was, it was all around me and was utterly inescapable. I could feel it ruining me. My slow recognition of the forces that were making me and so many other men feel like failures was the genesis of this book.

AMERICA IS in the grip of a soulless capitalism that is slowly destroying the American male and bringing down the American female and family with him. We all want money. We want to be successful. But we are paying for that success with our families. We men are broken. Our wives are becoming depressed and unhappy. A great many are actually leaving us. Our kids are uninspired, bored, and prefer the company of their friends to us. It's time we discover the causes of this downward spiral and take measures to counter it.

At no point in history was there ever a single criterion for success as there is today.

People have always wanted to make something of their lives. The human desire to distinguish oneself is innate. The German philosopher Georg Hegel called this drive "the thymotic urge," the will to seek recognition, the desire to earn the respect of our peers, the motivation to corroborate our uniqueness and humanity through achievement. In modern-day parlance, we would say that everyone wants to be a somebody. So how is modern America different? Because in every other period the definition of success included something other than money. In every other culture, money, fame, and power counted as markers of success—but never exclusively so. There was always something else. A man was expected to be enlightened enough to know to what purpose money and power should be put. There was always a need to cultivate virtues outside of power and wealth. Whether it was civic duty in ancient Greece, oratory and military service in ancient Rome, moral virtue and prophetic calling in ancient Israel, or patriotism in colonial America, money counted for a lot but it wasn't everything. Most of the founding fathers of this great nation were men of means. But they were not considered to be successful as men unless they heeded the calling of their nation and directed their resources toward the fulfillment of the dream of independence. In imperial Britain the landed gentry were expected to be educated, refined, and assume positions of leadership. In the Christian kingdoms of medieval Europe, wealthy and gallant knights were expected to defend the defenseless. It didn't make any difference how hypocritical these values and ideals were or how sincere the men were who purported to embody them. What was important was the expectation. The accumulation of money and power was never enough to determine a man's value. There was always something else.

Fast-forward to modern-day America where success is determined exclusively by money, power, fame, and preferably an amalgamation of all three. There is nothing else. The poster child for this destructive truth is Donald Trump, America's most famous businessman. By any measure but money, Trump is a failure. He failed at two marriages. As a shallow braggart who can never stop promoting himself and as someone who cannot stop ogling young, pretty females, he fails at being a refined gentleman. It seems he has not succeeded as a philanthropist. As the embodiment of the American dream, he has come to portray that dream as a soulless capitalist nightmare. And yet not only is Trump the most renowned businessman in America, he's the guy we all want to emulate. We all want to be his apprentice! What has made this man a guru who attracts tens of millions of students? Is it that he has class? Come on! A sense of personal honor, perhaps? Give me a break. Nobility of spirit, depth of purpose? Nope. Is it his hair, perhaps? I think not. So what is it then? He has money. Lots and lots of money. And he has buildings. He has fame. And all this gives him power. There it is. Mystery solved. There is nothing else. But that's okay, because those are the things that matter. So we watch Trump's TV show, attend his seminars, and buy his books in an effort to be just like him. And we do it without holding our noses. We're not turned off by his narcissism because narcissism, the singular focus on self, is that which makes you rich.

There are serious consequences to soulless capitalism for the American individual and the American family. Men who feel like failures—those who compare themselves to the Trumps of this world and feel like they have not accomplished much—are ruining their wives, who blame themselves for their husbands' brokenness and in turn feel permanently inadequate. And the biggest losers of all are our children, who are not being inspired by their parents and are largely raising themselves. My purpose in this book is not just to point out the problem but also to offer a solution. But this cannot be done unless we understand just how bad it has gotten. Amid the many challenges facing the American family today, soulless capitalism, along with its destructive effect on men and women, is the biggest problem of all.

Amid the many challenges facing the American family today, soulless capitalism, along with its destructive effect on men and women, is the biggest problem of all.

The unbridled lust for money and recognition drives fathers to become workaholics who spend precious little time with their kids. It creates men who neglect their home life in favor of office life. It also numbs men in their relationships as they are slowly transformed from people into machines. Soulless capitalism, as we'll see, also makes women depressed. The singular focus on money and materialism robs everything of depth and substance, reducing it to its most superficial shell. Soulless capitalism dictates that what determines the value of a thing is its price tag and its value on the open market. This means that men are judged by their net worth. And it means that women are valued for their packaging alone. Their beauty becomes a commodity with which they can purchase the love of a man, especially a successful man. An attractive woman becomes something akin to a superfast car, namely, an object that a man just has to have. Evolutionary biologists like to point out that the male search for feminine beauty is Darwinian in nature. Women are valued for their beauty and shapeliness because those characteristics indicate a capacity for fertility and child-rearing. But if this were the case then we would not see the hell-bent emphasis on women being superthin. On the contrary, big hips and not an emaciated, anorexic look are an indication of fertility. Without body fat a fetus has nothing to nourish it. No, the modern emphasis on the linear as opposed to curvaceous look of women is a product of women being created in the male, linear image.

The combined pressures of being married to a broken man who feels like a failure and living in a society that values them for their beauty and youth above all else leave most women feeling inadequate in every way. They fail at making their husbands happy, and they also fail, as time progresses, at remaining youthful and beautiful. The soulless capitalist environment that promotes women as trophies provides women one single criterion of importance: their looks. Beauty is to women what money is to men. And just as men are made to feel that they are never rich enough, women in our culture are silently assaulted on a daily basis for not being blond enough, tall enough, thin enough, and, of course, young enough. Consequently, they are nearly as broken as our men. And as our children witness broken fathers and inadequate mothers, they conclude that what they themselves should aspire to as they get older is not love—something they have rarely witnessed—but objects, material things that can be purchased with money. And slowly, soullessness becomes an American family heirloom transmitted from generation to generation.

And slowly, soullessness becomes an American family heirloom transmitted from generation to generation.

The American family is dying the cold death of neglect. It is ravaged by divorce. It is soured by strife. Built as it is on a broken male and an inadequate female, it has lost its center. It is disintegrating from boredom and listlessness. It is decentralized, lacking a nucleus around which it can revolve. Most tragically, it is lacking in love. And if we don't rescue the American family from its terminal decline, we will lose our country and our way of life.

Does a country with a 50-percent divorce rate deserve to call itself civilized?

Ask yourself this question: Does a country with a 50-percent divorce rate deserve to call itself civilized?

Will a country where most kids see their parents fighting rather than getting along raise a generation of healthy or damaged youths? And can we really hope to bring peace to the world if our own homes are filled with strife? Great fissures are already showing in our country. We are divided between right and left, conservative and liberal, religious and secular. We don't have peace on the inside, so how can we have peace on the outside? And it all begins with the family. The American family is rotting from the top down and is in desperate need of salvation. Saving the American family from collapse is our foremost national emergency. It is not terrorists who threaten us the most. They can hurt us, but they can never destroy us. But we can destroy ourselves. The Oxford historian Arnold Toynbee demonstrates in his classic *A Study of History* that great civilizations are never defeated from the outside. Rather, they crumble from the inside. The Romans were not destroyed by invading barbarians, Goths or Huns. Rather, they sealed their fate with political corruption, crumbling families, and self-serving civic institutions. The Incas were not defeated by Pizarro and the invading Spanish so much as by civil war, internecine fighting among the royal family, and fractured leadership. And the Ottoman Empire, "the sick man of Europe," collapsed from generations of strife in the governing family, bribery, and astounding moral and civic decay.

In America the problem is not government but society. Our government is strong, but our families are simply disintegrating. Do we really believe that a culture built on such a flimsy familial foundation can long survive? Do we believe that children who see more fighting than affection between parents are going to grow up secure and strong? Can our country long endure a whole generation of young people who, in their yearning to simply be noticed, have become exhibitionists who parade themselves in exploitative poses on YouTube? It is not normal for men and

> **It is not normal for a man to come home after a long day's work at the office and feel more comfortable watching TV than talking to his kids.**

women who once loved each other enough to marry and have children to fall out of love with such alarming frequency. It is not normal for a man to come home after a long day's work at the office and feel more comfortable watching TV than talking to his kids.

It is not normal for 30 percent of American women to be so depressed that they have to be medicated with the "miracle drugs" Zoloft, Paxil, or Prozac. It is not normal for most American parents and children to have family dinners together only on Thanksgiving and Christmas. It is not normal for teenagers to have more sex than their parents. And it is not normal for young teens to be so uninterested in their parents that they can only be kept at home through threats, bribery, and guilt.

IN SEARCHING for the corrosive influences that most plague the American family, we could identify several causes. We could focus on the instability created by a twenty-four-hour economy and the workaholic parents who try to keep up. We could look at modern media distractions—from TV, to movies, to iPods, to the Internet—that are causing families to cease to communicate. We could speak of the two-income family and how moms having to work outside the home robs the family of its most important nurturer. We could find hundreds of unconnected reasons for the breakdown of the American family.

Or we could find one main culprit, to which most of the problems can be traced. That problem is the brokenness of American men and the sense of inadequacy of American women.

2.

The Shattered Male Ego

THE ABSENCE of a healthy and stable father figure is destroying the American family. Men are not psychologically or emotionally at rest. They suffer convulsions of the mind and tempests of the spirit. They do not much like themselves and feel increasingly empty. Reduced in the eyes of his family and himself to nothing more than a provider and raised in a world in which only money matters, the American male today feels broken and lost, stripped of his humanity and robbed of his dignity. Feeling like a checkbook and an ATM, he doesn't feel necessary to his wife or a hero to his children.

On the TV show I hosted for TLC, *Shalom in the Home,* I traveled across America helping families in crisis. In each episode we looked for a new theme. One week we might focus on divorce, another on infidelity, still another on eating disorders, depression, and so on. Choosing new themes offered the audience something fresh every week. It was thus with considerable consternation that my producers and I kept finding, with virtually every family we visited, that their primary problem was a broken American male. Whether it was the husband who constantly criticized his wife, or the man who couldn't have sex with his wife, or the father who had no relationship with his teenage daughter, or the many dads who simply came home and slunk down comalike into the sofa in front of the TV, the common denominator was always the same. Dad was a mess. Men who are miserable on the inside will openly treat their wives miserably. Men with no self-esteem have little to no libido. Men who don't value themselves feel tiny in the eyes of their children and therefore make almost no effort to engage them. And men who live in constant pain will pursue any escape—most notably television—in order to break from reality.

The broken American male was not what we wanted to find on *Shalom in the Home*. Indeed, when we did, there was an "Oh brother, not this again" feeling among our crew. When we did an episode on unfaithfulness and adultery, it turned out that the husband had had an affair because he was a truck driver who felt like a failure and wanted to feel desirable again. When we did a story about a couple who had lost the romantic spark, it came down to a husband who was convinced that his wife would never be attracted to a loser like him—he worked as a clerk in an accounting office—so he made no effort to even touch her. And when we did a story about a construction worker who came home after twelve-hour shifts only to neglect his family in favor of picking up a hammer and fixing things around the house, it was because this man thought of himself as a human doing rather than a human being, a man whose family could appreciate only what he provided and never his human essence.

On one particularly moving show we traveled to the home of a fifteen-year-old girl whose life was being threatened by anorexia. She was down to ninety pounds, and if she lost any more weight she would have to be hospitalized for a second time. Now, what does a teenager's poor body image have to do with a broken male? Well, it turned out that her insecurities were somewhat exacerbated by her father feeling that he hadn't completely measured up, both because of a stutter and because he had not achieved the vast riches that society expected of him. He was an outstanding father, an extremely devoted husband, and a refined gentleman who loved his daughter with all his heart and never refrained from showing it. But he didn't love himself enough. He was self-conscious about how others perceived him, especially when he spoke. And his attempts to compensate for those insecurities, while being in no way directly responsible for his daughter's anorexia, influenced her to be overly concerned with image and what others thought of her. She developed an outward- rather than an inward-oriented life. A body that was perfectly thin became her goal. This innocent young girl wished to be esteemed for the slimness of her legs rather than the largeness of her heart. She wished to be judged by the flatness of her stomach rather than the content of her character. She wished to be esteemed for the smallness of her frame rather than the expansiveness of her spirit. Slowly but surely, she was robbing herself of content, rendering herself all cover and no book.

No one knows for certain what causes anorexia, and no one is apportioning blame. But there was no question that in this particular family there could be no healing of the daughter without healing the parents as well, and making them understand that the fact that they were extremely loving parents and compassionate people was good enough.

On another show, we visited a Rhode Island family in which the mother was very unhappy. For us, the show was about the increasing tendency of American women to be depressed (according to a May 2003 article in *The Washington Post,* one of three doctor visits in the United States on the part of women is for depression) and how it might be cured. But, as I expected, the story again became about her husband. He showed her little affection and indeed barely spoke to her. Not because he was a jerk. On the contrary, he was decent, kindhearted, and loved his wife deeply. Rather, as a construction worker, he felt that he was nothing very special. He did not value himself, and could not imagine that he held the keys to his wife's happiness. Why would his wife be interested in him if he wasn't interested in himself?

The only thing he could value about himself was his capacity for work. So he left for his job every morning at five and came home at six. He ate dinner, in near silence, with his wife and three kids, and then went back out to work on cottages the family rented out for extra income in the summer. This man was convinced that all his family valued about him was his ability to make a couple of bucks and pay the bills. He repeatedly told me through the course of filming the show that he was bad with words. He said he wasn't trained in expressing emotion. It wasn't his heart that he had worked to develop, but his hands. So he refrained from offering his wife any deeper part of himself in the belief that everything about him was sub par. But in the process, he never saw how lonely his wife had become. Here was a man who really was a success. He was married to a woman who loved him and had three great kids. But in his own eyes, he was a failure.

On yet another occasion, we visited Hershey, Pennsylvania, to focus on lost passion in marriage. The young couple consisted of a Jewish-American man and his Muslim Turkish wife. They had overcome their cultural differences and married because they were so excited about each other, only to find themselves, after nine years, in a sexless marriage with no visible displays of affection. The wife, a beautiful woman, had put on weight and occupied her time with her kids, virtually ignoring her husband. But once again, the story was hijacked by the larger issue of a fine family man and a great father who nevertheless felt like a failure due to being way down in the professional pecking order. He had wanted to be a screenwriter and producer but got stuck in a dead-end accounting job. He returned to his small home with his tail between his legs every day from a position that made him feel like a failure. I still remember Tijen, the wife, crying to me in my Airstream trailer: "He won't let me into his heart. He won't share his pain or show emotion." A broken man who cannot love himself has no love to give his wife and is incapable of inspiring his children.

The broken American male was not only the subtext behind

many episodes of *Shalom in the Home*. He also consistently comes up in counseling sessions I do with families in crisis. One woman from Texas called me in tears and pleaded that I meet with her and her husband immediately. Two days later they had flown to my home state and were sitting in my office, a handsome couple dressed in expensive clothing. She spoke first, describing how she was married to an emotionally closed man who showed her no affection. She said she could barely get him to speak to her. He spent most of his time giving her the silent treatment. When she entered my home she looked beautiful and radiant, young and alive. After ten minutes, her mascara was running and her eyes were red. She looked disheveled and unkempt. Her husband pounced. For the next hour, without respite, he shared everything that was wrong with her, from the way she picked her teeth in public, to how she was missing a tooth, to how she ate with her mouth open. He sounded thoroughly repulsed by her, and to listen to him was to believe that his devoted wife had no redeeming virtues. I listened in disbelief as he pummeled his wife with biting criticism while she sobbed her eyes out. And if this happened in my presence, what was taking place when no one was around?

When he finished, it was my turn. I began slowly. "Very often, couples come to see me because their actions within the marriage have alienated them from each other. Sometimes a husband stops loving his wife because she puts him down. At other times a wife stops loving her husband because he flirts with other women. But your case is different. You did not stop loving your wife because of anything she did. Rather, it's clear that you're consciously looking for reasons to hate her and finding justification in the most trifling of details. Your contempt for her began just as soon as you married her. And now you're just looking for ways to justify such negative emotions about a woman who is supposed to be your closest confidante in the whole world." He objected vigorously to my assessment. No, it was his wife who had turned his once warm heart cold. But after a few hours, the real story began to emerge.

This man came from a moneyed background and was raised in considerable privilege. The family business was entrusted to him by his father, who was semiretired, and he was running it into the ground. Try as he might, the business was disintegrating. He could not salvage it and felt like a miserable failure. The first generation had built the business. He came along and lost it. It was himself that he really hated, not his wife. But miserable people treat other people miserably. And husbands often take out their self-loathing on their wives because they can. A wife will put up with it when no one else will. And a wife is, after all, your very flesh. So if you hate yourself, you hate her for being part of you. So he showed his wife all the aggression that he really felt for himself. If his wife picked her teeth after eating dinner, he could simply have said to her, "Honey, I love you. You're beautiful. So I don't like it when people see things about you that aren't beautiful. Why not do that in a more private setting." Instead, he used a minor bad habit as ammunition to attack his wife and deflect all his inner-directed animosity away from himself. The only way this marriage was going to be healed was by healing a broken man of his feelings of worthlessness.

What this man shared with so many other broken men I meet was a near total blindness to his own self-hatred and how it was rendering him incapable of giving affection.

On another occasion a close friend asked me to meet a couple from Virginia who were on the brink of divorce. They came to see me a week later. When they walked in, the husband was subdued and tense; the wife, sad and anxious. It didn't take longer than ten minutes for me to discern their problem. I had seen this a thousand times before, a wife's unhappiness being the direct result of her husband's brokenness.

The wife began, "Please, Rabbi Shmuley, can you help us? We've been together for fifteen years, married ten. We have four young children."

"What seems to be the problem?"

"We don't get along, we only fight. We need you to help teach us how to communicate. Whenever we try and speak we only end up arguing." The husband seemed distracted as this conversation between me and his wife took place. He looked around, scratched his head, stared at his watch. I said to his wife, "Well, you have to be more specific." The floodgates opened, as they had with so many women before her. Sobbing through her words, she said, "My husband puts me down constantly. He finds fault in everything I do. Nothing is good enough. If I cook dinner, it tastes bad or it was late. If I take the kids somewhere, he asks why I was out of the house. If I don't take the kids anywhere, he calls me lazy. I can't do anything right!"

I looked at her husband and asked, "Is this correct?" He said, "Well, I was very happy with her until the past year. But now, it's true. I feel she is letting me and the children down in many ways."

I asked, "Can you think of one good thing about your wife?" He paused for what seemed a long while, then lifted his eyes at me and quietly said, "No."

"Not one redeeming quality?" I asked in utter bewilderment. He thought again. "No, I cannot think of a single good thing. My wife is disappointing me. She doesn't know how to be a mother. She doesn't know how to be a wife."

I looked at him and asked where he was from. He spoke with an accent that I could recognize, and I was asking the question for a specific purpose. "From South Africa. But why does that matter?"

"Did you come to the United States for economic opportunity?" I asked.

He said, "Yes. I came to open a business selling computer parts."

"Did your professional dreams pan out? Did you make the money you thought you would?"

He hesitated. "No, not really. The company I started went bankrupt and I now work for a friend."

I knew the answer before I'd asked the question. A husband who saw himself as a loser would look at his wife, who is his own flesh, as a loser as well. And a miserable husband usually takes out his misery on his wife.

In front of me was the quintessential broken American male—albeit with a South African origin—whose own feelings of failure were causing him to see his wife as a failure as well. After all, if you're a big nothing, then the woman dumb enough to marry you is a nothing squared.

Through the prism of his own brokenness, this man was seeing an inadequate wife. Through the looking glass of his own inadequacy, his own deficiency, his own self-loathing, he was learning to despise his life, and his wife.

I shared these observations with the husband. Remarkably, he didn't argue with me. As I spoke, he flashed the knowing look of quiet acquiescence. Another broken male had found a diagnosis for something he had always felt but could not completely comprehend.

But while he acknowledged the problem, sadly, he did not change. I did not succeed in getting through to him. He continued to belittle his wife and they ended up divorcing six months after our meeting. Which just goes to show you, it is far easier to diagnose the broken American male than it is to fix him.

I would not be exaggerating if I said that approximately 70 percent of all couples that come to me for counseling suffer to some degree from the Broken American Male syndrome. They exhibit the telltale symptoms of a suffering husband who is slowly undermining his wife and his children, a man who cannot accept the love his wife gives him because he is so worthless in his own eyes that he views the affection as patronizing at best and contemptuous at worst. He cannot believe his wife loves him so much as pities him. It is impossible for a wife to boost the flat ego of a broken American male because she is inflating a burst balloon. Whatever goes in quickly goes out.

It is impossible for a wife to boost the flat ego of a broken American male because she is inflating a burst balloon. Whatever goes in quickly goes out.

Since the man looks on himself as a failure, the woman who is his wife is by association an equal failure. If some big loser is your fan, will it boost your ego? In the world of TV, it is not enough to have people watch your TV show. It has to be the young people, the cool, trendsetting demographic with the disposable income. If it's just a bunch of what TV producers and advertisers dismiss as old geezers who are watching you, you're doomed, even if your ratings are high. It's not about having fans but rather the *right* fans. It's brutal, but true. The basic law of mathematics is that something without value cannot confer value on something else. When AOL took over Time Warner, it quickly deflated the value of the world's largest media company. Since AOL quickly lost its stock market valuation, Time Warner was pulled down with it. And this is why so many broken American males constantly put down their wives. They look to place the blame on those closest to them for pulling them down, even if such blame has absolutely no basis in reality.

3.

Failure

WHAT IS wrecking the American male? It's this simple: feelings of failure. Immersed in a culture obsessed with success through competition, the modern father and husband is trained to forever feel he doesn't quite measure up. Rather than peering inside himself to discover his own unique gifts and talents, he is forever looking outside. First he looks in front of himself to see who has surpassed him in the rat race of life. Then he looks behind himself to see who is gaining on him. He has become an external creature with no inner identity and little knowledge of his innate gifts. He does not value the unique contribution he can make to society, but only what the market deems advantageous. He does not seek to develop any unique understanding or insight into himself or his life. Rather, he is trained to be mechanical and practical, to acquire material things that will compensate for the emptiness on the inside. He lives for acquisition. He thinks inner value will not confer significance upon him, but rather external bells and whistles. And he judges his self-worth by the extent to which he possesses baubles that the world considers precious. Since there is always someone who has more baubles than he does, the modern American male has little self-esteem. He lives in a society resembling not a circle, in which all are treated more or less as equals, but a pyramid, in which only a tiny few are perched at the top and the overwhelming majority are at the bottom. The American male is immersed in a culture where the people at the apex of that pyramid, the top 2 percent, are endlessly paraded before him as models of achievement, even as he remains the paragon of failure. Every time he opens the newspaper, he reads of Michael Dell's billions and Bill Gates's zillions. He reads of LeBron James making tens of millions of dollars as he exults in the acclaim of fans and how David Letterman signs thirty-million-dollars-a-year contracts. He reads how Larry Page and Sergey Brin of Google came up with a fantastic idea that made them billionaires, and then he looks in the mirror and punishes himself for thinking so small. If only he could think big like these giants then he wouldn't be such a pygmy.

He is then invited to a class reunion, which turns out to be a low-intensity, scarcely subtle brag-fest, with each person trying to prove to the others how he has outdone them.

I still remember hearing about how an old friend of mine—several years younger than I am—built an Internet start-up that was valued at six hundred million dollars. I will never forget how much trouble I had sleeping that night. I know it sounds pathetic and yes, I am ashamed to admit it. But it's true. The friend's success haunted my dreams. He had just overtaken me on the ladder of life, he had obliterated my achievements. In a culture that puts a cash value on human worth, he was much more important than me. He had attained much more than I had, and didn't that mean that he was a better man? By every objective criterion my culture had given me to assess my worth as a human being, he had surpassed me and was therefore more valuable. I was a piece of garbage. A nothing. A zero. I also remember how, when I finally fell asleep and awoke in the morning, I was doubly down on myself. First because I saw myself as a loser, and second because, in my arrogance, I thought I was above such feelings of envy and was therefore disappointed to discover I was doubly ordinary.

FAILURE

To be sure, even my friend probably didn't feel like a success. Yes, he was a multimillionaire. But he read the same newspapers and magazines I did and knew there were Internet start-ups that had made their founders billionaires. Compared to them, he was a failure too. There is always someone on the list ahead of us, and it helps explain why the rich are not much happier than we are. Indeed, because they are already on the rich lists, they are even more conscious of how their value as human beings has a number attached to it, which depresses them even more.

There was an amazing study that proves this point. Winning a Nobel Prize, *NewScientist* reported (*The Week,* February 9, 2007), has a "health-giving magic" that usually adds about two years of life to its recipients. The study was done from the top-secret lists of nominees for each prize, which is released by the Nobel committee only fifty years after the prize is awarded. Of 524 men, the recipients as well as the nominees, it turned out that the winners typically lived about two years longer than their nominated colleagues. The researchers speculated that enhanced status conferred by the Nobel improves a person's health. We all want to be winners, and feeling important even has a bearing on our longevity and health. I don't deny that this is true, but it is equally true that the broken status of those who did not win the prize may have contributed to their not living as long as the winners. For modern men, status and prestige are the very stuff of life, quite literally.

For modern men, status and prestige are the very stuff of life, quite literally.

As the broken American male wades through an incessant assault on his value, and as he tries unsuccessfully to bolster his macerated ego, he is painfully aware that the recognition and respect of his peers will not come from assisting his kids with homework, or remaining faithful to his wife. All around him the culture glorifies men who have built businesses even as they abandoned the women who bore their children and their last names. Jack Welch, Donald Trump, and countless others are the heroes of the age, the men whose books we buy to learn how to be "successful," even as their personal lives crumble around them. Treating his coworkers with dignity, the American male notes, will never bring him onto the *Forbes* list of the four hundred richest Americans. Sure, it's nice to be nice. But everyone knows that nice guys finish last. What matters is how successful you are, even if you have to knife people in the back to make your way to the top. No one gives a damn that you said good morning every day to your coworkers. Nor do they care whether you had any real friends. The broken American male looks ahead to see who has surpassed him and behind to see who is catching up. What he is *not* trained to do is look sideways to find real colleagues and confidants. The corollary of soulless capitalism is that other men are your competitors rather than your compatriots, the guys who are angling to take your piece of the pie and for whom you should harbor distrust and suspicion. And without real friendship, the broken American male feels lonely and ever more broken.

Reading your children a bedtime story will not get you an invitation to the White House Christmas party, which is attended by people who have money and power rather than loving family histories. Money brings prestige, and power brings respect. Since the average American male has only a little of each, he sees himself as inferior to men who may be far less moral or selfless. His children do not make him feel heroic, and his wife struggles, but fails, to massage his perforated ego.

American men want to be important, and that's okay. Yearning for significance is a basic human aspiration. But their humanity gets in the way of their being important. They live in a culture that values their inner machine rather than their inner person. The culture punishes them for any time they spend on personal commitments. Any time wasted on romancing their wives or playing with their children means they're not building a business or making money. Just look at all these politicians who climb the political ladder by ignoring their families, pandering to constituents, cozying up to important

contributors, and flying around the country to network with important people. On the campaign trail they'll suddenly rediscover their
family. They'll pull their cute little kids out for photo ops. They'll
grab their wives in a passionate embrace under the television lights.
But the rest of the time, they're not even around. Their wives are political props who are extremely lonely. Their kids are often completely lost. Is this not the legacy of America's most famous and
illustrious political family, the Kennedys? A family whose third generation is ravaged by divorce and who have suffered the death by
drug overdose of Robert's son, David, not
to mention the continuing drug problems
of Teddy's son, Patrick.

When men are forced to perform constantly in order to succeed, they are slowly
stripped of sensitivity. Under that pressure,
even good men can go bad.

**When men are forced to perform
constantly in order to succeed,
they are slowly stripped of
sensitivity. Under that pressure,
even good men can go bad.**

When Tom and Cheri lived in New York City and came to see
me for counseling, Cheri told me that her husband embarrassed her.
He had a ferocious temper and regularly exploded at his workers.
When he attended his children's soccer matches he yelled at the refer-
ees from the sidelines. She told me that his repeated loss of self-
control made her hate him. Every night she purposely went to sleep
on the couch in order to express her contempt for him. Now Tom
seemed like a good man who patiently listened to his wife's biting
criticism. But he lost his temper at the workers in his clothing store
because work for him was a life-and-death gambit. Only by being
successful did he feel like he was alive. Like so many men, it was his
business and the money it made him that let him feel important. In his
own mind, he was treading water, and professional success was his lifeline. So when someone took away that lifeline, by making a mistake in
the office that could cost Tom money, he felt himself drowning again.
And he lashed out. He also needed his kids to be the best, to win
every soccer match. Since he feared that he was a failure, he feared that

his kids were failures too. So he yelled his lungs out on the sidelines of their sports matches to rescue them from the abyss into which he had sunk.

There are a lot of Toms out there, and they're crying out for help. They're not bad people. Most of the time they're good people, even if their spouses can't see it. But they are very broken. And they are in serious need of healing.

4.

The Escapes Broken Men Pursue

SPORTS
—

IN HIS distress and with his feelings of failure and forlornness, the broken American male turns to various forms of escape, designed to either make him feel better about himself or numb his pain. Foremost among them is an indulgence in sports.

Why, after all, are so many men obsessed with sports? How has sports become the new male religion and great athletes the contemporary male gods? It's one thing to enjoy sports as an entertaining pastime. But to be a professional sports fan seems the height of mediocrity. You're going to subordinate your entire life to someone else's stats? How can proud men choose to live vicariously through someone else's accomplishments? What propels men to come home from work, plunk themselves on the couch, and transform themselves from the animate to the inanimate, couch potatoes incapable of intelligent verbalization and anything more than monosyllabic grunts? How is it that this man who was so eloquent at work throughout the day arrives home and cannot even string together a sentence? *Monday Night Football* goes on, and his wife asks him if he wants to eat dinner, and he offers a groan in response. He has become an uncommunicative lower life-form. At any moment we might expect him to start pounding his chest and sniffing his armpits. Indeed, the only time he recovers the ability to speak intelligently is when his wife walks in front of the TV screen. Then miraculously he can put together a thought. "You're not made of glass, you know." Wow, the creature talks!

His children come to show him all the things they have made at school, or to ask his assistance with their math homework. But he is not even there. He is in a different time, a different dimension. He is with his team, in the arena. Only an empty shell of himself, a hologram, sits on the couch. His essence is elsewhere.

Many teenagers have told me that the reason they have stopped communicating with their dad is that when they try to speak with him, forget listening, he doesn't even hear them. He's far, far away. And they find his mental absence both insulting and infuriating. So they stop talking. Why bother? I have personally made this mistake on many occasions and deeply regret that I made my children feel insignificant.

Why the obsession with sports? Why is it that a man who shows little to no emotion in almost every other area of life suddenly shows such indescribable passion when watching football, baseball, or basketball? Because his team makes him feel good about himself. He may be a loser, but his team, well, they're winners. And by attaching himself to them, he achieves greatness by association. Being a sports fanatic allows him to live vicariously through his favorite team and feel heroic. Since they are winners, he, by his association, by his love and devotion to his team, is a winner as well. Their triumph is his triumph. Their supremacy elevates him from the dung heap to the high places. *I may be a cockroach, but my quarterback is Peyton Manning, the greatest player in the league. So by wearing his jersey, or by talking about his stats, or by watching every one of his games, I become the king of the jungle.*

WORK
—

The next diversion of choice for the broken American male is work. Many broken men are incurable workaholics, coming home at ungodly hours, and even when they're home, they're not at home. Their mind is still at work. They're doing e-mail. They're on the phone. They neglect their kids. They neglect their wives. They neglect themselves. And why? Because only when men are working do they feel good about themselves. It gives them purpose and definition. Coming home reduces them to their loser state. They're not good at home. They don't know how to communicate with their kids or be romantic with their wives. That involves a state of being. It involves the human, feeling side of their personalities rather than the practical side, which knows only how to perform. But they don't know how to *be*. Only how to *do*. They don't know what to do with themselves when at rest. They don't know how to rest. They get restless when they rest. Why can't they ever give themselves a break? Why can't they come home and *be* home? Because when they're at home they're not working. And when they're not working, they're falling. The broken male forever feels like he's sinking into the abyss of anonymity, into the eternal black hole of nothingness. He has weights on his legs, pulling him down into the unfathomable depths. The weights are the broken pieces of his soul that will not mend. He is haunted by voices that endlessly whisper in his ear that he is a failure. He is permanently at sea and has to tread water in order to survive. Telling him not to work is tantamount to telling him to disappear into the ether. He wants to make a name for himself. How can he do that if he doesn't work? He is certain that if he stops churning for even one moment, he'll go under. There's nothing to prop him up, nothing to make him buoyant. He does not work to live. Rather, he lives to work. He feels empty and vacuous on the inside, so he has to keep up limitless activity on the outside. He cannot let himself alone for even a moment for fear the demons will overtake him. That inner voice that will not be silenced, that haunting whisper that forever tells him he is nothing, can only be overcome through the clatter of constant activity.

He convinces himself that one more hour at the office will help him turn the corner and find extraordinary success that will finally give him the value he so craves. He is made of lead, and if he stops treading water for a moment, he will sink to the bottom. In his mind, he is not living but just surviving. No matter what he achieves, it goes in one end and out the other. He cannot be filled up with any appreciation of sense of success because he is a bottomless pit of failure.

This is why so many American men have become crack addicts, addicted to their "Crackberries." I own a BlackBerry too. Did you ever watch a man with his BlackBerry? He is pulling it out of its case several times an hour, even in the middle of a meeting, to look at the incoming e-mail. He is addicted to every message that arrives. He cannot live without checking his messages, because every incoming e-mail holds the potential promise of success. Every e-mail is a light at the end of the tunnel that might rescue him from his all-consuming darkness. He is a rat in a race, and even an insignificant packet of information, transmitted over fiber-optic lines, might signal the finish line, might finally herald his arrival into the circle of victory. Of course, even if it did, even if the next e-mail that came in told him that he'd won the lottery, or the Pulitzer, or the Nobel Peace Prize, that feeling of satisfaction would last for perhaps a day or a week. And then the demons would overtake him again.

WOMEN AND PORN

The biggest distraction employed by the broken American male is women. Feeling desirable to women makes broken men feel special and manly. More than anything else, the attention of a woman, especially a younger woman, and one to whom he is not married, quiets the demons for a time. Every minute of every day he hears a voice telling him he is not unique but ordinary, not successful but a failure, not desirable but unattractive. And then, suddenly, a woman flirts with him or glances at him and he feels like a million bucks. *Wow, I'm not a loser after all. I'm a sexy guy. I'm irresistible. That pretty woman keeps on giving me the eye.* Little does he realize that since women have become his drug of choice, it's bound to lead to an addiction. Soon, one woman will not suffice. Like any addict, he needs more. And more. And more. Because feeling desirable to women doesn't cure the problem, it only masks it. It takes away the pain momentarily. And when the pain returns, he needs another hit.

This explains the phenomenal explosion of porn in our time. The popularity of porn is directly linked to the degree of brokenness and unhappiness of American men. *New York Times* columnist Frank Rich wrote a cover story for the *Times Magazine* in May 2001, which asserted that porn is no longer a fringe business. It's mainstream. It accounts for about 70 percent of all traffic on the Internet. Its revenues are five times that of all Hollywood movies combined. Now why would something that is on the surface (*surface* being the operative word when it comes to porn) so utterly boring become so irresistible? Porn is not erotic, because eroticism is about the hidden and the mysterious and porn is all too revealed. It's not sexy, because watching women groan and moan to the hidden instructions of an off-camera director is pretty pathetic when you think about it. And it's not that exciting, because all that rolling of the eyes, feigning ecstasy, when really they look pretty distracted, is an insult to the intelligence. And every single porn movie is, in essence, exactly the same (not that I would know any of this stuff personally, but so my friends tell me). It's the same sexual positions, the same inane dialogue. Even the actors—if such pathetic performances can be called acting—look exactly the same. And then the breasts are fake, as is much else on the body. And you can't even see the bodies, covered as they are these days in a sea of tattoos!

So why do men watch this boring garbage? How has porn become an epidemic among American men? Well, it may be pathetic, but it gives men two things they can't live without. The first is a respite from their pain. Porn offers up women as a drug. Immersed as the man is in women as fantasy, he forgets that he is a failure. For one moment, with all those women contorting their bodies into pretzels for his pleasure and enjoyment, he is a king. He is the master of women. They will humiliate and degrade themselves for his erotic edification. The second is much more insidious. He watches porn to masturbate, because masturbation brings him the numbness and the emotionless nonfeeling that dulls his inner anguish. The broken American male doesn't want to feel, because whenever he does feel, all he feels is pain. This is the real reason that so many men masturbate, for the brief bliss that follows orgasm. The nirvana of nonfeeling is what the broken male seeks, and the deadness of nonstimulation is what he craves.

> **The broken American male doesn't want to feel, because whenever he does feel, all he feels is pain.**

> **The nirvana of nonfeeling is what the broken male seeks, and the deadness of nonstimulation is what he craves.**

FROM SEX ADDICT TO ORGASM ADDICT

—

We make a mistake in thinking that men watch porn, or try to bed as many women as possible, because they are sex addicts. Modern men are not sex addicts so much as orgasm addicts. There is a considerable difference between the two. The sex addict actually enjoys sex. He loves the friction of sex, the intensity of sex, the loss of self that comes through sex. He loves the strong emotions and the sense of closeness that sex conjures up. The sex addict loves the sensuality of sex as well.

He loves the feel of a woman, the scent of a woman, the sound of a woman, the taste of a woman, and the look of a woman. In short, he drinks in a woman with all his senses. Now, does this sound like any man you know? Most men today want to bed women, rather than enjoy them. These men do not seek to share them-

Modern men are not sex addicts so much as orgasm addicts.

selves with women so much as use them. The orgasm addict hates the strong emotions that sex conjures up, which is why he wants sex to be over with as quickly as possible. For him, sex is nothing more than a means to an end. Sex brings him to orgasm, and the quicker he gets there the better, because at the moment of sexual climax, he reaches his intended goal of nonfeeling, utter emotionlessness, followed by the oblivion of sleep. Presto. A world of numbness, just as he intended.

And why orgasm? Because, as the French call it, the orgasm is *la petite mort,* "the little death." After orgasm he is granted the pleasure, not of intense emotion, which the sex addict craves, but of nonemotion, which the orgasm addict seeks. Loving sex reflects a love of life. The

After orgasm he is granted the pleasure, not of intense emotion, which the sex addict craves, but of nonemotion, which the orgasm addict seeks.

whole pleasure of sex derives from the intense feeling of aliveness that is heightened during the act. But loving *only* orgasm reflects a love of death, because after orgasm we feel expended, finished. The aftermath of sexual climax is one of the few times that the broken American male feels liberated from painful emotion. He feels like the dead. Better yet, he sleeps like the dead. His wife is utterly at a loss to explain how a man could be so passionate and alive one moment and a virtual corpse the next. She is offended and humiliated that sex ends so abruptly. She is frustrated that he moves to his own side of the bed and falls into a deep sleep the moment sex is over. She takes it personally and sees it as rejection. But in reality, the deadness he seeks was never about her or the inadequacy of her body. It was always about him and the pain in his heart.

The orgasm addict also despises the sensual woman. He doesn't want women with curves or flesh. No, he wants them superthin, so it can't be argued that he really enjoys the feel of a woman. Because a bag of bones and a rib cage, lacking any curves or contours, is just not that pleasurable to touch. The orgasm addict makes love linearly. Like a line segment, sex has a beginning and an end, and it is the shortest distance between the two that he craves. Subconsciously, therefore, he makes his women into lines as well. The less sensual, the less curvaceous, the better. After all, the woman is there only to provide the friction required for orgasm. Hence, the broken American male wants a woman to wear perfumes, artificial scents that mask a woman's pheromones, her natural scent. Pheromones create connection, while perfumes merely increase arousal. And it is arousal rather than intimacy that he craves. He certainly doesn't want to hear a woman speak. The misogynistic attitude of the porn addict is "Shut up and spread your legs." Talk? "Fugedaboutit."

The sex addict enjoys the friction of two bodies in ecstatic embrace. So he prolongs sex. He's not running to the finish line. On the contrary, orgasm will indicate the end of the experience, so instead he prolongs the journey. Whereas the sex addict loves seeing the pleasure of the woman he is with and therefore focuses on her climax rather than his own, the orgasm addic selfishly shortens sex, leaving the woman he is with unsatisfied. The orgasm addict treats women as

It's the anonymity of her vagina rather than the specificity of her face and personality that he craves.

a means to his own selfish ends. A woman is there to get him off, to get him to climax. Her own boredom is none of his concern. And that's why the woman in question is not specific. She could be almost anyone. It's the anonymity of her vagina rather than the specificity of her face and personality that he craves.

Orgasm addiction is why men these days have so many sexual partners. Incapable of finding something novel and exciting within one woman, which would take work, they take the easy way out and simply switch women whenever they get bored. Mining a woman's depths takes effort. Buying a woman dinner and expecting her to put out as a trade-off is much easier by comparison. Even faithful husbands can be guilty of this insulting behavior when they think about other women while making love to their wives.

And nowhere is this obsession with variety better captured than in pornography. Porn is the male orgasm personified. It is not smart, it is not entertaining, and it is not erotic. But in the endless variety of disembodied and faceless body parts that it provides, it is pure sexual detonation.

In October 2003 *New York* magazine ran a cover story by David Amsden about the male addiction to pornography and how it is undermining male-female relationships (surprise, surprise!). Entitled "Not Tonight, Honey. I'm Logging On," the story was advertised with the following tagline: "Internet porn is everywhere; even 'nice' guys are hooked. So where does that leave their girlfriends?" The feature went on to say that Wall Street traders, the most manly of men (since they make the most money), have reached a point where they prefer to stay at home and masturbate to pornography rather than have sex with their girlfriends. If it was their wives they didn't want to have sex with, we might understand. But girlfriends? The story was scarcely believable. These guys are dating gorgeous women, but rather than mess around with them, the traders are staying at home and masturbating to porn. Because even sex involves an exertion. You have to woo the girl. Take her out to dinner. Heck, you even have to do the hard work of removing her clothes. And when it's over, just before you give her the reason why she can't stay the night and has to take a taxi home, you've got to at least say something nice and complimentary. Man, that's a lot of work. Why make all that effort when you can just go home and get straight to it?

When I published a column about the modern American male orgasm addict, which appeared in *The Jerusalem Post,* I received the following e-mail from a brave young American soldier stationed in Iraq:

> *I disagree completely with what you wrote. Men going to prostitutes and strippers, there's nothing new about that at all. That's what guys do. It seems to me that the three things that guys have to do is fight, have sex, and eat. When that's over, we're over. I'm amazed that a guy as worldly as you would believe this. When I first read this, I was very surprised it was written by a male rabbi.*

For those who, like my military friend, believe I'm way off the mark here, and that men always were, and still are, orgasm addicts, here's the $100,000 question: Why aren't they having sex with their wives? Why is it that when men get married, they often lose interest in sex? The American marriage is quickly becoming a platonic affair, with millions of married couples having sex a few times a year at most. Even *Newsweek* caught on, with a cover story in June 2003 about how 20 percent of American marriages are sexless. Completely and utterly sexless. On *Shalom in the Home*, of the twenty couples we worked with in our first two seasons, roughly half had not had sex in more than a year. The couples that come to me for private counseling routinely tell me that they don't share a bed or a bedroom and haven't had sex in months. When I first started marital counseling this really surprised me. It strained credulity. *What? You haven't had sex in a year? Are you guys human?* Nowadays, the opposite is true. If they tell me they have a regular and healthy sex life, I raise my eyebrows in wonder. "What, are you guys normal?"

The sexless couples we're talking about are, for the most part, young couples, not men on a Viagra drip. As for those couples that are still having sex, studies show that marital sex in America lasts for, on average, seven and a half minutes at a time. And that includes the time the husband spends begging. Sparse pickings indeed. And husbands being such impatient and goal-oriented lovers is slowly extinguishing their wives' libidos. This generation of bad lovers is slowly under-mining women's interest in sex. Women aren't sexier. They're slut-tier. And there's a big difference between the two, which I shall address later. But let me show you how much the perception of women and sex has changed over time.

In ancient times it was the women rather than the men who were considered to be obsessed with sex. That's why King Solomon keeps on warning the men, in the book of Proverbs, to watch out for vora-cious women who want to rob men of their virtue. Here's an exam-ple from Proverbs 5:

> *For the lips of a forbidden woman drip honey,*
> *and her speech is smoother than oil,*
> *but in the end she is bitter as wormwood,*
> *sharp as a two-edged sword.*
> *Her feet go down to death;*
> *her steps follow the path to Sheol;*
> *she does not ponder the path of life;*
> *her ways wander, and she does not know it. . . .*
> *Keep your way far from her,*
> *and do not go near the door of her house,*
> *lest you give your honor to others*
> *and your years to the merciless,*
> *lest strangers take their fill of your strength,*
> *and your labors go to the house of a foreigner. . . .*

Whoa! King Solomon, 2,500 years ago, is warning men to stay away from the sexually voracious woman before she gets them in her bed, then uses and dumps them. Now isn't this exactly the advice we give to women today, to stay away from cads who will use them and discard them? But in ancient times, the roles were reversed. It was the women who were the seducers. That's why kings and emperors locked their wives up in harems. It wasn't the men who were being locked out. After all, only a crazy guy would dare do something with one of the king's wives. He was bound to be separated from the very equipment he used to offend the king in the first place. Rather, the harems were designed to keep the women locked up, because in those days it was the women who were perceived to be incapable of living without sex.

Of course, all that has changed today. The conventional thinking today is that the husband turns to his wife at night and says, "Honey, how about some sex tonight?" to which she responds, "Not tonight, honey. I have a headache." But a man can have an ax lodged in his head and still he's ready. His wife will turn to him and say, "Honey, are you sure you want sex tonight? I don't know how to tell you this, but, um . . . er . . . you have an ax stuck in your head." And he'll turn around and say, "Really? Aha, so I do. An ax. But, um, that's nothing. Don't worry about it. I'm still ready to go. Can we also call your sister?" The modern cliché is that men love sex and women tolerate it.

Of course, that's absurd. A woman's libido is much stronger than a man's. Indeed, male sexuality compared with female sexuality is pathetic. Women are multiorgasmic while men are uniorgasmic. After sex a woman is still raring to go while the guy is practically a corpse. Women's sexuality is an internal experience. It is anchored in emotions. Like a home wired to an electric substation, a woman's libido is fully powered. Women feel sex incredibly deeply. But men find it easy to compartmentalize their bodies from their hearts. Their sex drive is battery-powered, easily exhausted, easily spent.

So why is today's conventional thinking that men are the sex-crazed ones? Because so many husbands have basically destroyed their wives' libidos. Men are like microwave ovens when it comes to sex. Their heat is artificial, and they think that nuking their wife is going to be a pleasurable experience for her. So they're in and out. And we know how long the heat from a microwave oven lasts. But women are real ovens. You have to take the time to heat up the oven. But once it's hot, man, it stays hot! And men, with their rush-to-the-orgasm approach, have made their wives so cold that women don't even enjoy sex anymore. And this is on top of all the other mistakes husbands make, like neglecting their wives during the day but suddenly expecting them to rev up in bed at night. In my twenty years of counseling, wives have constantly complained to me that they don't enjoy sex with their husbands because it's so abrupt. Who could enjoy an experience where your husband is essentially using you?

This does not mean that husbands who have become orgasm addicts began that way. A great many were at first extremely passionate about their wives and felt intense desire for them. But as the years went by, the passion waned. Yes, I know that there is an innate male orientation toward novelty and new flesh. And in my books on relationships, most notably *Kosher Adultery,* I have written a great deal about how men can find vertical newness in their wives' personalities in place of the horizontal newness of new flesh. But the real reason that these men slowly stopped making love to their wives was a loss of emotional connection. Immersed in a society that converted them from humans into machines, they learned how to make money but not how to make love. Men know how to conquer women but not how to share themselves with women. And once

> **Immersed in a society that converted them from humans into machines, they learned how to make money but not how to make love.**

they conquer women, they quickly become stymied. From physical intimacy they're supposed to move on to the next stage of emotional intimacy. But many men find it too challenging. Emotions are too alien to them. So they choose false eroticism through porn instead.

When Larry and Susan came to see me for marital counseling, Susan shared with me that she harbored unnatural rage toward her husband. "I don't want to be an angry person. I never was like this.

But I'm not important to Larry. Everything in his life comes before me. He doesn't talk to me. He shares nothing with me. He comes home and ignores me. At night he barely touches me. We have perfunctory sex. I feel ugly and unattractive. My marriage is a rip-off. I give everything and get nothing in return."

She spoke of Larry as if he were a bad person. I said to her, "Susan, just think about this. Your husband goes to work every day for ten hours. There, he isn't allowed to be human. He is trained to produce and not to feel. He knows that however much the boss may tell him he's a great guy, he's still only valued so long as he is productive. His humanity be damned. He is trained to sweet talk and to sell, to win people over with charm rather than sincerity. He can never express his frustrations or disappointments. He's a warrior in the office. He has to show a stiff upper lip. And then he comes home and he's expected to suddenly become human again. He's expected to talk about his feelings, share his frustrations, tell you how his day went. Really, what he needs is a decompression chamber that allows him to get all the robotics out of his system so he can be a husband again. Instead, he finds it easier, not to mention more comforting, to just sink down in the couch and forget all his problems by escaping them. You're trying to pull him back to reality. But reality is simply too painful. Your husband's not a bad guy. He's just a broken guy."

Many broken American men share the inability to love a woman. Each one of them comes home a shell of a man, a defeated creature whose modest surroundings reinforce his permanent feeling of failure. Because he doesn't love himself, he cannot love his wife. His marriage is reduced to a series of meaningless and monotonous gestures, coldly functional, bereft of warmth or intimacy. The compliments his wife offers him bounce off him. Since he doesn't believe in himself, he treats her attempts at comfort as patronizing. Later he will complain that his wife does not lift him up when he is down, even as he has pushed her away on countless occasions when she has sought to offer comfort.

I have met many men who cannot accept their wife's love because they mistake it for pity. They think to themselves, "I'm this giant loser who struggles just to meet his mortgage and credit-card payments. I can't afford that new car my wife needs. Who would love someone like me?" So when the wife reaches out to caress a broken man at night, or tells him how special he is to her, he cannot accept the sincerity of her words. He assumes she must feel sorry for him. *Why not make this poor wretch feel good about himself?* So he finds it challenging to make passionate love to his wife. He doesn't feel very masculine. He doesn't feel passionate about who he is. So what passion does he have to give to his marriage?

5.

Premarital Sex Reinforces
the Brokenness of American Men

I HAVE FOCUSED on soulless capitalism as the principal engine behind
the collapse of American manhood. Unending competition prevents
men from ever feeling truly comfortable or content with themselves
or with anyone else for that matter. Men feel that they are being constantly weighed and evaluated in order to be found either worthy or
inadequate. They are set against one another in a never-ending race
for material supremacy. Most of the time, they are made to feel not
victorious or successful, but rather that they can never measure up.

One of the areas in which this has happened, quite literally, is sex,
where most men are with women who have in turn been with so many
other men that the modern American male feels that his very anatomy
is being measured against some standard that he cannot attain.

Much has been written about the negative effects, beyond STDs
and pregnancy, that premarital sex has on young women, of the emotional scarring left on girls as they go through a series of casual sexual encounters. All too little, by contrast, has been written about the
scars left on men.

In few areas of our lives are we as vulnerable as we are in the
realm of sex. Sex, by its very nature, involves a loss of inhibition and

self-protection that leaves us utterly exposed and quite literally naked. Sex reveals a human being at his or her most natural, not enhanced or magnified by clothing, money, a fancy car, or any other accoutrement of success.

Imagine that you are with a woman. You take off all your clothes, your Rolex watch, and all the things you normally use to mask your insecurities and tell the world you're a success. You're in a sexual environment where you want to love and be loved. Nothing more. You're a man, and you live in a culture that is constantly evaluating you for your performance, for what you do rather than who or what you are. And this is your sole respite, to be held in a woman's arms and feel that you are nurtured, that you are enough just as you are, in your most natural state.

Aha, but it's not so simple. You see, the woman you're with is like you. She has been with about twenty men before you. Like you, she has become an expert in the body of the opposite sex. She has encountered firm muscles and soft muscles, flat stomachs and rotund stomachs. She waits to see what kind yours will be. Most of all, she has encountered the central male sex organ on so many occasions that she can tell whether yours is impressive or not. So when you take your clothes and armor off, your inhibitions are turned on. You feel ashamed. Maybe you're nowhere near what she's used to. And then, of course, there is the sexual performance itself. She has been with other men, men who probably went out of their way to make an impression. Not by being soft and tender and loving, but by being rough, by showing just how manly they were. You may want to make her feel secure and appreciated. But they made her scream. So you've got to compete here as well. And you especially have to compensate for any physical shortcomings that you perceive about yourself.

All this just increases male self-loathing. There is no place men can escape the yardstick. It also alienates men from women. As it is, men complain that whenever they meet a woman, the first question she asks is "What do you do?" It's his profession, his status in society, rather than his essence, that she is most interested in. Now, even his body and his sexual technique are put under a microscope.

So after you come home from work, you have to go to the gym. There is no rest for the wicked. And you don't go to the gym because you're focused on your health, but mostly because you're focused on your appearance. The external orientation of your life continues. When will it ever end?

Of course, truth be told, it is the men themselves who are most responsible for this state of affairs, focused as they are on getting casual sex from women. Rather than searching for real connection and commitment with a woman, men often capitulate to their basest instincts and lust after orgasms instead. And so the cycle continues. A culture that has lost its sexual innocence works against men in the long run, and only adds to the male sense of inadequacy and suffering.

6.

The Death Wish

THE MOST corrosive escape mechanism of the broken American male is the indulgence of a death instinct by which he seeks to deaden pain through extremes of nonfeeling. Foremost among these death mechanisms is alcoholism. I am amazed at how much men today drink. A lot of guys I know who are incredibly serious and responsible at work go home and drink a quantity of whiskey that could sink the *Titanic*. And why do men love to drink? Because it helps them stop feeling. Drinking, like drugs, is all about numbing pain, killing off the heart, and deadening emotion. Drink and drugs are just other versions of *la petite mort,* the little death of orgasm. Orgasm rockets a man into a state of bliss and nirvana where he feels utterly quiet and numb. It silences the haunting voices that tell him endlessly of his failure. Alcohol does this even more effectively, which is why men are even bigger drinkers than they are sex addicts.

The broken American male has a death wish. It's not that he wants to die. He's not stupid, after all. It's just that he wants to numb the pain of life. He wants to be alive without feeling. He strives to be the walking dead, the Tin Man from *The Wizard of Oz,* all machine and no heart. He wants his suffering, brought about by feeling unworthy, to go away. He wants to quiet the demons that haunt him every day, telling him he's a big nothing. Notice that, very often, the more successful the man, the more he takes risks and plays with his life. The more competitive the man, the more he seems to court death, taking huge risks that can spell disaster at any moment.

Richard Branson spends every Monday and Wednesday jumping out of an airplane or hot air balloon. Bill Clinton played Russian roulette with his presidency, virtually assassinating his place in history. To have sex with an intern in the Oval Office—arguably the most guarded space on earth—is to court the death of your career and your family. Why do successful men take such big risks, putting their lives and careers on the line? Because the demon of ambition so haunts them that they want to kill it. And that means killing themselves along with it. Without even being aware of it, men who push themselves so hard harbor a death wish—death is the only thing that will bring them peace.

To be sure, thrill-seeking need not be a bad thing. We all enjoy an adrenaline rush, and pushing ourselves beyond our limits can be healthy. But the stunts pulled off by many supersuccessful men go beyond normal thrill-seeking or risk-taking and constitute the deliberate courting of danger that could lead to an early demise.

Hence, we see many hugely successful men die an early death—either figurative or real—after gambling with their lives or developing destructive patterns that ultimately bring them to self-immolation. What people as different as Elvis Presley, Johnny Cash, Michael Jackson, Kurt Cobain, and Jack Kennedy have in common is a certain recklessness that bespeaks a contempt for all that they achieved. Because what they achieved brought them not joy, but pain. Kennedy was one of our most charismatic presidents. But he lived on the edge, bouncing from bed to bed and woman to woman. He did so to feel desirable to women, to get an ego boost. But wasn't he the most powerful man in the world? Wasn't that enough of an ego boost? Not really. He had a father who made him, and his siblings, feel that they only mattered if they were supersuccessful. In their natural, everyday state, they were zeros. So they had to work constantly to win recognition. Imagine living with that kind of burden. Feeling valueless unless you win power, prestige, and money. And wouldn't you want to feel desirable to other people, especially women, in order to prove that you really were special? And when you did that, would you still feel good about yourself? Or inside, would you always feel like a failure? And if you still felt like a failure, even after all that acclaim, would death not seem just a little bit inviting? It is well known that President Kennedy overruled his secret service agents to ride in an open limousine on that fateful November day in Dallas. I am not suggesting that he wanted to make himself a target for an assassin. I am suggesting that, like so many other Kennedy men, the president's attitude toward death was "Bring it on, and give it your best shot." We have all witnessed the terrible tragedies of this illustrious family made up of so many successful yet highly broken men whom only the grave could grant peace.

One night I lectured about inspirational parenting at Dalton, one of New York's most famous and elite schools. Tuition is in the crazy range—over $30,000 a year—and, while the school has an admirable policy of diversification and scholarships that fund that diversity, most of the parents are obviously very wealthy. When I was signing books after the lecture, a woman came over to me with red eyes and her mascara running. She told me that, although she had children in the school, the real reason she came to the lecture was to speak to me about her marriage. She and her husband had been together nineteen years. They had four children. He had just celebrated his forty-fifth birthday, only it wasn't a celebration. He quickly spiraled into a textbook case of a midlife crisis. He grew his hair down to his shoulders. He bought a snazzy sports car. And he started going out every night with friends to bars and clubs, leaving his wife and children at home. It tore the family apart. The eldest son, who was twenty, developed a deep loathing for his father, whom he viewed as immature, selfish, and pathetic. The mom cried herself to sleep most nights, wondering where her husband was. When I asked her if there were other women involved, she said, emphatically, that there were not. But since she could not possibly know, I took her denial as her way of coping with a marriage that was going down the toilet.

What the woman could not understand, however, was why her husband was having a midlife crisis when he was so successful. She told me his net worth was over a hundred million dollars. I answered that none of that mattered. There were other guys out there, his acquaintances from Manhattan, who were worth ten times that. So he felt like a failure whose life was headed toward the grave, and he was grasping for a false sense of youth in order to reinvigorate himself.

Another New York hedge-fund manager with whom I am friendly came to see me to discuss a shocking secret. Married for twenty years, he was in the midst of a destructive affair from which he wished to extricate himself. He was asking me how to do so and how to tell his wife. I had always thought he had a very happy marriage. This is a man who makes, without exaggeration, about fifty million dollars a year in fees from his fund. He is enormously successful. "What was missing in your life that you felt the need to do this?" I asked him. He told me that one day he was reading the *Time* 100—the magazine's annual list of the one hundred most influential people in the world—and saw one of his acquaintances on the list in the business category. Like him, his colleague was a hedge-fund manager. "Shmuley, I felt like a failure. I'm forty-eight years old, and here is this guy I know who's voted one of the hundred most influential people in the world. And who has even ever heard of me? I guess, after that, I was really vulnerable. My secretary saw my depression and we started talking every day, and one thing led to another." Incredible. A man with everything was throwing his blessings away because he wasn't on a magazine list.

I had something of a reverse experience with lists. In April 2007 *Newsweek* magazine published a list of the fifty most influential rabbis in America. The list put me at number nine, and then added that I had been called "the most famous rabbi in America." That day media calls poured in for comment. What did it feel like to be the best-known rabbi and among the top ten in influence? Truth be told, it felt good, but also horrible, and I said so. I mentioned that the list was probably corrosive. And why? Because I knew that now I, and the forty-nine others on the list, would feel enormous pressure to make sure we were on the list the following year as well. Our value as rabbis, as spiritual leaders, had been given a number value, a quotient. The list would also ensure that we chose to do the kind of work that got noticed so that we would be on the list the following year, as would all those unnoticed rabbis who had not made this year's list. What would happen to all the unspoken, quiet acts of kindness and counseling that rabbis do every year, which are the true stuff of greatness? Would they just be lost? I write these lines just two months after the list came out. It's done nothing for me other than give me a brief ego boost and leave me in anxiety about my standing in spiritual America. But our country is obsessed with lists. We love them, we live for them. Everything in America has a price tag, everything can be given a numerical value, especially human beings. There's one problem. People are of infinite value, and when they are reduced to a place on a list, even when they are at the top of the list, they are regressing.

In fact, the more successful the man, very often the more broken he is. He is still broken even after he becomes immensely successful, because he never internalized a feeling of real self-worth. And that happens especially in fields like rock music, where the locus of your self-worth is held in the hands of screaming fans. G-d help you if they ever stop screaming.

I was Michael Jackson's rabbi for about two years. I tried to heal him and repair his life. For a time I met with considerable success. I got Michael to take his life more seriously, to lecture at Oxford University and Carnegie Hall, to surround himself with serious and responsible people, and to reconnect with his family. But ultimately, I failed. What most people think ruined Michael's life was the charges of pedophilia and molestation. But that's not true. Others have been accused of serious wrongdoing and survived. The difference with Michael was that when he was accused of those things, people immediately believed them because he was so weird. A weirdo like him had to be a pedophile, went the thinking. And why was Michael so strange? What made such a mockery of his life? People pointed to the mask he wore in public, the story of how he bought the bones of the Elephant Man, and Michael's walks around his neighborhood with a chimpanzee and a giraffe. Indeed, all that is pretty darn weird. But my opinion was that much of this was deliberate affectation. In the two years that I knew him well, I saw very few things that could be construed as weird. Sure, Michael's life needed a lot of repair. He was a recluse. Like Elvis, he stayed up at night and slept a lot of the day. But there were no giraffes following him around, he never wore a mask while speaking to me, and there were no Elephant-Man bones in the closet. He slept in a normal bed and not in a hyperbaric chamber.

So where did all this nonsense come from? I believe that Michael did these things and had his people put out some of those ridiculous stories to keep the public interested in him. The greatest fear he lived with was that the public would forget him. From his earliest years he was a performer. That's all he knew. He was never taught how to be, just how to do. Performance was something central, rather than peripheral, to his life. And something of his humanity was lost in the process. He acquired love by pleasing people, by singing and dancing, wowing his fans and making them smile. His entire identity lay outside of himself and was firmly ensconced in the palms of his fans. The secret of the pain of his life is that, like so many other celebrities, the locus of his self-esteem is not in his own hands but in someone else's. And that's a terrible way to live. If the fans were to forget him, he would, to his mind, cease to exist. But if he could keep himself on their minds at all times, even when he wasn't singing and dancing, he would always be alive.

So he made his entire life into one big performance. He built Neverland, he got a zoo, he changed his appearance so many times that people just had to talk about it. But what he didn't realize while he was doing all this was that he was detaching himself from all that was healthy. What Michael never understood was that he was the quintessential broken American male, a man whose entire identity hinged on one thing only: professional success. There was no man under the performer. He had *become* a performer. In the same way that a tap dancer cannot choose to simply walk off the stage in the middle of a performance without risking permanent professional ruin, Michael could not stop dancing even when he wasn't on the stage, because his whole life had become a stage.

Once, when I took Michael to England to lecture at Oxford University, we were walking outside his hotel in central London. Camped outside were hundreds of German fans who had come to lay eyes on their idol. Michael turned to me and said, "Isn't it beautiful? Look how much they love me." Later, I responded, "Michael, they don't love you. Rather, they love what you do *for them*. It's all about them and not about you. You are the thriller. But G-d help you on the day that you stop thrilling them."

The great Jewish philosopher Maimonides wrote, about nine hundred years ago, that each of us possesses two natures. There is our inborn, congenital nature. Some of us are born calm, some tense, some happy, some slightly morose. Today's scientists would call this genetic predisposition. But then, Maimonides said, there is a second nature, the nature we acquire through repetitive action. So even if you're born angry but train yourself time and again to be patient, you develop a patient personality. What begins as something you do ends up as something you are. Habit becomes second nature.

> **What begins as something you do ends up as something you are. Habit becomes second nature.**

In Michael's life, performing began as something he did. It ended up as a second nature that could not be escaped. I am convinced that this is the reason he developed his much-publicized addiction to prescription drugs. It was not a physical ailment that plagued Michael, but a spiritual one. He always used to tell me how something or other was hurting him—his foot, his back, his head. But really he was afflicted by tremendous torment of the soul. He never knew any rest. He could never quiet the inner demons that told him he was intrinsically worthless so he better put on his dancing shoes and get out there and make something of himself. For Michael, prescription drugs were the one escape from the horror his life had become, a pain that vastly increased once his fans began to abandon him in droves with the second round of molestation charges that finished him off in the public mind.

But while Michael might be the ultimate broken American male, the rest of us are not too far behind. How many of us, if we want to be honest, have also become performers? How many of us only feel alive when we're working? How many of us live to impress other people and create admirers and fans? And how many of us have allowed our families to fall apart, as the Jacksons did, in pursuit of professional success?

Alcohol is huge. Enormous. And it is especially prevalent among young men at college, as they experience their earliest exposure to what life has in store for them. How desirable will they be to women? The world will grade them by the kind of university they attended and their performance at that university. What kind of job will they get after they graduate? When your self-worth depends on all those external things, which are to some extent outside your control, it's no surprise that you enjoy drinking yourself into oblivion.

At Oxford, where I served as rabbi for eleven years, I was amazed at how many students—both men and women, but overwhelmingly the men—got plastered on a regular basis. We lived on Cowley Road, about a mile from our student center, which was in the city center. Every Friday night I would walk back from our large Sabbath evening meal and have to literally step over drunken students passed out on Oxford High Street. There was vomit on the street, and it was disgusting. Then there were the debates at the Oxford Union, one of the world's most prestigious lecture venues. It was not uncommon to see one of the student debaters, or student officers, especially in the last week of term, getting up completely hammered to deliver an incoherent address.

What always puzzled me was how this could happen at an elite university, where you would expect so much more. But in lecturing at leading universities around the United States, I discovered that the drinking there was nearly as bad.

Now why are so many young people drinking? And why are they taking drugs? What could have happened to them already in their short lives that could cause so much pain? We rarely ask these questions, seeing drugs and alcohol rather as a youthful rite of passage or some benign form of youthful rebellion and experimentation. I disagree. The only people who drink themselves into oblivion, or take drugs, are those who want to escape something, usually unhappiness and pain. Drinking is about numbing feelings, usually feelings of anxiety and depression. And we don't want to accept just how unhappy young people are today. Come on. Do the typical American teenagers look alive to you? Or do they appear to be in a near catatonic state, hidden as they are behind their iPod earbuds and endless technological connectedness.

But what is it? Why are young people in pain? If a guy comes back from Vietnam traumatized and in pain, I get it. If a soldier returns from Iraq having lost his buddies, I understand that he is suffering. If a man loses all his money in a bad investment, I understand his anguish. If a woman's husband runs off with another woman, she's going to be in agony. But what could possibly have happened to our young people that they are in so much pain?

I suggest the reason is that our educational system and child-rearing techniques are all based around fear. The fear of being a big nothing is how we get our kids to perform. Without even realizing it, we have made our kids circus performers designed to earn attention and love from us based on achievement. From the earliest age, we make our kids feel that they aren't special unless they achieve. They better get good grades or they'll be ordinary. They better do well on their SATs or they won't get into a good college. They better graduate on the dean's list or they won't get a good job. The fear goes on and on. Of course, this process is augmented by a punishment-based discipline system employed by most parents, which is also about fear. Kids, of course, need discipline. But this will never compensate for a program of inspiring our children not with the fear of failure but with the promise of their future. In the course of scaring the living daylights out of our kids, we have made them into frightened monkeys who perform for teachers and for college entrance officers, as well as for their parents. And then we wonder why they drink and take drugs? Fear is entirely unpleasant. Feeling like a loser sucks. Young people will go a long way to escape those kinds of negative feelings, and the bottle is just an arm's length away.

The fear of being a big nothing is how we get our kids to perform.

The reason why parents cannot enforce discipline among their children today is threefold. The first is physical exhaustion. Since we define success today primarily through our professional endeavors, that is where we exert our energy. There is very little of us left by the time we come home. And it is easier to give in to our kids and let them do their own thing than to lay down the law. The second is guilt. Many parents do not give their children the attention they need, so they give in to them as a way of compensating for the neglect. The third is the most interesting of all. In an age when so many parents have bad marriages, they depend on their children as their principal source of affection. Would you punish or alienate your only source of love?

In an age when so many parents have bad marriages, they depend on their children as their principal source of affection.

That's why one of the fundamental solutions to the lack of parental discipline is a more holistic definition of success, which embodies both the personal and the professional, and more passionate and intimate marriages.

The absence of intimate relationships and an inspiring institutional structure explains why deadening ourselves to life has become the all-American pastime, embraced by all strata of society. We're just not very happy with ourselves or with our lives, so we choose various forms of escape, the drugs of choice being TV, movies, alcohol, marijuana, the Internet, pornography, impulse purchases, and celebrity gossip.

There is, of course, the ultimate form of numbing pain from which there is no return: suicide. Tragically but understandably, it is becoming more and more common among American men. According to the Centers for Disease Control and Prevention "Suicide: Facts at a Glance" (posted online at www.cdc.gov), suicide is the eighth leading cause of death for all U.S. men, and males are four times more likely to die from suicide than females. Of the total number of suicides among young people fifteen to twenty-four in 2001, 86 percent were male and 14 percent were female. That's a lot of pain.

All this bespeaks a terrible malaise among modern men. Depression among American men is reaching epic proportions, and it often goes unrecognized—by themselves, by colleagues, by family, and even by physicians. Yet some researchers estimate that the depression rate among middle-aged men approaches 40 percent—considerably higher than the rate among women (33 percent)! Statistically it takes ten years and three health professionals to properly diagnose depression in men. Often depression is not recognized until men are in their sixties or even seventies.

Why is depression in men so often undiagnosed and undetected? The symptoms are different from the "blue mood" that typifies it in women. Many men sink into a state of noncommunication and emotional nonresponsiveness that often expresses itself in a loss of libido and general inability to connect. Worse, men typically resist seeking help, and their male friends and colleagues don't ask in-depth questions. Brokenness among American men accounts for both the reason they are depressed and the reason they don't seek help. They get depressed because they feel like failures. And they refuse to seek help because any guy who needs help is an even bigger failure. The macho image of the successful guy who is invincible is killing today's men, literally. And in cultures where the macho stereotype is more greatly ingrained, they seek even less help. Hence, 92 percent of depressed African-American males do not seek treatment, a number so high that it is as tragic as it is shocking (D. F. Bailey and J. L. Moore III, "Emotional Isolation, Depression, and Suicide Among African American Men: Reasons for Concern," in *Linking Lives Across Borders: Gender-Sensitive Practice in International Perspective,* edited by C. Rubin).

It turns out that brokenness is not just depressing. It's a killer.

7.

Hero Without a Spotlight

THE BROKEN American male is doubly tragic. Tragic because he lives an uninspired life, seeing himself as a failure, and tragic because all along, for the most part, he is actually a hero. In reality he is a man of considerable, unsung greatness. He is the only one who never sees it.

The average broken American male, who punishes himself for being a loser, goes out every day and kills himself to feed his children. He gets up at the crack of dawn, sits in traffic, takes abuse from bosses, works to tight deadlines, and travels on red-eyes, all in an effort to support his family. He compromises his dignity to sell his wares. He will accept the abuse of customers in order to do his job and take home a paycheck. He struggles with temptation yet comes home to his wife and tries his best to remain faithful. He gives his hard-earned money to complete strangers in charitable gifts. He thanks G-d for his blessings and prays and goes to church or synagogue. By every meaningful definition of honor and nobility, he is a great man, sacrificing of himself so that others might profit. Only he can't see it, because he has absorbed the poisonous lie that because none of this will end up in a newspaper, because none of it will give him the money for a palace in the Hamptons, because it won't earn him an invitation to spend the night in the Lincoln bedroom, it just doesn't matter. Because no epic movie will be made about his life, it is as if he has not lived. Because no twenty-one-gun salute will be fired in his honor, he has failed at becoming important. The broken American male feels that his existence is analogous to that proverbial tree that falls in the woods. If no one heard it, did it even fall?

On our very first *Shalom in the Home* episode, I found myself counseling a Latino truck driver whose wife had left him after he had an affair. Why would a man throw away the wife he loved, the bride of his youth, and his four children for another woman? Well, he did it because he suffered from low self-esteem. He was approaching his fortieth birthday and he was still a truck driver with a modest income. He had a beautiful young wife who adored him, and his children saw him as a hero. But that wasn't enough for him, since he lived in a culture that judged him by his occupation alone, and where the truck driver was pretty far down the ladder of success. He started going to clubs and bars at night with his friends and leaving his wife at home. One night he met a woman who made him feel good about himself. He felt desirable. The loser now felt like a winner and he started an affair. He was caught by his teenage daughter. His wife, in her humiliation, left him and took the kids. I was called in to see if there could be a reconciliation. I sat with him and this is what I said: "Luis, you see yourself as a loser because you drive a truck. In truth, I am in awe of a man like you. You get up every morning at the crack of dawn and you sit behind that wheel. You drive hundreds of miles and you continue to sit. And you get up the next day and you do it all over again. And why? Because you love your children. You do all that just to feed your babies and put clothing on their backs. That level of sacrifice is awe-inspiring. You're one of the great men of history. Who would even believe that a man could love his children that much? And the tragedy of your life is not only that you cheated on your wife and lost her, but especially that all along you were a hero. You were never ordinary. You were always extraordinary. Your wife saw it. Your children saw it. That's why they loved you so much. You were the only one who didn't see it. And in your blindness, you turned to another woman to feel good about yourself. But how can a man as great as you have succumbed to a fleeting passion? It's completely out of character. You are not a regular guy. You are a man of greatness. And a man of greatness doesn't do lowly things. So go back. Go back to your wife. Beg her forgiveness. Tell her that you now understand that as long as you were devoted to her, you were a big man, as big as the truck you drove. And now that you have betrayed her, you're a small man. Not because you drive a truck, but because you completely mistook that which made you great. And you want her back. And you're sorry. And you'll never do it again."

Such are the consequences of the current epidemic of soullessness in America, an epidemic so widespread that the greatest heroes of all—the brave soldiers of the American military who risk their lives so that others might live—have some of the highest rates of depression, suicide, and spousal abuse. In fact, in June 2007, the *Journal of Epidemiology and Community Health* published a horrifying report that showed that male military veterans were twice as likely to die of suicide as their civilian counterparts. According to a summary of the study by CNN.com (posted on June 11, 2007), for twelve years, more than 104,000 veterans who had served in the armed forces at some time between 1917 and 1994 were compared with more than 216,000 nonveterans. At biggest risk were veterans who were white, those who had gone to college, and those with activity limitations, according to the study.

It is said that tragic statistics like these reflect the horrors of war. No doubt this contributes heavily. But those horrors could perhaps have been mitigated if the veterans at least came home to a grateful public who treated them as actual heroes rather than political pawns. There can be no doubt that one factor that greatly increases the brokenness of our soldiers is that once they take off the uniform—and sometimes while it is still on—they are not treated as the heroes they are in real life. They come home, after risking their lives, to their small houses and their pile of bills, and they feel like failures too.

Imagine that you're an American soldier who spent a year trying not to get blown up in Baghdad just so that complete strangers who don't even appreciate you might live with democracy and freedom. Then you come home. You feel distant from your teenage kids who have become strangers. A whole year of their lives has passed by and you haven't been a part of it. And although they know it's not your fault, still they quietly blame you. And as if bridging that gap weren't enough, you walk into their rooms and they have posters of stupid rock stars and teen heartthrobs on their walls. People with little virtue, who often lead profligate and selfish lives, are your kids' heroes. You try to talk to your kids, but the conversation is drowned out by the noise of the TV and video games, all of which seem more interesting to your kids than you do. You were in the real video game. You experienced war firsthand. But your kids don't see that as particularly heroic. How would they, immersed in a culture where the guy who sings in a stadium and the woman who acts in a movie are considered the real heroes?

You say to yourself, "Wait a minute. I'm these kids' father. I do everything for them. So I ought to be on their wall, not some shallow woman like Jessica Simpson. Second, I'm a soldier who did some real important stuff out there. I risked my life for the American dream of people living free. And I've been replaced by these shallow narcissists?" And you end up feeling not like a hero on his homecoming, but like a loser in whom no one is particularly interested. America rewards not heroism but success.

On the final episode of *Shalom in the Home*'s second season, I was sitting with a twelve-year-old girl in her Rhode Island bedroom. There were posters of teen idols on the wall—movie stars, recording artists, and famous models. I asked her who these people were. One by one she started to name them. I responded, "Oh, I know what their names are. They're famous. I was rather asking who they are to *you*." She looked confused. So I continued. "Here's what I mean. They're on your wall. So no doubt they're related to you in some way. Your uncles, aunts. No?" She laughed and told me that surely I knew that they weren't related to her. So I then asked her the clincher. "Where is the picture of your father on your wall?" Of maybe twenty pictures, her father was nowhere to be found. She acknowledged as much and shrugged her shoulders. It never even occurred to her to have a picture of her dad on the wall. And yet her father was a construction worker who got up every morning at 4 A.M. in order to put in a twelve-hour day to feed and clothe her. And all of it went utterly unnoticed by his twelve-year-old daughter, whose heroine was Lindsay Lohan. No wonder this guy haunted rather than inhabited his home. He had lost any real capacity to inspire his children. In the week that I spent with him, he wandered through his home and interacted with his family like an empty vessel bereft of pride or self-esteem. Because he had little money and had to struggle to make ends meet, he saw himself as a failure, even though he was a hero whose character was orders of magnitude above the shallow attention-seekers on his daughter's bedroom wall.

The ancients regarded the man as the sun and the woman as the moon. Like the sun, the man bestows his light on the woman, who in turn reflects his love and illuminates the night. A man who loves and inspires his wife makes her comely and radiant, and she in turn lights up the entire home. Whenever my wife and I have an argument, which thank G-d is rare unless I do something really stupid, she always reminds me of the adage "A happy wife is a happy life." But what happens when the sun runs out of light? What happens when the husband is just a broken potsherd, bereft of joy or inspiration? Then his wife becomes a

> What happens when the husband is just a broken potsherd, bereft of joy or inspiration? Then his wife becomes a dark planet. And the kids, the little moons who orbit around those large planets, lose their gravitational pull to the large bodies and are cut loose.

dark planet. And the kids, the little moons who orbit around those large planets, lose their gravitational pull to the large bodies and are cut loose.

The family is decentralized as the kids do everything to get out of the house and hang out with their friends. The decentralization of the American family is a direct product of the broken American male. If there's one thing we know about kids it's that they love having fun. They are naturally joyous. They laugh, play, and sing. But when a dad comes home broken and bitter, and when a mom seems permanently on pins and needles, the kids see their home as cold and lifeless. The home becomes a prison, filled with rules and bereft of inspiration. Of course they want out. Every day I receive e-mails from parents around the world asking for advice on how to deal with teenagers who have little interest in being around them or communicating with them. They argue that these kids seem to have no concept of family. But how hypocritical of us parents to blame our children for losing interest in home and family. Were they the ones who made their parents workaholics? Were they the ones who brought the money-is-everything-and-love-is-secondary credo into the home? What are they supposed to do? Sit at home and hang out with the nonfamily?

We have succeeded in creating a culture that makes men feel like achievement machines, measured solely by how much they produce or how much money they make, and in the process we have created a generation of broken men married to lonely women and raising insecure children. And the cycle is intensifying. The self-esteem of each successive American generation seems to be diminishing, such that each becomes more dependent on external accoutrements to make them feel valuable.

As our children pursue flimsy objects and empty titles to prove that they really matter, they too will enter loveless marriages, producing limp and anxiety-ridden children.

As our children pursue flimsy objects and empty titles to prove that they really matter, they too will enter loveless marriages, producing limp and anxiety-ridden children.

We must drill into the hearts and minds of today's men that what makes them special is being a child of G-d. Possessing a spark of the divine, a fragment of the infinite, confers value upon us. Money does not make the man. We are not oxen born to the yoke. We are men, created in the divine image, beloved of the Creator. We are husbands and fathers. We are loved for the quality of our relationships and not the quantity of our bank accounts. Communities must learn to honor men who are devoted husbands and fathers rather than rich businessmen.

I believe that American men are quickly rushing to a precipice from which it will be difficult to pull back. In the immediate future, American men will continue to go to college and find meaning not through being conquistadors of the mind but through being conquerors of women. Tom Wolfe chronicled this brilliantly in his novel *I Am Charlotte Simmons,* a searing indictment of the grotesque and appalling misogyny on the American college campus. Men will continue to delay marriage mostly until their early thirties, as they put career before commitment and the pursuit of wealth before the pursuit of a worthy companion. They will become fathers much later in life and grandfathers nearly at the end of their lives, thereby greatly compromising their ability to connect with children, so great will be the age gap. They will eventually marry women whom they will not be able to fully appreciate and love, bereft as they are of real love for anything other than great material success. When they read they will read business books with the potential to expand their wallets rather than historical or philosophical works that can expand their minds and enrich their spirits. They will continue to lack core convictions that could serve as an inspiration to their children, since all they will crave in life is to impress their neighbors. Their families will continue to crumble without leadership, since the man of the house expends all his imagination and creativity on work and arrives home a vacant husk, good only for vegging in front of ESPN. And in the absence of any real masculine presence, the wife will be forced to become the man of the house, as so often happens in single-parent homes, thereby robbing the home of its essential nurturing presence.

The masculinization of women, which we'll discuss later, is another crisis of the family. Children are being raised in a harsh environment, one run by threats and guilt rather than love and caring. Wives are learning to close their hearts out of the pain of not feeling loved by their husbands. They are deducing that to be vulnerable and open is not virtuous but naïve. They are learning to be as hard-edged as their husbands, embittered by the belief that they give much more than they receive.

In many homes, the father is the disciplinarian and the mother is cast in the nurturing role. It need not be so. The roles can be reversed. But both roles must be present if children are to receive the twin advantages of strength and tenderness, iron resolve accompanied by a soft and understanding heart. But what happens when both father and mother parent out of harsh discipline and a lack of patience? What happens when both are embittered by life and lack the inner reserves to parent with patience? The kids are going to recoil from their parents' sternness and sink into themselves. They'll appear like zombies and offer their parents monosyllabic responses to questions. The parents will then feel rejected, and the cycle will only intensify.

In an unhealthy home, children witness parents who have ceased to be lovers and who have instead become partners, treating their shared life as a chore rather than a gift, a burden rather than a blessing.

In a healthy home, children witness affection between father and mother. In an unhealthy home, children witness parents who have ceased to be lovers and who have instead become partners, treating their shared life as a chore rather than a gift, a burden rather than a blessing.

The home continues to decentralize and disintegrate, as father teaches mother and children to find satisfaction outside of the home rather than in it. All this will only get worse. Divorce and infidelity will increase beyond their already impossibly high numbers as husbands and wives drift apart, become strangers to each other, and find comfort and validation in the arms of strangers. Already between two-thirds and three-quarters of all divorces in the United States are initiated by women, so dissatisfied are they with husbands who can neither love nor appreciate them, and that number will continue to escalate. Likewise, the number of wives having affairs—seeking other men within their marriage because, for whatever reason, they cannot divorce—has gone up higher than ever before. They either pursue or agree to be drawn in by men who show them attention, desperate as they are to feel special to someone, yet convinced that that someone will never be their own husband.

8.

The Curse of Ambition

A FEW summers ago I visited Yellowstone National Park with my family and my twenty-one-year-old nephew. We all went to bathe in the mineral hot springs of the Boiling River. It was toward dusk. When we arrived, three men were sitting together in a crevice of the river and we joined them. My nephew told them that he was from Miami and they said that they were from Chicago. The four immediately broke into a discussion of the recent NBA play-off game between the Heat and the Bulls. I was fascinated to watch what ensued. Here were a bunch of men gathered in a natural hot tub, strangers to each other. There seemed to be no immediate point of connection save that of sports. There was no other place they could meet. We men were sitting in one of the most beautiful places on earth, but we could not connect through the wonders of nature or the inspiration of exotic wildlife. We could connect only as combatants. Each side bragged about how good their team was. In this case, my nephew and I were the victors because our team had recently defeated their team in the play-offs. But no doubt we would meet on the battle-field again in the future, either directly or through our proxies. Because duel we must.

The American male is broken because he is trained to feel good about himself only in relation to his colleagues. He is in a permanent race to be well regarded by his peers—better yet, to surpass his peers. His self-esteem is established not through some congenital gift but from having overtaken some of his colleagues in the rat race of life. He is entirely dependent on external markers. He cannot point to something intrinsic within himself that gives him joy or pride. He cannot identify anything permanent that makes him special or establishes his uniqueness. Rather, his identity comes from the place he occupies in society, in juxtaposition to others.

Even winning cannot be enjoyed, because it is always accompanied by the knowledge that competitors are gaining on him. He lives in the permanent fear of being overtaken, which causes him to race harder until he drops. Calvin Coolidge famously said, "The business of America is business." America is the greatest capitalist power on earth, and the essence of capitalism is competition. Fair enough. But when capitalism comes to dominate all other human aspirations, it becomes soulless and makes men into nonfeeling machines. The loss of an inner identity, the inability to feel good about oneself regardless of one's external condition, is completely toxic. First it denies the broken American male any real possibility of companionship and guarantees his isolation and loneliness. His companions are his competitors. When they succeed he cannot be happy for them. Indeed, it kills him; as Gore Vidal confessed, "Whenever a friend succeeds, a little something in me dies." When others pass the broken man by, becoming more materially successful, it makes him feel even more unimportant. So he becomes consumed not with making himself successful but with wishing others ill. He cannot abide other people's success, and therefore he cannot have any real friends. Which leads to the second toxic result. The broken American male spends more of his time talking about other

> When capitalism comes to dominate all other human aspirations, it becomes soulless and makes men into nonfeeling machines.

people and scrutinizing their lives than mastering his own. The more his peers go up, the more he goes down. Their success is his failure. He becomes a gossip because hearing, or sharing, bad news about other people makes him feel good about himself. But his enjoyment of other people's travails, however venomous, is not what ultimately pulls him down. Rather, it's the fact that he spends so much time obsessing over others' misfortunes that he ends up neglecting his own inner potential.

There are three levels of discourse. The lowest is a discussion of things. The middle is a discussion of people. And the highest is a discussion of ideas. But what profit will modern men find today in a discussion of ideas? Will it lead to more money? Will it bring them a Ferrari or a yacht? Will it win them the respect of their peers? I once saw a bumper sticker that said, "The greatest things in life are not things." How true, but how alien to the broken American male, for whom things define his self-worth and for whom the discussion of the neighbors has become an obsession.

Once, in the old country of Russia, a tailor came to see the rabbi of the town. "Rebbe," he said, "it's not fair, and you have to do something about it. Mottel, a new tailor from Kiev, moved into our town and he's stealing all my business. And as if that were not bad enough, he's a *ganiv,* a thief. For every inch of tailoring, I put in four stitches, but he puts in only three. I use pure wool, he uses a blend. I spend a full hour doing hems. He does the same job in a rushed twenty minutes." The rabbi looked at the man and said, "It seems to me that if you spent as much time focusing on your own business as you do on his, the success of your business wouldn't be in doubt."

> The voice of ambition admonishes rather than inspires, bullies rather than encourages, degrades rather than sustains.

Male ambition in our time has become an angel of destruction. Whereas once ambition was something that beckoned a boy to distinguish himself in some great enterprise and become a man, today that same voice terrorizes men, emasculating them and making them feel like boys in an arena of men. The voice of ambition admonishes rather than inspires, bullies rather than encourages, degrades rather than sustains. It does not inspire us to develop our potential but mocks us for having failed to do so. Once, ambition was something that went before a man, showing him visions of his own potential grandeur and beckoning him to follow. Today, ambition lies not in front of man, as if it were a rope pulling him up, but behind him, like a cattle prod pushing him from behind.

This transformation took place when ambition stopped being about developing one's gifts and became instead about competing to outstrip one's peers. In previous generations, ambition focused on making the most of our uniqueness. But in our day it has become about amassing property. I have seen **Quantity has come to define quality.** this in my own work on numerous occasions. Whereas once I was happy to write books that changed lives, even if they were not huge sellers, I have since come to understand that the market values only books that sell. Quantity has come to define quality.

I have always been ambitious. And some might say that's a good thing. But for me ambition results not only from a desire to leave a positive mark on the world, but from a desire to prove myself to the world. There is a world of difference between them. The former is liberating, the latter incarcerating. **What profit is it to a man to feel that without profit he is not a man?** The former is selfless, the latter narcissistic. The former invites others to make their mark as well. The latter seethes with envy upon witnessing another's gifts being recognized.

Ambition is a demonic spirit that haunts men from their earliest days, telling them that if they don't achieve, they fail, if they don't stand tall among their peers, they are pygmies. What profit is it to a man to feel that without profit he is not a man?

Yes, there is healthy and unhealthy ambition. The healthy variety comes from strength and from a belief that each of us is born with a unique gift to bequeath to the world that we have an obligation to contribute. The unhealthy variety is when we feel that we are internally dark, with nothing to contribute, and therefore are always seeking the external spotlight. We are ambitious out of weakness. We seek to substantiate ourselves out of a sense of our own nothingness. The man who experiences the luminescence of his own soul will never feel dark. Rather, he will seek to share his light with the world. But the man who feels dark will forever be dependent on the external spotlight in order to feel alive. And this is unhealthy ambition of the worst kind.

It was this kind of ambition John Milton wrote about in *Paradise Lost:* "But what will not ambition and revenge descend to? Who aspires must down as low as high he soared."

9.

The American Dream
Becomes a Nightmare

SINCE I was a small boy growing up in Los Angeles, I have heard the expression "the American dream." My father, an immigrant from Iran, came for that dream, as did millions of immigrants before him. The American dream held out for many the promise of a bright economic future. America was the country of limitless possibilities where a man or woman could come with nothing and support a family with dignity and material aplenty. Unlike Europe, with its class-ridden society, in America it didn't matter how you were born. Noble birth paled beside the true virtue of the self-made man. America had no aristocracy but was a meritocracy where a man, by the sweat of his brow, could raise himself up from poverty and live like a king.

But the American dream has become perverted into the endless pursuit of material success. To be sure, the American dream still works. Like you, I know many people who started with nothing and ended up wealthy. And even if we're not all superrich, the American dream has allowed our country to have the highest standard of living in the history of the world. But what is often overlooked is how, in our time, that dream has been translated into a *purely* economic vision. The ugly underbelly of the American dream is the insatiability it fosters. How enough is never enough.

The ugly underbelly of the American dream is the insatiability it fosters.

At the beginning of the Bible, Adam and Eve are placed by G-d in the Garden of Eden. But what makes the garden paradise is not the beautiful trees, flowers, and waterfalls. Rather, it's paradise because Adam and Eve are satisfied with the life they live inside it. Their satisfaction with their station in life, and indeed their satisfaction with each other, is what makes the garden perfect. G-d tells them that they can eat the fruit of every tree in the garden save one. They focus not on what they can't consume, but on what they can. And they are happy.

But along comes the serpent and injects his cold poison into this idyllic life. He says to Eve, "Well, it's pretty cool that you get to eat from every tree. But what about that tree over there that's off-limits? Don't you want to know what that fruit tastes like as well? How can you be content with one tree being forbidden?" He gets her to focus not on what she has, but on what she doesn't have. Eve in turn passes on this insatiability and lack of contentment to Adam, and soon enough the two of them are utterly corrupted, unable to be content. They are cast from the Garden of Eden. But this need not be understood as a physical eviction. Rather, the Garden of Eden ceased to seem a paradise to them because suddenly enough was not enough.

The ancient rabbis point out that the serpent represents insatiability because snakes eat the dust of the earth. There is plenty of it, but it is never filling. Similarly, the serpent represents the American consumer who devours everything and still never feels full. It is the man who is given unending love by his wife but still never feels satisfied and ogles other women. It is the man whom G-d has blessed with a comfortable life and income, who focuses not on what he has but on what others have and lives in envy and covetousness. For many American men, the American dream has become a reincarnation of the ancient serpent, permanently poisoning them with the venom of insatiability and discontent.

How could we have so corrupted the American dream? How can we have so debased this beautiful country by defining its highest aspirations as the incessant grasping for money? Do we really believe that George Washington bravely crossed the Delaware for a mutual fund? Did Jefferson write in the Declaration of Independence of the incessant pursuit of riches or of the pursuit of happiness? Did Revolutionary War troops walk barefoot in the frozen wasteland of Valley Forge in the hope that they would eventually wear Ferragamo loafers? And did the brave GIs of D-day storm the beaches of Normandy in Higgins landing craft in the belief that they would eventually drive Lexuses? The American dream was a dream not of cash but of freedom. Not of stocks and bonds but of liberty and democracy. How could we have so defiled that dream by making ourselves slaves to purchasing power alone?

> Do we really believe that George Washington bravely crossed the Delaware for a mutual fund? Did Jefferson write in the Declaration of Independence of the incessant pursuit of riches or of the pursuit of happiness? Did Revolutionary War troops walk barefoot in the frozen wasteland of Valley Forge in the hope that they would eventually wear Ferragamo loafers?

10.

Soulless Capitalism

THE EVISCERATION of the modern American male has been exacerbated by the corrosive forces of modern, soulless capitalism. At its heart, capitalism is a system that thrives on and exploits human insecurity by fostering incessant human competition. It pits every human being—but especially men—against one another in a never-ending race for status and riches. It is a system that both lures and taunts men with a vision of potential success. Immense treasure can be yours if only you work your guts out to earn it.

Capitalism is a system in which men are judged by what they have and not what they are. Its basis is the unending amassing of property. It breeds dissatisfaction and fosters insatiability, promising that we will all feel better about ourselves if we just submit to a little more accumulation and ownership.

I once counseled a fifteen-year-old girl who suffered from life-threatening anorexia. Her fragile body was down to eighty-seven pounds. She was thin as a stick. Still, she barely ate. When I was called in to help reverse this potentially fatal trend, I asked her why she wanted to be thinner still. She explained that, like many anorexics, she heard a constant voice in her head whispering that if only she lost a couple more pounds, she'd look great. She'd be beautiful. She'd be loved. She called this voice ED, for Eating Disorder. ED spoke softly, with the tone of a comforter, even as it ravaged her body and destroyed her health.

Anorexia afflicts mostly women. But it struck me as I listened to this innocent soul that we men were not much different. We too hear a constant voice that gives us no rest and no peace. It is the voice of capitalism forever promising unparalleled rewards for effort. If only we put in one more hour at the office, we too will be special. We too will be loved. Like ED, the voice sounds comforting and reassuring, even as it destroys our lives.

The genesis of this voice is the idea that each man begins life empty—undistinguished, anonymous—and will acquire a name for himself by placing himself at the center of an ever-expanding circle of possessions. It posits life and human existence as a race to the finish in which the man who ends up with the most money wins. In so doing, it also pits all men against each other in financial combat, thereby subverting the religious message that all humanity is one family and all are equally G-d's children. Capitalism also creates a system of haves and have-nots, those who are talented at making money and those who are not. And it is based on a deprivation mentality: The world consists of limited resources, finite wealth. Wealth is amassed by taking it from those who have it by outperforming them in the sectors in which they have been successful. Since the world is a pie of limited resources, grab as big a piece of the pie as possible, because there isn't enough to go around. It is a system of inequality in which, at best, the haves will condescend to support the have-nots with handouts.

Now don't get the wrong impression. I am a capitalist and believe in capitalism as the only viable economic system. But I recognize that the reason capitalism works, and has been the most reliable engine for human advancement in the history of the world, is because it admits that most people feel empty on the inside and are prepared to compensate and find human significance through the acquisition of property. In order for capitalism to function, it needs the broken egos of those who feel inadequate. That's why capitalism has never inspired saintly figures to amass wealth. True religious saints, or sincere philosophers, for example, don't give a toss for money. They're not broken on the inside, so they don't need compensation on the outside. There is the famous story of Alexander the Great and his meeting with the philosopher Diogenes. The philosopher was reading on the side of the road when Alexander the Great walked up to him and said, "I am Alexander, king of all the world." Diogenes replied, "I am Diogenes, the Cynic." The celebrated conqueror asked if there was anything he could do for the renowned thinker. Diogenes responded, "Get out of my light." All he needed was to continue studying, not the gifts of kings. If your life has spiritual or intellectual meaning, then it doesn't require a yacht or a limo to lend it significance.

Capitalism has never inspired saintly figures to amass wealth.

Capitalism is not about survival or having enough, which is why the most successful people in a capitalist society continue to amass wealth well after they have more money than they could ever spend. As Aristotle Onassis said, "After a certain point, money is meaningless. It ceases to be the goal. The game is what counts." And by the game, he meant, of course, the constant competition to outdo your neighbor.

The consumer society exists as a layer just above capitalism. It heightens insecurities and feelings of inadequacy by subtly reminding you that if you don't have valuable objects you will be empty. The two, of course, feed off each other. Without money you can't buy things. And without things, you're nothing, or no-thing. The purpose of money is to acquire those things that will make you important. Capitalism addresses, therefore, what anthropologists term the *reptilian brain,* the least developed part of our psyche, which determines value by size alone. The bigger the better.

A capitalist consumer society can only survive if people spend money. Now, how do we get people to spend money? Well, they will always spend money on life's necessities. They require food, clothing, and shelter in order to survive. But a reliance on staples is only the beginning. What is needed to keep the capitalist engine running is people who live for luxuries, or better yet, people who feel that luxuries are actually necessities.

What is needed to keep the capitalist engine running is people who live for luxuries, or better yet, people who feel that luxuries are actually necessities.

A man may need a watch to tell the time. But what if that man, in addition to needing to know what time it is, also has low self-esteem? The watch he buys will not only tell the time but will also be made of gold so that he can impress his friends. His ownership of an expensive timepiece tells the world he's a success. Without the gold watch, he feels naked, as if he doesn't exist. He has no dignity. No one recognizes his name. But if he turns his name into Rolex, if people know him not as Harry but as the guy who drives a Bentley, then he feels like a million bucks. Without fancy designer labels with Italian or French names, he feels bare and exposed. So he buys expensive things in order to make himself feel clothed, and for him these things are not luxuries but necessities. They are the currency with which he purchases self-esteem.

Thus, in order to keep people spending, we have to continue to make them feel inadequate. If they feel satisfied and happy, they won't need to continue exerting themselves to be happy. If they feel permanently empty, then they'll stuff themselves with the latest fashions, cars, and electronics whether they need them or not.

Capitalism has people replacing things that are not worn out or broken. It's about feeling needy even when you're not in need.

Our society is built around making people feel small and unimportant so that they'll kill themselves working and buying those things that will make them feel substantial. Capitalism has people replacing things that are not worn out or broken. It's about feeling needy even when you're not in need.

Central to capitalism, therefore, is instilling within the individual a feeling of permanent insignificance. It shows you the *Forbes* 400 list. Which you're not on. It shows you the newest Lexus. Which you can't afford. It shows you that perfect model on the catwalk. Whom, if you're a man, you can never date, or, if you're a woman, you can never resemble. In short, it keeps us in a permanent state of longing. It fosters within us a permanent sense of inadequacy, which in turn leads to a permanent state of insatiability. *That little house you live in, how could you ever be happy with it? Come on. That's not living. A small house means you're a small man. Why, just look at your friend Bob who lives in a mansion. And look at how fat and ugly you are. But if you buy this diet book and have that cosmetic surgery, you'll be a winner.* The voice whispers, "Just one more hour at the office, just one more hour on the treadmill, and you will have made it." And the voice never shuts up.

Once again, I believe wholeheartedly in capitalism. I am not a socialist, and much less so am I a communist, G-d forbid. Communism is an ineffective and often evil system that erases individuality, leaves people in poverty, and subjects them to governmental surveillance and control. But because capitalism by its very nature preys on human weakness, it *must* be balanced by spirituality. The capitalist society that has killed off G-d can become as dark and as toxic as a communist system that has done the same.

For every capitalist whisper that we are nobodies who must work to become somebodies, there must be the balancing voice of religion thundering the belief that we are born children of G-d and are therefore of infinite value. For every capitalist sentiment that tells us that we are created in the image of our job titles, there must be the

> For every capitalist sentiment that tells us that we are created in the image of our job titles, there must be the overriding voice of religion reminding us that we are created in the image of G-d.

overriding voice of religion reminding us that we are created in the image of G-d.

The subordination of spiritual pursuits to capitalist interests is where America has gone seriously astray and broken the flower of masculine youth. Who among us today can really say that we strive for enlightenment as much as we strive for enrichment? Who among us can claim that we wish for spiritual growth as much as we wish for the growth of our stock portfolio? And who among us would be so brash as to deny that we define security as a comfortable retirement nest egg rather than strong family bonds?

Who among us today can really say that we strive for enlightenment as much as we strive for enrichment?

I became rabbi at Oxford University at the tender age of twenty-two. Two months later my first child was born, and over the next few years many more children were born, thank G-d. I had little time to focus on financial security. I worked my guts out on behalf of my students, putting on exciting programs, lectures, and classes. Then one day my wife came to me and said that our financial situation was in crisis. I was responsible for raising all the money for our organization and I wasn't keeping up with our expenses. I was numb with worry. We were running out of cash. We had to pay rent on a large student center and didn't have the money. I couldn't sleep. In desperation, I called a rabbi I respected and virtually cried on the phone that I had no security. I'll never forget his words. Very calmly he said to me, "You need money, I understand that. But don't confuse that with security, for money cannot provide security. The only security we have in this life is knowing where our children will be in ten years' time." What a brilliant response. He was right, and I was comforted.

In America today we have just the opposite of security: money in the bank, and our kids out on the streets.

In America today we have just the opposite of security: money in the bank, and our kids out on the streets. We live with the illusion of security. For all our stocks and bonds, we don't even know if we'll be married in a couple years' time.

America is a religious country. It believes in G-d and even proclaims that belief on its currency. That amalgamation of G-d and capitalism is the formula by which capitalism might be saved. America needs a soulful capitalism. In a soulful environment, men are made to feel, from their earliest years, that they have something of infinite value within them. So they don't have to work their guts out in order to become important. Rather, because they are born with such infinite potential, they have an obligation to both themselves and the world to translate that potential into actuality. This is an empowering message because it places the locus of the male's importance squarely within himself. The soulless capitalist message, however, begins from the opposite view. Men are born undistinguished and unimportant. They are vacuous and empty on the inside. At least little girls are born pretty and with the power to attract a man. They are genetically worthy. But the man is born empty. And what he does on this earth, and especially what he accumulates, will determine the extent of his significance. This is a soul-destroying message that guarantees not only that the man in question will live with lifelong insecurities, but also that what he achieves will never bring him contentment and happiness. How could it? There is no bottom to the hole inside. There is no intrinsic self-esteem or innate sense of self-worth that could serve as a foundation upon which his later achievements can rest. So it all sinks straight into the eternal quicksand of self-doubt.

The American victory in the Cold War and the disintegration of the Soviet Union proved communism to be a vulgar and empty lie. When I grew up in 1970s America, we all lived in mortal fear of the Soviet Union. America fought a long and soul-destroying war in Vietnam in the belief that if we didn't stop the spread of communism, its cancer would permeate the globe. Then one day, the whole communist house came tumbling down with barely a push from the outside and we discovered that, for all its lofty rhetoric, it was a house of cards. People need a personal incentive to produce. A system that robs them of individuality and makes them into an indistinguishable mass will never inspire them to maximize their potential. Worse, communism leads to tyranny. But unbridled capitalism, bereft of the religious message that man is possessed of an infinite soul—which must be nurtured not only through worship, community, and family, but also through being made to feel heroic by attaining personal and not just professional greatness—is nearly as destructive. Like communism, it too robs men of their uniqueness and individuality by emphasizing that it is what they own rather than what they are that is significant.

The principal cause of the ruination of today's men is a culture that teaches them to use money as the currency by which to purchase self-esteem. Capitalism is a system that recognizes that the most effective engine of economic advancement is one that rewards individual effort and achievement. Communism may be a more moral economic system insofar as it provides according to need rather than ability. But its immorality, not to mention its ineffectiveness, lies precisely in its inability to recognize the human desire, indeed the human need, for recognition. People work not just to eat, but also to distinguish themselves.

> **The principal cause of the ruination of today's men is a culture that teaches them to use money as the currency by which to purchase self-esteem.**

Capitalism is limited by its failure to recognize that man is not just a body but a spirit. Man is not *Homo sapiens* but *Homo spiritus*. Capitalism that is soulless, that only caters to the material needs of the body rather than the spiritual needs of the soul, will destroy humanity as thoroughly as communism. Which explains why America is a land of such profound contradiction: the greatest and richest country in the world with the most shallow and vulgar culture; a place with the highest standard of living but also some of the highest rates of depression.

For about a year I hosted a radio show that aired in Utah and was geared toward women. We were able to deal with issues that few others explored, especially on a monster 50-kilowatt station. I talked often about the effect of soulless capitalism on men. The discussion resonated with the women listening, especially the married ones. One by one they would call in to speak of how their finances directly impacted their husbands' happiness. When it came to the women, if the family did not have a lot of money, they felt the squeeze. Theirs was a practical concern about how to pay the bills. But for the men, it was different. Financial problems ate away at their very selves. Their confidence eroded. They did not question their professional acumen but their entire existence and they sunk into a depression from which their wives could not easily lift them.

Then one day I took this idea of feeling worthless further. The Talmud relates how the two scholarly academies of the House of Hillel and the House of Shamai had a debate on the question of whether it was good or not for man to have been born. I asked my listeners, "If you had a choice whether or not to have been born, what would you choose?" Three calls from women in rapid succession all affirmed their desire to have been born. But the fourth call was from a man and it was easily the most memorable moment I have ever had on radio. He related how, at that very moment, he was perched on a cliff in his car and his plan was to drive off and kill himself. Just as he was about to floor the accelerator, he decided that he would turn on the radio and look for a sign that might bring him back from the brink. Improbably, he found us, a women's station! He heard the discussion and decided to call in. "I'm standing here moments before I kill myself, and I'm not bluffing. I would never have chosen to have been born, and now I'm choosing to die. I was a cop. I did everything right. I risked my life for other people and I got paid very little for it. I always struggled financially. And then one day the department downsized and they let me go. And for the past four months I have looked at a mountain of bills that I can't pay and I have slipped to a very dark place. I have a loving wife and she's done everything to get me to believe in myself. But I'm a failure who can't even support his family. I have no reason to live and I'm going to kill myself."

He was forty-four years old. What a waste of a precious life! More important, he had a wife and three children he needed to take care of and who loved him. I proceeded carefully. I told him he sounded like a good and honorable man. A hero. "Right now, you're an inspiration to all of us for the choice you made to serve and protect others. G-d bless you. But if you kill yourself, you'll substantiate the big lie that a man is only worth as much as the amount of money he makes. If you take your life, you will have let down not just yourself and your family, but all us men who struggle to find self-worth in a life devoted to something other than the endless pursuit of capital. But if you back your car up and choose life, you will be a hero to your wife and your children and an inspiration to the rest of us struggling men. You will show that you have infinite value as a human being and infinite worth as a child of G-d, which no pile of bills can ever take away. And you will give that lesson to your children." While still on the phone he promised me to go home and seek help.

Three weeks later I received a letter from his wife telling me that together they were seeing a counselor several times a week. She thanked me for saving her husband's life. I wrote back to her that the idea that I saved him was absurd. She had saved him. It was the knowledge that he was not just an empty bank account but a man who was loved by a devoted woman and their children that had brought him back from the brink. It was just a matter of reminding him how precious he was.

11.

Two Great Lies

WHY CAN'T women save the men in their lives? Why are so many women failing at boosting their husbands' confidence and self-esteem? The answer lies in the fact that nearly all women today feel inadequate. And one sinking ship cannot rescue another.

American culture in modern times is built on two great lies. The first lie is for men. It says you're only important if you have money. The second is for women. It says you're only special if you're young, thin, and beautiful. With both sexes consuming such lies wholesale, you have one messed-up society.

> **American culture in modern times is built on two great lies. The first lie is for men. It says you're only important if you have money. The second is for women. It says you're only special if you're young, thin, and beautiful.**

Just as soulless capitalism preys on men's insecurity by making them feel like failures, it preys on women's weaknesses by attacking them where they are most vulnerable: their perception of their own looks.

Just as the consumer society needs to make men feel that without expensive baubles they are worthless, it requires women to feel permanently inadequate so they will do anything to look and feel better about themselves. Our society inspires women to shell out cash constantly by telling them their very being—their appearance—is not good enough. Not thin enough, not pretty enough, not young enough, not tanned enough, not fit enough, not trim enough, and not toned enough. The assault on women is particularly mean-spirited and below the belt because it strikes at a woman's very person. It tells her that she is just not attractive, that no one is naturally drawn to her, and that many women look much better than she does. Why shouldn't she be ashamed?

As an American Jewish boy, I was raised on images of the Holocaust. From my earliest years I remember watching documentaries at school and seeing picture books filled with the emaciated inmates of Auschwitz, Buchenwald, and Bergen-Belsen. The hideous sight of bellies bloated in starvation and rib cages that jutted out underneath shriveled skin was enough to make a lifelong impression on a boy who would have liked to believe that the world was innocent.

Who would have thought that the richest country in the history of the world would be producing young women who look like concentration camp victims? According to a 2001 booklet published by the National Institute of Mental Health, about 4 percent of all women in America suffer from an eating disorder. This means that about four out of a hundred women in this country of boundless plenty are starving themselves, sometimes to death. Is it possible that this country has so undermined a young woman's confidence in herself that she would allow her body to wither to Nazi-death-camp proportions in order to somehow become worthy?

Is it possible that this country has so undermined a young woman's confidence in herself that she would allow her body to wither to Nazi-death-camp proportions in order to somehow become worthy?

And there's more than just alarming stories about teenage girls with eating disorders. America is a country where grown women, at an age when you would expect a certain measure of wisdom, hate themselves so much that they inject poison—literally—into their foreheads in order to erase lines. Lines on a woman's face were once a badge of honor. They represented experience—having lived and having loved, having learned and having felt emotion. But in today's culture of permanent aesthetic inadequacy, they represent ugliness.

Years ago, when I was rabbi at Oxford, a husband and wife came to see me concering a big argument they were having. The husband wanted his wife, who was committed to looking completely natural, to wear a touch of makeup. The wife adamantly refused. I told the wife, "Marriage is important and being attractive to each other is important. If your husband told you to do something that isn't you, something highly unnatural, like have a nose job, you could tell him he's a shallow man. But makeup is different. It doesn't change who you are, but just highlights your beauty, so long as you don't put too much of it on. And if drawing attention to your beautiful features makes your husband happy, then so be it."

The procedures that women are getting today are very different. They do not enhance beauty; they mask personality. Botox is not a neutral beauty enhancer. It is insidious because it compromises personality. It is the personification of the lie that a woman is beautiful through her skin rather than through her charm and character. Botox makes it impossible for a woman to show emotion in her face. She can't raise her eyebrows when she is surprised or furrow her brow when she is perplexed.

> The procedures that women are getting today are very different. They do not enhance beauty; they mask personality.

Often I appear as a guest on other people's television shows. Now the art of being a good TV guest lies in being able to read the facial expressions of your host. Do they want you to join in? Do they want you to stop and listen? Is the question they are asking rhetorical? You can't know those things without studying the face of your host. So, there I was on a TV show in Canada. The host was a woman in her fifties. She was Botoxed to death from her hairline down. Her skin was as smooth as a baby's. But it was also completely dead. I was promoting one of my books. She looked at the camera and said, "Are Canadian families as troubled as American families?" I looked right at her for guidance. Was it a question? The beginning of a statement? I had no idea. I could not read a single thing from her face.

Botox procedures may compromise a woman's natural grace and subvert expressions of personality, but face-tightening surgeries make women resemble aliens from another planet. I have seen women whose eyes have been pulled to such opposite sides of their heads that they look like characters out of *Star Wars*.

I believe wholeheartedly that no group in America hates itself more than women. No group in America is as prepared as women are to cut themselves and injure their bodies in order to conform to an externally imposed standard of beauty.

Sociologists have long pointed out how, over time, persecuted minorities internalize the hatred shown them. This self-hatred often manifests itself in the form of contempt for ethnic features. Jews getting nose jobs and blacks bleaching their skin are classic cases in point. A few years ago my wife and I traveled to Dakar, Senegal, in sub-Saharan Africa, the poorest region on earth. And yet as we traveled on the roads we saw giant billboards advertising skin bleach. That's how much these poor souls had absorbed the lie that their dark skin made them ugly.

> I believe wholeheartedly that no group in America hates itself more than women.

But American women are even more tragic. No group embodies self-loathing more than they do. They are even prepared to surgically implant foreign packets filled with silicone or saline into their chests in order to make them heave a few more inches for men. In many instances, these implants can kill them. And still women spend thousands of dollars for breast-augmentation surgery. And don't tell me they do this for themselves rather than for men. If it weren't for the male obsession with large breasts, what woman would feel self-conscious about having small ones? Women are prepared to reduce the sensitivity in their nipples and breasts and lessen their ability to experience sensation in a vital sexual organ just to make them larger. Wow. That's a lot of hatred.

When I was close to Michael Jackson I asked him the obvious question. Who told you you were so ugly that you would feel the need to forever tinker with your appearance? He told me, as he has told others, that when he was a teenager his father made him feel very self-conscious about his looks. And it always amused me that society held up Michael as an example of a troubled individual, what with all the plastic surgery he's had. Perhaps it's true. But doesn't that mean that women are just a small step behind the King of Pop?

In the winter of 2006 I was invited to address a women's philanthropic convention in Florida. I lectured about the need to reverse feminine self-loathing. I decried the Tupperware-style Botox parties and all the chin lifts women were undergoing. When I finished and stepped down from the podium, the organizer of the event said to me, "Don't you know who you're talking to? Every single woman in this room has had work done. You'll just alienate them." I responded, "Better that they be alienated from me than be alienated from themselves. Better that they hate my guts than hate their own guts. For how much do you have to hate yourself if you're going to have surgery when you're not sick?"

> How much do you have to hate yourself if you're going to have surgery when you're not sick?

And it starts so young. Few women in society are as self-conscious about their looks as coeds on campus, which undermines their whole reason for being there: it's about their brains, not their busts. Most of us believe that sending our daughters off to college will safeguard their future and increase their self-esteem. In fact, for a great many young women the campus environment serves to foster

> This constitutes the great American lie for women: that their value is inversely proportional to their dress size.

permanent anxiety about their looks and concern that rejecting the sexual game-playing will label them as unpopular prudes.

In March of 2007, DePauw University took the extraordinary step of expelling the national sorority Delta Zeta after the group kicked out twenty-three of its members for being overweight and "socially awkward." Universities are supposed to be places where women can get an education. But these students were more concerned about becoming the Barbie cutouts that campus men supposedly prefer. This constitutes the great American lie for women: that their value is inversely proportional to their dress size.

12.

Twin Brokenness

How can women who live with a permanent sense of inadequacy possibly heal men? They can't. Is it any wonder, then, that relations between the sexes are at an all-time low? Can two people who have no love for themselves possibly love each other? Can a man or a woman who is cracked and splintered possibly make their spouse feel whole?

To be sure, the brokenness engendered by our soulless society affects men and women differently. For men, the sense of personal inadequacy strikes to the very core of their being. Feminine inadequacy still allows a woman to feel that she is beautiful on the inside, while men are taught to feel that their entire existence is a big zero. The man who is not professionally successful and commercially triumphant is ugly on the inside and the outside. For what woman would date a man who is a loser, even if he is handsome? The man without money is taught to feel ugly in every respect. People like him but don't respect him. They pity him. He's invisible. He may as well not exist. Which is why men today find it so hard to bond with one another.

We rarely see men actually talking to one another. When was the last time a woman heard her husband say, "I'm going over to Chuck's house to talk about my life"? On the contrary, men only *do* things together. They watch football together, they go to Atlantic City together, they go fishing together, they have a drink together. But share their emotions with one another? Fugedaboutit. And why won't men talk, even to each other? Because when you think you're a loser, all you ever feel is pain. So better to bury it in incessant activity and the numbness that comes from watching a screen.

But women, even if they feel ugly and inadequate, still find comradeship with one another. Women love unburdening themselves emotionally to one another.

Why does the capitalist sense of inadequacy affect men and women so differently? It has to do with how men and women are judged.

Even after decades of feminism, women are still judged primarily by their appearance. Men especially are drawn to women by their physical looks. A woman can be sitting with her friends in a restaurant. A man looks across the room. He knows nothing about her. Not her name, not her hobbies, not her beliefs, not her passions. But he is drawn to her by her appearance alone. In this sense, women are afforded the freedom of being human beings. They can just be. Even as they sit utterly passive and idle, doing absolutely nothing but breathing, the world is still drawn to them. Feminine comeliness is itself a magnet.

But men are afforded no such luxury. They are not allowed to just be. They have to do. The world is not drawn to men by their appearance but by their success. A guy might be sitting in a bar and look really handsome. But if he comes across as a loser, women will run as if he had the plague. On the contrary, it is the balding billionaire holding an outsized cigar (after all, size does matter) to whom women are drawn. Danny DeVito can get virtually any woman he wants. But what woman who looks like DeVito can do the same with men? Men become attractive, enhance their magnetism, and appeal to others through what they do rather than through what they are. And this is why the subtle capitalist message that they are giant zeros strikes so deep. Without success, they have nothing going for them. Only if they prove themselves by making a lot of money, amassing power, and achieving fame will they begin to matter.

From their earliest years men are stuck in this constant loop of having to achieve. From proving themselves as boys on the sports field to being assessed by how pretty their girlfriends are in their early teens, young men are always judged by what lies outside of them. As they get older, it only gets worse. Soon, the university they are accepted to will determine how important they are, as will their first jobs out of college. And when they finally settle down (I love that expression, as if marriage were the first step into the grave), they become providers and breadwinners, feeling that their first responsibility toward their children is not to love them but to feed them.

Hence, even if men are successful, they are still broken, detached as they are from their very humanity and sense of self. This explains why our culture produces so many men whose success does not lend them dignity but only makes them into shallow braggarts.

13.

Donald Trump:
The Most Broken Man in America

MANY PEOPLE make the mistake of believing that broken American males are only those who have failed at life. In truth, it's all of us men—both rich and poor—who are made to feel like failures. We are all equally dehumanized when our worth is determined solely by how much money we have. We can have all the gold in Fort Knox, and still soulless capitalism, like the serpent in Eden, will tell us we don't have enough.

Donald Trump is the most broken man in America. For all his wealth and for all his fame, no one is a bigger failure than Donald Trump, and no one has more succumbed to the destructive effects of soulless capitalism. Why is Trump so famous today? How has he become America's best-known businessman? Could it be because of his personal sense of honor? Nope. He's the shallowest man around. Perhaps his humility and grace, then? *Puuuuleeease!* Perhaps his reputation for philanthropy? Uh, er, there doesn't seem to be much of that reputation to speak of. Then it must be his respect for women! Fugedaboutit! So what is it then? It's the fact that he has money. Pure and simple. That's it. There is nothing else. Donald Trump is the ultimate proof that men in America are valued and achieve status and envy for their money alone.

I do not dislike Trump. In fact, I find him entertaining. He is the court jester of American business. I have no feelings of hostility toward him whatsoever. And less so am I jealous of him. Rather, I pity him. I too am a broken American male just like Donald Trump. But there is one important difference. I am well aware of my own brokenness.

Trump is utterly clueless. He brags about himself endlessly to try and impress others; he sticks his name on every building he buys; and as he trades one buxom beauty in for another, he isn't even aware that he is a walking billboard for brokenness. He is the poster boy for my book (but since he's rich enough as it is, I'll refrain from offering him royalties).

Would it be asking too much for America's most famous businessman to behave like a gentleman? With great wealth comes great responsibility, and foremost among the responsibilities of a powerful man is the proper treatment of women.

But Trump is a narcissist for whom attention is as necessary as food and water. Indeed, Trump represents a completely new paradigm in the evolution of male honor, with grave repercussions for those who aspire to be gentlemen today.

Men begin life with superficial dreams: to make money, to be powerful, or to be famous. But as we get older and wiser, those dreams tend to evolve and mature into something more wholesome. Bill Gates crushed Microsoft's competitors and became the world's richest man. But then his passion was transformed from selling software into giving away his billions and saving tens of thousands of lives. A similar transition happened to Gates's good friend Warren Buffett. Bill Clinton aspired to power and influence as president, but later launched an impressive array of international initiatives to help the downtrodden.

Trump, however, has never outgrown his obsession with unbridled self-aggrandizement. Indeed, he has not evolved but devolved. His narcissism and boastfulness scrape the skies, just like his buildings. Enlightenment seems utterly beyond Trump, who continues to believe that self-glorification is life's only purpose. If wisdom's highest manifestation is the human ability to discern a cause greater than oneself, then Trump is mired in an abyss of self-absorbed darkness so thick that it blights any ray of hope.

Normally, such monumental flaws would be the business of no one but Trump himself. Indeed, one of the Jewish religion's strongest prohibitions is that of *lashon hara,* "the evil tongue," or speaking badly of someone else. I intend no such personal slight. Rather, what Trump represents is leading directly to the vastly increased brokenness of American men and as such must be rebutted and repudiated. Trump's success-through-boastfulness augurs ill for the rest of us.

Ancient codes of honor dictated that while man should aspire to greatness, he should do so with a whisper. Let others speak of his feats of daring. A gentleman is not crass and is certainly not a braggart. Indeed, boasting of one's achievements undermined them, since boasting betrayed insecurity rather than confidence, weakness rather than strength.

Troubadours and minstrels could create your legend, as Homer did for Achilles and an unnamed bard for Beowulf. To crow of oneself, however, was the height of vulgarity.

But Trump has built his reputation and brand name through sheer and unending braggadocio, and has made it challenging, if not impossible, for the rest of us not to follow suit. After Trump, if you want to build your brand, you have to brag and talk about yourself constantly. Humility be damned. Those in American society who seek to live modestly will forever be dwarfed by those who seek success at any cost.

The ancient code of male honor dictated that a gentleman was judged first and foremost by his treatment of women. Trump's nauseating attacks on Rosie O'Donnell's weight, in their ugly public feud of early 2007, betray a man who denies women an independent identity and creates them solely in a man's image. Who determines how women should look? Trump and his testosterone. Rosie, who lacks an hourglass figure, fails to entertain and is therefore a primate. Trump had every right to respond to Rosie's criticism of him. But to bring her weight into it was a sign of a man lacking in gentlemanly qualities. He can criticize her opinion, but not her size and shape.

The hallmark of the misogynist is the conviction that all women belong to him and that he retains the right to pass judgment on every aspect of his servants. During slavery, black women were put on the block and studied for the health of their gums and teeth. Trump's beauty pageants are slightly more elevated, focusing instead on the shapeliness of a woman's breasts and the length of her legs.

What Donald Trump has brought to new heights is a new kind of rich man. The man who has money but no class. The man with a million bucks but a penny's worth of manners. The man who lives in high society but whose behavior is in the gutter.

> **What Donald Trump has brought to new heights is a new kind of rich man. The man who has money but no class. The man with a million bucks but a penny's worth of manners. The man who lives in high society but whose behavior is in the gutter.**

Trump is proof that a man can be immensely rich but feel extremely poor. Nothing will fill him up. All the money in the world will not grant him the self-esteem that has permanently eluded him and for which he must compensate through boasting.

Trump is a billionaire businessman. And yet you and I own him. We are his masters. He lives in our small pockets. Everything he does is calculated to impress *us*. If he buys a building, he needs us to know of it. If his show has high ratings, he needs us to read of it. He does not merely crave our approval, he is utterly dependent on it. Amazing. To be worth billions, and still be the slave of the public.

Listening to him boast, you can tell that this poor man is broken into a million little pieces. Earth to Trump: Character, rather than money, is the real currency by which we purchase self-esteem.

This is not to say that there is no good in Trump. Indeed, the broken American male is not a bad man, just an insecure man. Trump has many laudable qualities. He seems to be a loving father and he occasionally engages in acts of philanthropy. And there is hope that perhaps one day he will take his responsibility as a public role model seriously and aspire to be a true gentleman. But for now he represents all that is wrong with soulless capitalism and is the poster boy of broken American manhood.

14.

Ready to Be Broken:
The Inherent Fragility of Men

I HAVE argued that modern cultural factors have broken the American male. The soulless capitalism of modern America makes men feel that they are only successful if they have money, power, or fame—and preferably all three at once. But truth be told, there is something inherently broken in men that transcends even cultural factors. Yes, America with its soulless capitalism expedites the brokenness of men. But there seems to be something *within* men, something innate, that already lends itself to brokenness. Just look at history. Men always seem to be messed up, fighting stupid wars for thousands of years just to gain some prestige—to wear medals on their chests, to conquer a castle—and to feel good about themselves by overpowering others.

My favorite hobby is history. I read many history books and take great pleasure in traveling to historic sites and showing them to my children. But you don't have to be a connoisseur of history to come to one overwhelming conclusion. Insecure men, in an effort to prove their worth, have brought untold misery to our world, over and over again. Whether it was Alexander the Great, who had to conquer the world to prove he was the worthy successor of his illustrious father,

Philip II of Macedon, or Julius Caesar, who expressly declared his desire to compete with Alexander's historical legacy, or, in the more modern era, Napoleon, who sought to mitigate his noble family's loss of position by conquering Europe, or Kaiser Wilhelm II of Germany, who engaged in a senseless arms race with Britain to compensate for physical defects, insecure men have brought the world incessant war. And in the twentieth century it gets much worse, of course, with the ghastly spectacle of the monster men of modern times like Hitler, Stalin, Mao Tsetung, and Pol Pot, who combined killed over one hundred million innocent people. It seems that history is a tragic sequence of events brought about by men with serious self-esteem issues.

The modern American male, immersed in a soulless capitalist environment where he is judged by a single criterion of success, is extremely insecure. But haven't men always been that way? Is it nature or nurture that makes men broken?

It's undeniable that regardless of environment there seems to be a congenital flaw in men. As a man, I have always felt that my nature required refinement. I often joke with my friends that I'm embarrassed at how men often behave and should have been born a woman. Now, that doesn't mean that in my spare time I put on my wife's undergarments and call myself Sally. But it does mean that I have spent a lot of time thinking about the underdeveloped character of men, and why they are often so vulgar, unfaithful, and brutal.

When I was a young yeshiva student studying in Israel to be a rabbi, I was waiting at a bus stop in Tel Aviv late one Saturday night to travel to Jerusalem. There were about five other men waiting with me. A young woman with a low-cut blouse walked by. I watched as all the heads followed her, in unison. There we were—a bunch of guys in heat. I couldn't help but think how pathetic it was to be a man. A man seemed a tragic figure, ruled by his hormones, incapable of reaching for spiritual heights, so tethered was he to the carnal earth.

Is it that simple? Was evolution right? Are we nothing more than sperm donors, led by our genes to take up with the first woman who walks by? Is there nothing potentially honorable about us: an ability to share love, practice faithfulness, and be noble?

To better understand the male nature, it is helpful to use a kabbalistic model of masculine and feminine energies. Kabbalah, Jewish mysticism, has recently achieved mainstream adherence in modern American culture, and it is particularly insightful in discussing the differences between men and women.

Before the Judeo-Christian religions, the ancients looked at the world and were amazed at its multifacetedness. What could be behind the world's vast variety? The answer to that question was paganism, the belief that there are many gods, each responsible for a different element of the universe. Why were there so many different earthly properties? Well, because they all emanated from a different heavenly source. There was, for example, a god of water, Poseidon, and a god of the sun, Apollo. Men and women, masculine and feminine, were antithetical, which is why the Greeks ascribed their origin to male and female gods, like Zeus or Jupiter, Hera or Juno.

Monotheism came along and obliterated the belief in many gods in favor of one. But with the rise of monotheism and the attribution of the creation of all living things to a single, indivisible source, the big question remained: Was G-d masculine or feminine? If G-d is a man, where do women come from? If G-d is a woman, where do men come from? How could one G-d be responsible for such duality?

Kabbalah explains that there is both a masculine and a feminine energy within G-d. There is the masculine G-d of history and the feminine G-d of creation. In kabbalistic geometry, the masculine G-d of history is represented by a line and the feminine G-d of creation is represented by a circle, which is why the male anatomy reflects a line and the female anatomy reflects a circle. The masculine side of G-d is the aspect of the divine that we often encounter in the Bible, which is why G-d is called "He" in scripture. It is the personal G-d of history who rewards the righteous, punishes the wicked, and communicates with prophets. This aspect of G-d is masculine and linear because, like a line, it comes from above to below. The masculine side of G-d descends from on high to govern human behavior. This G-dly energy is stern and disciplinarian.

The feminine aspect of G-d is represented by a circle because it is the infinite aspect of G-d that gives birth to the universe. It is the side of G-d that serves as giant womb, birthing all existence. Since it is infinite, it also encompasses the universe, enveloping it like a circle. Rather than being disciplinarian, it is nurturing. Whenever we speak of the all-enveloping nature of G-d, we use maternal terms like Mother Nature, in whose nest we all exist.

The masculine and feminine aspects of the divine serve as the celestial origin for men and women. Men are goal-oriented, like a line. They spend their lives in competition, rushing to the finish line. They use linear standards to judge themselves and each other. Who is higher on the totem pole?

The masculine can be rigid and inflexible, like a line. Swords, rising Wall Street graphs, baseball bats, hockey sticks, the gridiron, field-goal posts, and other lines are the tools of choice for men who wish to distinguish themselves. Men even judge their very masculinity by a line. For men, size does matter! Women, by contrast, are cyclical and are means-oriented rather than goal-oriented. Unlike men, who get bored when they come to the end of the line, as in a relationship where they become restless once they attain the prize, women do not focus on a beginning and end. They find it easy to discover novelty within the everyday. They also gravitate toward circles of intimacy. They are not looking for novelty so much as for emotionally fulfilling relationships. Men get claustrophobic in relationships. Women thrive in relationships. Like a circle with no end, women, unlike men, rarely experience midlife crises.

Since men stem from the more rigid, linear divine energy, they lack the wholesomeness of the circle. They are broken from birth. The circle has a flexibility that the line lacks. The circle is more robust, more able to withstand shock, than the line, which is so easily broken.

There is a harshness to men that belies their underlying vulnerability. Numerous studies have shown that testosterone makes men aggressive. And to an extent, it's what makes men successful, even attractive to women. Women like "the man who can take care of them" and "the man with a plan" because he is robust, sturdy, and protective (or so it seems). Women like the fact that men are strong, reliable, and dependable. But the guy whose false notion of masculinity doesn't allow him to show emotion or cry or depend on a woman turns women off.

The G-d of history is an unpredictable G-d. He is a G-d of seeming contradiction, a G-d that at times can appear to exercise harsh judgment. As seen in G-d's destruction of Sodom and Gomorrah in the book of Genesis, or G-d's drowning of Pharaoh's legions in the Red Sea, the masculine G-d of history appears aggressive and seems to betray the notion of the divine being as compassionate and long-suffering.

We observe these inherent contradictions in human nature as well. Men love their families, but often betray them. Men love the idea of being successful, but they rarely *feel* successful. They project confidence, even while they feel wholly inadequate. Contradictions are part of being masculine.

Men's brokenness doesn't just come from the culture; it's in their nature. Men are not as sturdy as women. They are more compartmentalized, more naturally fragmented. Our culture has broken men further. But they were fragile from the beginning and ripe for breaking.

This is not necessarily a bad thing. Men's natural fragility is meant to be healed by family, community, and society. This is why a man seeks to share his life with a woman who nurtures him, bolsters his ego, and loves him unconditionally. Had men been truly made of steel they would seek out a Lois Lane.

But while fragility is a good thing, complete and total brokenness is a terrible thing. And our culture, with its single criterion of professional success, has crushed the male egg and made it into an omelet. The men in our society consist of pieces of crushed shell.

15.

How Women Heal Men

BROKENNESS, WHILE greatly exacerbated in modern times, is built into men. And it's why men seek out the warmth and gentility of women. Women don't need men. They love men. But men *need* women. Numerous studies have been conducted that demonstrate the debilitating effect of remaining a bachelor. Men without wives often end up walking into oncoming buses simply because there wasn't a wife to tell them to watch out. They are more prone to illness, depression, and disease, and they die a lot younger. In short, when a man doesn't have a wife, he often doesn't last very long.

Judaism has always recognized the dependency of men on women. A wife is not a luxury for a man but a necessity. In the Jewish religion, a man is obligated to marry. It's a divine commandment. Unlike Catholicism, there is no celibacy in our religion. Indeed, the book of Proverbs declares, "A man who has found a woman has found goodness."

For Christians, the suggestion that Jesus married is not just doctrinally unsound, it is positively blasphemous. On Good Friday of 2007, I debated Theodore McCarrick, former Cardinal Archbishop of Washington, D.C., on CNN. We discussed recent movies and TV shows, like *The Da Vinci Code* and the Discovery Channel documentary *The Lost Tomb of Jesus,* which suggested that Jesus had married and had children. I told the cardinal that I understood why Christians would take issue with something that directly contradicted scripture, like the idea that Jesus married Mary Magdalene. But even if the suggestion was heretical, why was it so deeply offensive? On the contrary, seeing that Jesus was a Jew who lived by Torah law, it would have been completely against his religion *not* to marry! Of course, the cardinal disagreed. He himself has taken a vow never to marry.

In the Bible G-d explicitly commands that the masculine must always be balanced by the feminine. The very first time the Bible labels something as "not good" is when G-d creates Adam alone, looks at his loneliness, and says, "It is not good for man to be alone." Justice can never exist without love. The line must always be enveloped by the circle. And when men and women make love, the line is encompassed by the circle—literally.

Men are redeemed and fulfilled by the presence of a woman in their lives. It is the woman who sorts through all the inner confusion and turmoil, as well as the contradictions, that are inherent in the masculine. Women make men feel worthy. And women give men the impetus to become noble. In the course of aspiring to win over a woman, a man ennobles his character and becomes a gentleman in order to be worthy of her. Women heal and refine men, bringing out their best qualities. Men need women to survive, not just to procreate.

I have counseled thousands of men in my time. I believe that men who remain bachelors for too long—and I know men who date hundreds of women and still in their forties and fifties cannot commit to one—become slightly odd. Rather than sharing their lives with a woman and finding healing within the feminine, they instead become slaves to women. They cannot commit to one woman since no one is good enough. They become victims of their own arrogance. They fall in love instead with womankind, which in reality is a mask for their own narcissism. It is a way of saying that they are so special that no one woman can suffice. It takes all the women of the world to satisfy them. There are few things as pathetic as the modern male womanizer. I would even say that without a permanent woman in their lives men become tragic. Their quirks and idiosyncrasies find no balance. There is no woman to ground them.

I used to debate this issue with Bill Maher, who is a perennial bachelor, on his former Comedy Central and ABC TV show, *Politically Incorrect*. He took umbrage at my suggestion that marriage is a far better way for men to live than bachelorhood. Maher, who was always friendly to me both on and off camera, would nevertheless lash out at me on TV as judgmental and primitive for my assertion that marriage is a great blessing for a man.

But aside from the obvious benefits of having a life companion rather than existing alone, numerous scientific studies bear out the supremacy of marriage. Indeed, studies show that bachelors experience far more physical ailments than married men. People who have never married are more likely to die—at all ages—than people who are married and live together. "It's the 'never-married penalty,'" suggest University of California researchers Dr. Robert M. Kaplan and Dr. Richard G. Kronick, in the August 2006 issue of the *Journal of Epidemiology and Community Health*. Kaplan and Kronick extracted data from two sources: a 1989 national health interview survey and the 1997 U.S. national death index. They had sufficient data to analyze information on more than 80,000 Americans. Single men are more accident-prone and are more susceptible to disease. There is no one there to nurture them or to offset the rigidity in their lives. Women teach men manners and soften the hardness of men's nature. Men who live without the appreciation of a feminine partner have an undomesticated lifestyle, which is why male dormitories at places like universities are almost insufferable.

Why have women lost the ability to heal their men? I receive hundreds of e-mails every week from women around the world telling me just how broken their husbands are, and how they are powerless to do anything about it. Here is an example from a woman who wrote to me following a lecture I delivered in Los Angeles:

> *There is a particular man that I need, a man that I am dependent on. And that is my husband. I have not been happy and I have been thinking of leaving. Sadly, you ended up reinforcing for me all of the reasons why I should just pack up and leave. I fear that my marriage is lost and the situation is hopeless. My husband is a broken man. Nobody can fix him. His head is somewhere else, anywhere but our marriage. I don't feel that he is in love with me. My husband and I are way too bright to be wasting our lives like this. I deserve to be happy. The only thing that keeps me in this marriage is my kids.*

Tragic e-mails like this arrive by the boatload. Women don't understand why their husbands are so broken and why they are powerless to heal them. They each tell me they show their husband extravagant affection but it doesn't help. He doesn't heal. He still just sits there watching TV, barely talking, never sharing his emotions.

Why have women lost their influence over men? One of the principal reasons is that women have bought the great American lie about women hook, line, and sinker. They only matter if they're beautiful. They are only important if they are stunningly attractive.

But the other reason is that men are slowly destroying the women in their lives. If a man is broken, and sees himself as a giant zero, then the woman dumb enough to marry him is a zero squared. She is a far bigger loser than he is. So how can he possibly be healed by someone he sees as beneath him?

And this is how the broken American male sees his wife. He feels he has no value. So as soon as his wife marries him, paradoxically, she loses the ability to inspire and comfort him because she loses all value as well. She is an extension of him, bone of his bone, flesh of his flesh. And one loser can't uplift another. The wife becomes puzzled at her inability to make her husband feel good about himself. She hugs him, but he is robotic and unresponsive. She tells him she loves him, and he offers a barely audible, monosyllabic response. She begins to blame herself. Why can't she make him happy? Why can't she satisfy him? *There must be something wrong with me,* she concludes. *No doubt it's because I'm not pretty enough, or smart enough. If only I were thinner, then he would love me. If only I were younger, then I could sustain his interest.* Little does she realize it is the very fact of her having married him that ensures that she cannot lend him value. Ironically, it is her very devotion and her union with him that subverts her ability to make him feel satisfied.

But another woman, a stranger, well, that's different. The very fact that she is not married to him makes her appealing. She never merged with someone without value. She still has great worth. She's the woman you can't have, the one outside your loser grasp. She is a winner. So when the stranger shows an interest in him and makes him feel desirable, the broken American male suddenly feels special. To be sure, the value he feels won't last. But he pursues it nonetheless because it temporarily silences the demons inside. This is why so many otherwise decent men cheat on their wives. Not because they don't love their wives. Very often they do. But they are looking for that ego boost. *Anything* to feel valuable.

One of the truly cruel things about adultery is that the devotion a woman has for her husband works against her. Because the other woman is not married to her husband, she is appealing. Had she been dumb enough to marry this loser, she would be treated like garbage too. And of course that ends up happening. As I've discussed in detail in a previous book, *Kosher Adultery,* the vast majority of men who leave their wives and marry their mistresses end up divorcing their mistresses within a few years of the new marriage.

Of course, the cheating husband just makes his wife feel even more inadequate and the cycle continues. But even if a husband doesn't cheat, his inability to love his wife fully makes it impossible for her to feel whole.

The problem is much broader than the contempt that husbands often show their wives. Let's face it. Men today don't respect women. Even when they live with and marry them, they seem to have trouble appreciating them. Our society treats women as a means to an end. Men are conditioned to see women as the walking satisfaction of their male hormonal needs. Indeed, men deprive women of their cyclical, circular qualities that would otherwise prove so healing to them. They make them into lines. To such a man, a woman is not Cindy. Rather, she's a 36-24-36. She's a measurement, a collection of body parts. How does he classify the women he is attracted to? Not by their nature, but by their measurements. She has long legs. She has large breasts. In other words, even when a man shares a life with a woman these days, it is no longer automatically redemptive, and it does not cure him of his brokenness. Indeed, the reverse happens. Men today are destroying women and creating "the inadequate woman," the woman who questions her very worth because she cannot understand why she can't heal the man in her life. She asks herself constantly, *Why can't I make him feel good about himself?* Slowly, she begins to blame herself. If she can't comfort him, she blames herself for not being warm enough. If he won't touch her or make love to her—and remember, one out of three American marriages is entirely platonic—then she blames herself for not being attractive enough. And if his eye begins to stray, she blames herself for growing old and wrinkly. Of course, the problem lies with him and not with her. But she has never heard of a broken American male.

Ten Ways to Identify a Broken American Male

1. He comes home after work and immediately slumps down in front of the TV.

2. He watches TV for more than two hours a night.

3. He doesn't ask about your day or the children's day.

4. He has three or more drinks a night.

5. He barely hears you when you or the children speak to him. You have to repeat yourself several times before getting a response. When he does respond, he doesn't make eye contact. He offers monosyllabic responses even to detailed questions. He appears to be in another world.

6. He is uninterested in sex and seldom touches you as a woman. Even when you undress in the bedroom at night, his eyes are still glued to the TV. You have not been intimate with him in months. Or,

7. He is an orgasm addict in bed. If he does touch you during sex, it's perfunctory and mechanical. You could never construe what he is doing as making love, but rather as using your body to achieve sexual climax. During sex, he closes his eyes and does not communicate. He retreats into a world of fantasy.

8. He is into porn, especially in private, and especially on his computer.

9. He gets depressed whenever he hears about one of his friends doing really well professionally. He feels challenged to be happy for others' success.

10. He never shares his emotions or pain. You ask him how he feels about things and he brushes the question off or changes the subject.

16.

The Inadequate American Female

MEN ARE transferring their insecurities onto women, causing even more anxiety in the American female. This casting of self-doubt on a whole generation of women has resulted in a higher incidence of depression among women, poorer self-images, and a towering rise in dangerous plastic surgery procedures, just in order to conform to the beauty ideals of the broken male. Women today never feel good enough, supportive enough, smart enough, or attractive enough to sustain the interest of a man. Rather than women healing men, men are breaking women. This extinguishes the light and inspiration that should be found in the American home.

It is not only the American male that is broken. The family is broken as well. It consists of constituent parts that all spin in their own orbits. It is made of husbands and wives who are not intimate. And it is producing children who are not secure.

It beggars belief that sixty years after the advent of feminism, women are more unhappy than at any other time in recorded history. Which does not mean that men aren't miserable as well, just that women, remarkably, are by some standards even more unhappy! The use of antidepressants by adult Americans nearly tripled in the last decade, according to figures on American health released by the federal government (*The Washington Post,* December 3, 2004). *Newsweek* reported that in 2003 more than two hundred million prescriptions for antidepressants were filled in America. What is especially surprising about these high numbers is the massive percentage prescribed for women. The latest studies show that approximately one in three women has been treated for clinical depression, and that one in three doctor's visits by women is to seek treatment for depression. Furthermore, psychiatric disorders disproportionately strike females. Anxiety disorders—which include panic disorder, phobias, and obsessive-compulsive disorder—affect 16.4 percent of Americans, and twice as many females as males. Mood disorders such as major depression afflict an estimated 7.1 percent of Americans. However, women between the ages of eighteen and forty-five make up the majority of those with major depression ("Women's Health Week Focuses on Minority Females," Health Link.com, Medical College of Wisconsin, May 10, 2002).

In general, you are more likely to suffer from major depression if you are a woman. In fact, twice as many women as men will have a depressive episode during their lives (Psychdirect.com, Psychology info.com).

In our pseudosophisticated society, we point to how oppressed women were throughout the ages, and how they were treated as little more than property. Women once had few educational opportunities and were treated as glorified baby-making machines that were born to serve men. In many cultures of the world, this is still largely true, which is why feminism's emphasis on women as the equal of men is so important. I don't support everything in the feminist agenda—like the suggestion on the part of some radical feminists that women should wean themselves from the need for men. I am in the business of increasing love and getting men and women to acknowledge their interdependency on one another and help them avoid drifting apart. But feminism's central premise of getting men to respect women as their intellectual, emotional, and spiritual equals is something that is holy. I want my five daughters brought up in a world where they are respected and cherished by men for their minds and hearts.

So here's the obvious question. Since things have gotten so much better, and women today enjoy many of the rights and opportunities of men (there are even more women in college today than men), why are women so unhappy? What is the cause of their deep discontent?

Furthermore, why are women so deeply unhappy in their marriages? At least two-thirds of all divorces today are initiated by women. Some researchers put the incidence even higher, at 75 percent. David Popenoe of the National Marriage Project at Rutgers University, who came up with the two-thirds figure, says that the high rate of women initiators is probably due to the fact that men are more likely to be "badly behaved." Husbands, for example, are more likely than wives to have problems with drinking, drug abuse, porn addiction, and infidelity. Another key factor is the emotional quality of the relationships. Few men today truly respond to their wives' emotional needs.

But this staggering divorce statistic becomes even more startling when you consider the circumstances. Studies show that when a man leaves his marriage, the vast majority of the time he is leaving his wife for another woman. Men—especially those who have already been married—don't function well on their own. They need to be taken care of. So it is rare for a man to leave his marriage unless he is leaving it for someone else. In his mind, he may be "trading up" for someone who is younger, more submissive, more compatible, or more attractive. But for wives, the opposite is true. Remember the days when little girls grew up dreaming about a knight in shining armor whisking them off their feet to live happily ever after? That's all over now, as women abandon men in droves and learn to find happiness completely on their own. Ninety percent of all women who leave their husbands are not moving on to other men. They are simply leaving their husbands and accepting what is often lifelong single status. Statistically, the odds are against them to ever marry again. We are all familiar with the famous statistic that single women in America over the age of thirty-five are more likely to be in a terrorist attack than to marry. (One friend of mine, a woman thirty-nine years old, was in the terror attacks of 9/11. She called me a few weeks later and said, "Now, Shmuley, let me get this straight. I've been in a terrorist attack. So does that mean that I'm now going to meet my soul mate?") The statistic has been disputed, but its theme has not. Women who divorce are more likely to remain single for the rest of their lives than to remarry.

Why do so many wives leave their husbands and go out into the wild blue yonder? Why are they abandoning their husbands and even the idea of remarriage? Because *they would rather be alone than stay with a man who does not appreciate them.* They would rather live by themselves than with a husband who doesn't speak to them, who won't share his inner self, and who chooses the company of the TV over theirs.

The single woman may live in loneliness. But she also lives with the hope that one day she will find a soul mate who cherishes her. What does the married woman who is abandoned by her husband within the marriage have to look forward to? In my twenty years of counseling, I have discovered that the loneliest women of all are married.

Sigmund Freud famously said that he could not answer the question, What do women want? Indeed, Freud is the scourge of feminists because he denied women an intrinsic identity. For Freud a woman was a castrated male with lifelong penis envy. Surrounded by a wife and five daughters, I think I have an answer for Freud.

Think about what a bum deal marriage is for a woman. She takes her husband's last name, thereby compromising her identity. She bears the children, thereby disfiguring her body. She works outside the home and then comes back to even more work in the home, thereby compromising her peace and rest. Why would any woman agree to this? And the answer is that marriage provides a woman with the one thing she wants and the one thing that so eluded Dr. Freud. Marriage provides a woman with a man who makes her the center of his world. She becomes the sun around which a planet revolves. She obtains a man who not only loves her but also basks in her light. What a woman wants is to be the center of her man's world. Whereas a man can cheat on his wife even if he loves her (he's a man, for goodness' sake), women only cheat if they are neglected. And that explains why so many women are leaving their marriages. All work and no love makes Jane an unhappy woman.

A shocking statistic was reported in January 2007 by *The New York Times*. For the first time in American history a majority of women are living without a husband. The *Times* reported that 51 percent of all women are living without a spouse, up from 35 percent in 1950 and 49 percent in 2000.

Women are beginning to give up on men. Whereas they once harbored hope that men could satisfy their needs and make them feel appreciated, today they are finding far greater satisfaction in a career than in male companionship and from female friends than from husbands.

These are the consequences for a culture that for half a century has mercilessly exploited women as men's playthings.

Beginning with *Playboy,* which coined the phrase "Entertainment for Men" in the early 1950s, and ending with the monsoon of smut that pours through the Internet daily, men today have been conditioned to see women as their subordinates. Women exist to satisfy men. They have no will other than to look pretty for their male counterparts. They will starve themselves into thinness and submit their otherwise healthy bodies to the surgeon's scalpel, all in an effort to get men to notice. And when they commit the terrible crime of aging, they will inject poison—literally—into their foreheads to rid themselves of the lines that were once proud symbols of life's experiences.

Men have developed a sense of entitlement toward women that precludes them from making any honest effort to be worthy of them.

The result is that the average man has no idea how to please a woman. He doesn't even know how to talk to her. On a date he uses compliments not to make her light up, but to make her lie down. After marriage his purpose is not to attend to her emotional needs but to get her to attend to his domestic wants, as she slowly becomes his maid instead of his helpmeet.

Quickly, however, she tires of this raw deal. Marital sex becomes a chore as he selfishly focuses on his own pleasure. And as for conversation, the most she can expect is boring exchanges related to practical matters, like taking the kids to after-school activities.

Unless a woman is a complete toady or sycophant, this is not something she's going to put up with for long. So she's dumping her husband and abandoning the whole concept of marriage.

It is revealing that the three most accomplished women in America—Oprah Winfrey, Condoleezza Rice, and Hillary Clinton—all have one thing in common: their choice not to share their most intimate selves with a man. (And yes, I know that Hillary is married to Bill, and I don't doubt that she loves him. But she is now truly married to her career.)

A woman from Minnesota corresponded with me at length about how her husband showed her no affection and how it was killing her. One day she wrote me the following tear-jerking e-mail:

Okay, so John had a meeting last night and I tried to stay up and wait for him, because I wanted to talk with him about the affection issue, or the lack of it. I was really tired and ended up falling asleep.

So, I just really needed to get it all off my chest because I feel as though every day that goes by, I get more and more depressed about the whole thing. So I sent John an e-mail telling him that he needed to make a decision. He was either going to show me affection or he was not. I needed him to make a decision. If he decided no, then I would just move on because I just cannot keep hoping and praying and need him to show me affection. I have had four months of a roller-coaster ride of emotions with this and I just feel as though I cannot do it anymore. I told him if he says he is going to do it, then this time, he just needs to do it. I just need to be done with this. Every time he and I talk about it and he says he will do better and he does not, I just go deeper and deeper into a dark hole that I feel I am eventually not going to come out of. I feel like it would be easier to just have him say no, he is not going to show me affection like I want him to, and move on. I truly believe now after four months of this that he is not going to do it. I do not at all understand why he cannot do it.

So, I called him after I was fairly certain he had read it and he is very, very upset. He is crying and just not doing well at all. Which of course makes me regret saying anything. He says it is not as easy as saying yes or no, he will or will not do it. I just do not get it. To me, it seems simple. Whatever, I just cannot do it anymore. I love him and I am willing to bury the feelings once again and not expect affection from him. I did it before and I will do it again. It is going to take me some time, but I will. I am not going to bring this subject up to him again. I cannot put him through this any more than I can put myself through it.

Here is a woman who, based on my prodding her, had exerted every effort to squeeze some emotion out of her broken husband. In the end, she just gave up. Loneliness within her marriage would become her lifelong lot.

Such feelings of forlornness are far from uncommon among American women. Husbands who do not love themselves cannot love their wives. And husbands who do not love their wives end up not just breaking their hearts but also destroying their sense of self.

All this is exacerbated by other factors that are creating the inadequate American woman.

There is the work-too-hard burnout of the modern mother and wife. Working outside the home to provide the family with the all-important second income and coming home to children who are domestically lazy and rarely help, Burnout Mom is overwhelmed with a deluge of responsibility that saps her energy and crushes her spirit.

In trying to keep up with her ever-mounting responsibilities and making every effort not to fail her family, Burnout Mom slowly loses her soft edge as she becomes either a shouter—browbeating her children to do their chores—or a martyr, forever lecturing her kids about everything she does for them and how she receives no appreciation in return. She quickly gives up the attempt to inspire her children to be actively involved in the home and is reduced to using guilt and pressure to get them to do simple chores. A broken record, Burnout Mom repeats herself constantly, while her children never internalize her instruction.

Burnout Mom develops resentment toward her husband because he works hard at the office but not in the home. And as she drags her haggard frame from kitchen to bedroom, she is expected to look attractive and youthful and to retain a trim figure, even as the woman inside her has gone into hibernation. Something has to give, and it is usually a sense of self, as she slowly loses her individuality and morphs into a chauffeur, chef, and sheriff. To add insult to injury, her husband will later use her devotion to the family against her by asserting that they have no time to be a couple and that she has lost any romantic impulse, obsessed as she is with domestic responsibilities.

The second season of my *Shalom in the Home* TV show took me to a family in New York where, ostensibly, we were brought to repair a broken father-son relationship. However, it quickly became apparent that the individual suffering most in the family was the mother. She was married to a man who had an unhappy childhood and felt that he was not succeeding sufficiently in his career, and therefore he was emotionally distant and removed from his family. His wife told me how lonely and inadequate she felt. When I asked her why she felt she wasn't good enough, she said that if she wasn't able to take away her husband's pain and make him feel valuable and happy, then how special a woman could she be? I then asked her if she felt that her husband was attracted to her. Without waiting an instant she said no, she did not feel that her husband found her at all exciting and that their intimate life was virtually nonexistent. This did not mean that she did not believe her husband loved her. She was convinced that he did. Rather, she just felt utterly inadequate as a woman.

For a year, I hosted a radio show aimed at women for a station based in Salt Lake City, Utah, and owned by Bonneville, which is owned by the Mormon Church. I created a strong rapport with my tens of thousands of female Mormon listeners. More than any other subject, they wanted to talk about why they were so unhappy and depressed, which surprised me. Mormon women may have the highest rate of depression of any female group in the United States, a problem that has been much remarked upon. I would always ask them to tell me why. They said that a lot was expected of them as religious women. They were expected to have large families with many children. They were expected to be a source of comfort and support to their husbands. And, since large families usually need two incomes, they were also expected to work outside the home. The straw that broke the camel's back, however, was that amid all those pressures, they were also expected to look fantastic. Great emphasis was put on their physical appearance. Don't believe it? Just go to Utah and you'll understand. Despite all their daily pressures, these women felt inadequate because they didn't think they looked fabulous. If they put on a couple of pounds after having a baby, they had somehow failed. That's where the depression began to set in.

The Utah women's experience is a concentrated version of the pressures American women are under. And that's not *all* the pressure they're under.

Just think about what it's like to be a woman in America today. Everything around you says you're not good enough. You're not pretty enough to be on the cover of *Vogue*. You're not thin enough to fit into that sexy outfit, so you better go on some new diet. You're not fit enough to run the marathon, so you better get on the treadmill.

Your legs are not long enough to saunter down a fashion show runway. Your breasts are not large enough, so you consider mutilating your body by implanting foreign objects in order to make them more bouncy. Your hair is not blond enough; your eyes are not blue enough. Even your brain, according to the former president of Harvard University, lacks the "aptitude" to compete with a man's brain in the important disciplines of science and mathematics. And what you certainly aren't ever as a woman is young enough. We've created an environment where women are ashamed of simply living because living means aging, and aging means being rejected for being unattractive. I know women who at the drop of a hat would share the most intimate details of their lives, even their sex lives, with strangers. But they would never share their age. Indeed, it is seen as an act of rudeness to even ask a woman her age, so ashamed are women of simply being what they are. The nurturers in our culture are not being nourished by love and have precious little to offer as a result.

The nurturers in our culture are not being nourished by love and have precious little to offer as a result.

All this has got to change before we destroy a whole generation of American women and completely undermine the American wife.

We need to emphasize to women and girls from the earliest age that they *are* good enough. Their eyes are bright enough, their minds are sharp enough, their bodies are shapely enough, and their personalities charismatic enough. We need to allow women to feel good enough so that the nurturers in our culture can be restored to us whole and unbroken.

17.

The Man Who Shuts His Wife
Out Emotionally

COMPOUNDING BOTH the brokenness of American men and the sense of inadequacy of their feminine counterparts is the diminished state of males' emotional self-realization. Simply put, men today have a real challenge feeling and opening themselves up emotionally. This is especially true about opening up to their wives.

Perhaps half the men who appeared on *Shalom in the Home* were decent husbands who just didn't know how to be intimate with their wives and their children. Anthony Vacarrela was one such husband—an honorable man, a reliable provider who loved his wife deeply. His work involved overseeing a team of workers at an engineering firm. But he had little idea how to show emotion, and his wife was very lonely as a result. Chris Page was the same. A thoroughly good man and a volunteer fireman with a ferocious sense of patriotism, he was capable of telling his wife through the day that he loved her. But when it came to *showing* it when he came home, he was at a loss. In both these cases, the wife's repeated badgering to open up and be more intimate just drove the husband further away.

I witnessed this again with Mike Burke, a fire captain from New Hampshire. Mike was a real hero, beloved by his community and friends. He loved his wife, Becky, and their three children very deeply. But he was almost completely emotionally closed toward his family. I should mention that all three of these stories occurred within a few weeks of each other on the second season of *Shalom in the Home*. To be sure, we didn't go out looking for husbands who were emotionally unavailable. Indeed, we looked for new stories every week. But try as we might to focus on something new, we kept coming back to the husband who locked his emotions in a fortress. The story of the husband who wouldn't open up to his wife was inescapable. And this, more than any other interaction, is what makes his wife feel so inadequate. The wife reasons, "If I can't get my husband to show me affection or even talk to me about his emotions, there must be something wrong with me."

This comes up time and again in counseling: the distraught wife, crying over her husband's inability to open up to her emotionally. I hear the questions all the time. "Why won't he let me in? Why does he shut me out?"

Of course, the wife has little to do with it. From their earliest years men are trained not to feel. Emotions hinder success. The man who can bury his emotions and train himself not to feel is going to go far. Soldiers are sent into battle and witness the most unspeakable carnage. Feelings? They have to put them aside in order to get the job done. Could they really fight and kill if they felt their hearts?

In a sense, every man is a soldier. Men go out into the battle for existence to prove their mettle and their worth. Emotions are cumbersome baggage. The guy that makes money on Wall Street is the one who doesn't feel. He remains calm while everyone else is volatile. The successful investor buries his natural butterflies when the market tanks and sticks it out. The guy with the queasy stomach—the emotional guy, the guy who overreacts—is going to get buried. The same is true for the successful doctor. Sure, he has to care about his patients. But it's really his ability to remain utterly objective in the face of misery and suffering that allows him to heal his patients. If he becomes too emotionally invested, his patient has had it. (And the same applies to female doctors who, in this situation, have to develop their masculine grit.) In virtually any significant field of achievement, emotions do not play a significant role. From boxing to professional football to being a police officer to being a fireman, the emotional guy is likely to fail. The fire captain I mentioned earlier, Mike Burke, told me a story when I was with him in New Hampshire that illustrates how difficult it is to remain emotionally involved when doing the toughest masculine jobs. One day he was called out onto a street where an eight-year-old boy who was riding a bicycle was struck by a car going sixty miles per hour. Mike told me, "The car mauled the boy into little pieces. He was all over the street. I had to scrape up his arm, his jaw. How do you do something like that without burying your feelings? And then I'm expected to come home and discuss that with my wife? Can anyone reasonably expect me to talk about that?" As Mike said this, his eyes were filled with tears.

Capitalism is generally about subordinating emotion. The successful capitalist entrepreneur lays off employees even when he knows they have families to feed. It's not that he doesn't care. It's that he has to overcome his feelings of compassion in the name of the health of the business. He can't personalize his relationships with his employees. He may like them, but that's not why he hired them. He brought them on board to do a job, and if they can't do it, he has to let them go. Likewise, the successful capitalist cannot personalize his relationship with the competition. He may like his competitors, but no matter. He has to try and outdo them because if he doesn't he'll be out of business. The moment he allows them to catch up is the moment the red ink will begin to pile up.

This explains why even great humanitarians like Bill Gates can be so utterly ruthless in business. On the face of it, it doesn't make sense. Bill Gates is arguably the most charitable man in the history of the world. He has saved tens of thousands of lives in the Third World with his program of vaccination and has promoted education throughout the world. On the other hand, the company he runs, Microsoft, is a ferocious competitor that has faced one of the largest antitrust actions ever brought by the U.S. government for its efforts to beat its competition. But that's the whole point. Bill Gates as humanitarian has a heart that the rest of us can only envy. But Bill Gates as businessman is a different story.

This natural closing off of the emotions is greatly exacerbated by the brokenness of today's men. Men won't allow themselves to feel because when they do feel, all they feel is pain. Encumbered by a permanent sense of loss, they would rather not feel at all than entertain feelings of failure. So they pursue an endless variety of distractions and numbing agents to dull their senses and deaden their emotions.

But this is the ultimate killer for their wives. A woman is deeply emotional. She does not marry a man only for functional reasons but for reasons of the heart. There is scarcely anything a man can do that is more harmful to a woman, or more sure to destroy her self-esteem, than to shut her out emotionally. Emotional coldness for a woman is like kryptonite to Superman. In the same way that a hurricane needs warm water to strengthen and a fire needs wood to burn, a woman needs emotional connectedness to remain alive in a marriage. Once that disappears, she slowly begins to shrivel. Which explains why two-thirds of all divorces are initiated by wives. They would rather be alone than be with a man who gives them no warmth in an emotional blizzard.

Yes, some women marry men for money. But the vast majority go into marriage, with all its inherent sacrifices, in order to be at the center of their husbands' lives. When they are denied that, they become as broken as their husbands. And slowly but surely, the whole family ends up in pieces.

18.

The Uninspired Child

BEREFT OF inspiration, the broken American male fails to inspire his children. He does not parent them so much as admonish them. He does not connect with them so much as police them. He loves his children but inhabits a different world than they do. Forget about being on the same page—he is in a different book. While his children are playful and wish to interact with him, he is locked into a cold, distant world. While his children are zestful and filled with life, he is half dead. After a while, his kids no longer turn to him for play or talk. They are reduced to searching for substitute heroes, from sports figures to rock stars to vacuous pop icons. The company of their friends soon becomes far more satisfying than their father's company, further compounding his feelings of isolation and bitterness.

Their mother, meanwhile, is haggard, emotionally raw, and physically and emotionally exhausted. After giving so much of herself to work and then coming home to more domestic responsibilities, she looks in vain to be rejuvenated and resuscitated by her husband's affection. Since he cannot offer it, she slowly withers and is unable to inspire her children either.

To look at American youth today is to witness squandered potential

and promise. Our kids are lost. They waste their time in an endless array of inane pursuits. They live for movies, video games, impulse purchases at the mall, and an unending stream of unsatisfying male-female
relationships. They have sex at an age when they cannot even enjoy it
and thereby lose their ability to use this most intimate expression of
human closeness to achieve emotional attachment later in life. And
they seem lifeless as they go about their everyday responsibilities and
chores. The American teenager especially is a walking zombie, the living dead, who only seems to come to life for the most worthless of
pursuits, like celebrity gossip and movie talk. They are dead in the
home and are only revived when they leave its stultifying air. The life-
lessness and numbness exhibited by today's youth, especially teenagers,
is more redolent of those who have been through wars than those
who ostensibly are innocent and have never suffered trauma. With
their ears tuned to iPod headphones, and the culture pumping incessant decadence straight into their cerebral cortex, they are cut off from
all that is natural and most of what is healthy.

Passivity, born of endless hours of sitting in front of the TV, has
become habit; idleness, second nature. Childhood exuberance has
been replaced with apathy, youthful innocence with cynical weari-
ness. Even if they are not on Ritalin—and one out of seven American kids is prescribed a stimulant drug these days—they are still
addicts, with movies, video games, and shopping being the drugs of
choice. They need constant stimulation just to feel alive. Noise is a
substitute for conversation. Hollywood heroes replace parents as objects of admiration. Friends have become the new family. With parents tuning out in front of the TV or on the Internet, their kids
develop a preference for the company of school pals and find any excuse to abandon the home.

The decentralization of the American home, in which kids have
replaced their parents with their peers, is among the greatest challenges
to the modern American family. And rather than rising to the challenge, mothers and fathers have capitulated, accepting that as parents

they bear the mark of Cain, that it is natural for teenagers to feel ashamed of them and not want to be with them. And slowly the friends supplant the parents as the principal influence in the child's life.

Where did we get this destructive idea that friends can ever be a healthy substitute for family? Friends can never provide the unconditional love that is the most essential ingredient in raising secure and stable kids.

The teenagers I meet on *Shalom in the Home* are deeply ashamed of showing affection to their parents. Often, I'll achieve a breakthrough of reconciliation between a distant child and a previously neglectful or angry parent. And just when you think that the father and his teenage daughter are going to hug, even though her face is streaming with tears, she pulls back and will not allow her father to show her affection on camera. Why? Because her friends might watch the show later and she'll be embarrassed. Teenagers are not allowed to show vulnerability to parents. On the contrary. It's the kid who doesn't need his mom or dad who's really "cool." For many teens, displaying love has become something to be deeply ashamed of. Love, the most natural emotion in the world, frightens them.

In one of our TV episodes, in an inspired moment brought about by counseling, a mother turned with tears in her eyes to the teenage son from whom she felt estranged, hugged him, kissed him, and told him that he was the best thing that ever happened to her. Utterly unmoved and with a blank expression on his face, his arms at his sides in his refusal to hug her back, he responded, "Come on, Mom. This is getting corny." I was astonished at how any expression of love between parent and teenage child had become something to be ridiculed, something "corny." When I politely admonished the boy off camera for being so cold to his mother, he told me that he loved his mother but that he wasn't going to be caught dead crying and hugging his mother on TV. Here was a boy who would reject his mother's affection because it might humiliate him in front of his peers.

I heard a highly respected New York talk radio host describe how he took his thirteen-year-old daughter, along with two of her friends, to see a Harry Potter movie. He described how he and his wife intuitively sat by themselves at the very back of the theater, knowing that their daughter wouldn't want to be seen with them while among her friends. He described this as the most natural thing in the world. He had taken his daughter to the movies, but only in the most abstract sense. In reality, he understood that he had to give her "her space." To be aware of how uncomfortable his daughter felt being around him and to accommodate that feeling was, in his view, responsible parenting.

Chris Page, the volunteer fireman I described earlier, is a very loving father. But our *Shalom in the Home* surveillance camera captured him arriving home from a long day at work, taking his dinner into the bedroom where he has his Internet-connected laptop, and eating dinner completely alone. When one of his daughters comes in to tell Chris about an argument she's having with her sister, he tells her to lie on the bed and just relax. Then, with a look of satisfaction on his face, he turns to the computer and surfs the Internet while eating. Is Chris a bad father? Of course not. This is a man who would destroy anyone who hurt his children. But by the time he got home, there was simply nothing left of him to share with his family. He had given it all at work. Domestic altercations were just not something he could deal with. He needed to escape. And his computer took him to a place where he could forget his pain and forget his problems. Of course, his wife was then left with the double responsibility of having to work during the day and take the entire burden of the home on her shoulders at night.

Parents don't appreciate kids the way parents once did. We don't talk to them as much, interact with them as much, guide them and discipline them as much. Heck, we don't even *have* them as much. We have tiny little families so kids can't drain our financial resources. So unappreciated are kids in America that the birthrate itself is plummeting. In the United States, the birthrate of the more affluent white population is 1.83 babies per family, well below both the replacement rate of at least 2.1 and the black and Hispanic birthrates of 2.2 and 3.0 respectively. This means that within a few generations America's white majority will diminish and disappear. Whiteness is inconsequential and meaningless. So who cares? But as an indicator of how prosperity in America has led us to value big cars over cute infants, and plasma TV screens over baby pictures, these statistics expose our soullessness.

Since my Oxford days, and now in the world of TV, I have always been surrounded by liberal friends, even though some of my own views are more socially conservative. But along with whites, liberals are also disappearing—quite literally—less due to the efforts of Rush Limbaugh and conservative talk radio than to a lost appreciation for children. The magazine *The Week* reported that "people who describe themselves as socially conservative are having far more babies than those who consider themselves liberals . . . differences in fertility rates accounted for 70 percent of the decline in mainline Protestant church membership . . . and the simultaneous rise in conservative church membership."

How ironic that we in America have bred a culture in which the more ostensibly enlightened the individuals, the less they value children, and the more progressive their political ideology, the more they tend to find purpose through career rather than family.

And let's not think for a moment that our kids don't notice. Let's not pretend that our kids are unaware that in our estimation they are of secondary importance. They are placed behind work, career, material objects, and sports. Sure, we parents love our kids and in an emergency would do anything to save them—spend any amount, move any mountain. But what if it's not an emergency? Why is it that only the possibility of loss awakens us to the preciousness of our kids?

I believe that there is an innate sensor within children that tells them if they're valued or not. Don't ask me how, but kids just know. And I believe that the numbness children today exhibit—especially once they become teenagers—is really silent rage. They rage against the neglect. They storm against the disregard. They seethe at the desertion. And they silently mirror their parents' contempt.

Every time you try to speak to your teenagers, and they respond with iPod buds in their ears and rolling of their eyes, they're telling you something. They're telling you to go to hell. They're telling you that they don't want a relationship with you. Now, since kids are born innocent, where did they learn such contempt? Perhaps their iPod is a miniature version of your TV. Perhaps their friends are the equivalent of your colleagues at work. And perhaps their school has become like your office: an escape that supplants the home.

On *Shalom in the Home* there was a father who was simply never home with his children. He got home from work at about seven, had dinner by himself, and then went out to a second job. On weekends he would go to motorcycle shows and sports events. Once a month he went with his buddies to gamble for an entire weekend. He had no relationship with his daughter. When he walked into her room, she would yell at him that he did not knock. He complained to me that his daughter was shutting him out of her life. "She won't even let me in her room," he said, "which is crazy because I pay the mortgage." I told him, "What's worse? A daughter who shuts her father out of her room, or a father who shuts his entire family out of his heart?" Her closed room was a mirror of his closed soul.

Another family I was called in to help boasted to me that they had family dinner together every night. Indeed, it was impressive to watch how the parents and kids, both teenagers, sat down every night to eat together—that is, if you could call it that. Throughout the dinner, the TV blasted away. It was incredible to watch a family as they sat down for a family meal but didn't even look at each other. The only thing that unified them at that meal was that, at the very least, they were all looking in the same direction—at the TV. And as I watched them, the full tragedy of the American family hit me. It no longer consisted of kin, people of the same blood and the same flesh, but had become a collection of disconnected individuals, dorm mates. They had nothing in common. They bored each other. Even as they sat together, they required the TV to give them something in common.

Many of the parents who come to me for counseling tell me that the family does a lot of things together. When I ask them for an example, watching TV together is often at the top of the list. Astonishing. Since when did sitting and barely interacting with one another pass for a shared family experience?

I don't claim to know a lot of things, but I do know this. The American family as it is currently constituted cannot continue. Something's got to give. Something's got to change. Just as the rot began with the shattered father figure, the cure must begin by healing the broken American male and gluing back together his splintered parts. Once that is accomplished, wives and mothers will feel valuable and self-assured, confident that the men in their lives are drawn to them and admire them. And once the men and women are whole, it will be possible to illuminate the home and inspire the child.

Let the healing begin.

The Five Most Broken Men in America

1. **DONALD TRUMP.** Trump is the quintessential broken American male. For all his success, he still sees himself as a colossal failure who must forever brag to all within earshot of how rich he is and how much women want him. How pitiable to be a billionaire and still live to impress complete strangers.

2. **BILL CLINTON.** Clinton was a successful president and remains one of the most popular men in the world. But none of that success has brought him any measure of peace. He remains reliant on the spotlight and finds it hard to stomach any level of criticism. It was his brokenness that led him to fall for a young woman who knew exactly how to play men like him—cater to his insatiable need for attention and make him feel good about himself.

3. KOBE BRYANT. Kobe Bryant dismantled a championship basket-ball team because he couldn't share the spotlight with others who might diminish his own radiance. When you are one of the greatest and most highly compensated athletes in the world and that still isn't enough, you are just insatiable. That's why Kobe nearly destroyed his life with a brief sexual encounter with a woman who later accused him of rape. (The charges were later dropped.) Broken men seek sexual conquest as a way of feeling desirable and good about themselves.

4. BARRY BONDS. Poor Barry Bonds. He has, as of this writing, just broken what is arguably sports' greatest records but is anathema to much of the nation. That in itself would not make him one of the most broken males. It's rather his lust for success at any cost—even at the cost of his reputation and good name. Even if you're not the home-run king, you're still valuable. But Barry seems driven by demons that are simply overwhelming. He does not seem to be a bad man, only a broken man.

5. MICHAEL JACKSON. This one seems like a no-brainer. There was once much good in Michael Jackson, including a meek spirit and a kind heart. But all that has been eviscerated by his inability to cure himself of a shattered spirit. No man in America defined himself more by external success than Michael. And no man in America lived more for the adulation of the masses than Michael Jackson. And therefore, no man in America became more of a prisoner of public acclaim than Michael. Once the crowds abandoned him over allegations of pedophilia, there was no one underneath the mask. He retreated into seclusion because without a stage he did not know how to exist. Michael's entire life depended on external success. And when it disappeared, he disappeared along with it.

19.

A New Definition of Success

BROKEN THINGS can be fixed; the American family can be mended. How will we do it? What will repair men, cure women, and inspire children? Just as the American family rotted from the top down, it will have to be mended from the top down. And that will begin with a new definition of success and with the understanding that success in life is measured not by the quantity of our bank accounts but by the quality of our relationships. That to be human is not to acquire, but to connect. That to make something of yourself does not involve accumulating things but appreciating people. That real achievement comes from a life devoted to service. That real triumph comes with victory over the ego.

> **Success has to incorporate the personal as well as the professional. And it must be about character rather than property and possessions.**

The beginning of healing American males involves a fundamental redefinition of what constitutes an accomplished life. The single criterion of success—the accumulation of wealth, fame, and power—has to change. We must reverse this most corrosive of all American lies. We will never repair the broken American male until we establish a better definition of success. Success has to incorporate the personal as well as the professional. And it must be about character rather than property and possessions.

Healing the American male must be based on this simple understanding. Yes, we all want to be successful. Yes, men want to prove themselves and make something of their lives. And yes, men take great pride in being able to point to something outside themselves and say, "I made this," "That belongs to me." But first and foremost, let the thing they point to be their families. Let them point to a happy, smiling, and contented wife. Let them point to sturdy, enthusiastic, and well-balanced children. The man who can point to a well-ordered family and a contented wife is a colossus. He is a success for the ages. He should be the envy of his peers and a model for all his acquaintances.

Let us create a new generation of American men, secure in themselves, comfortable in their own skin, who do not measure their importance in relation to their peers' bank accounts. Let us create an American male who is able to identify the unique gifts that G-d gave him, and defines success as the extent to which he maximizes those gifts rather than the extent to which he erases those gifts to conform to a uniform standard of success. Let us create an American male who does not live to impress others but to do the right thing. Let us create an American male who works to live rather than lives to work.

I am sick and tired of being a broken American male. I'm tired of feeling that because I sometimes have to struggle to support my family, I am therefore not worthy. I'm tired of hearing about acquaintances being supersuccessful and feeling envious rather than happy for them. I'm tired of not hearing my kids speaking to me at the dinner table because I'm thinking about a mounting pile of bills. I'm tired of hearing that one of my TV episodes has a low rating and then feeling like a failure and worrying that the series may be canceled. I'm forty years old, at midlife, and I know it's time to change. I also know that I am capable of change.

I know that I can be a man who accepts that life is about struggle and who therefore welcomes the struggle. The fact that I have to fight in order to support my family and the fact that I am prepared to struggle shows just how precious they are to me. I have a friend who makes about twenty million dollars a year on Wall Street. He doesn't have to struggle to pay college tuition or afford a family occasion. I am a middle-class man with a large family and I have to struggle. I work hard to support my family, and because it isn't easy but I don't give up, I have the capacity to become a man of greatness. This struggle is the object to which I have devoted my life. Not to the pursuit of wealth or acquisition. Not to the pursuit of power or fame. But to the pursuit of supporting and loving my wife and children. That is the stuff of greatness. And it is time that men like me— the tens of millions of ordinary men like me—stopped seeing themselves as ordinary. We are *extraordinary*. We get up every morning, tired and wishing we could stay in bed, and we go to work to support our families. We put up with the humiliation of

> It is time that men like me—the tens of millions of ordinary men like me—stopped seeing themselves as ordinary. We are *extraordinary*.

having to be salesmen and facing rejection. We put up with loss of dignity that often comes from having to do thankless and tasteless jobs. And we do all this to put clothes on our children's backs and food on their plates, and to purchase little trinkets to please our wives. If that isn't greatness, I don't know what is.

I remember the incredible story shared by Martin Luther King Jr., of an elderly black woman who was worn out from walking to work during the Birmingham bus boycott of 1955. A carpool passed her by and they asked if they could give her a ride. She declined and said, "My feets are tired, but my soul is rested." Yes, I am tired. But it is not a physical tiredness that has overtaken me. It is a tiredness of the spirit. I am tired of feeling like a failure. I am tired of comparing myself to people who sell more books than I do, whose TV shows are more successful than mine, who are quoted more than I am, and who have no financial worries. I am tired of living a life that is not me. In essence, I am tired of my *soul* not being rested. And the time has come to give it a break.

Now is the time for males in America to stand up and become men. Real men reject the lie that money is the commodity with which they purchase self-esteem. They reject the lie that unless jobs pay a lot of money, even if they are worthy and virtuous, they are not valuable. They reject the lie that quantity counts for more than quality. They reject the lie that if you're not famous, then you may as well never have lived. Real men do the right thing because it is right, no matter how unpopular or unprofitable the undertaking. And finally, real men take real pride in their real accomplishments. They don't walk around with their tails between their legs feeling lonely, sad, and sorry for themselves. When they feel down, they reject the lie that it's unmanly to feel depressed. They go and speak to their wives about their dejection and they invite their wives into their hearts. When they don't feel that attracted to their wives, they reject the lie that it's their wives' fault and refuse to turn to Internet porn to get an erotic thrill. Rather, they blame themselves and their moods for the lack of attraction, and they push themselves to interact with their wives until a spark of passion and attraction is slowly reignited. And when they feel bored with being a family man, bored with their lives, and uninterested even in their kids, they don't turn to professional sports to live vicariously through champions with a more glamorous existence. The real man does not pursue meaningless escapes. Rather, he invests himself with his family—even when he doesn't feel like it.

I remember when I was a young rabbinical student in Sydney, Australia, studying ancient Jewish texts for twelve hours a day. Sometimes my mind wandered and I felt bored. I blamed the texts, I blamed Judaism, I blamed G-d for not being sufficiently interesting. Why couldn't G-d be as interesting as one of the stupid movies that

I occasionally watched? Why couldn't G-d's law be as interesting as some of the sports that I occasionally played? And then I studied a verse from the book of Deuteronomy in which Moses tells the Israelites: "For G-d's word is not something empty from you." The Talmud interprets his pronouncement as follows: "And if it *is* empty, if it feels boring, then know that the emptiness comes *from you.*" Whoa. Moses was right. The emptiness came from me. The beautiful texts I was studying that dripped with wisdom were never boring. It was *I* who was bored. And I never forgot that lesson and try to apply it to every other area of my life. I love my wife with all my heart. She is the bride of my youth and we have been married since we were both kids: I was twenty-one and she was nineteen. But there have been times when I did not feel as drawn to her as I normally am. She is beautiful and kind and wise. Still, I blamed her for my distance. I know now that this has nothing to do with her and everything to do with me. My own listlessness, my own restlessness, my own feelings of failure were responsible for my seeing my wife as being as worthless as I felt.

Success for men must be redefined as the ability to be a human being and not a human doing. To succeed in things that foster being instead of focusing *only* on possessions and money. They say that real wisdom can often be captured in a bumper sticker. "The most important things in life aren't things" about sums it up. Men have to stop judging themselves by the things they acquire on this earth.

> Success for men must be redefined as the ability to be a human being and not a human doing.

Any thing can be taken away. And success must be defined by those things that are permanent rather than ephemeral. Love of knowledge is one permanent treasure. In the Jewish community men are expected to maintain study groups well after they have married and ceased being students. They are expected to define part of their worth by the level of knowledge they obtain. Every synagogue offers study classes for men that meet several times a week. An Orthodox

Jewish man is also expected to study the Bible every single day, completing it on a one-year cycle. He is expected to be conversant in the important Jewish texts. Many men, including myself, study the Talmud on a seven-year cycle, completing all five thousand pages by studying two pages a day. Each man is expected to read passages from the book of Psalms on a daily basis, until he is able to recite much of it by heart. And he is expected to derive pride from what he knows rather than what he has. It is part of his being.

Let us get men to study, learn, and read again. Let us get them to enjoy other wholesome pursuits such as reading, studying, inquiring, guiding, and gaining wisdom.

Inner directedness work wonders in marriage. Most husbands and wives go to their bedroom at night and interrupt the first few moments they have alone by immediately putting on the TV. But I advise many couples to reject the shared experience of watching and engage in the shared experience of reading. When a husband is reading a great book or magazine article, and he stops in midpage to read aloud to his wife something that he finds interesting, it serves as a springboard for conversation and thus to connection.

The new definition of male success should also incorporate the degree to which a man is involved in his community. The ancient rabbis taught "Do not separate yourself from the community." But soulless capitalism not only pulls a man away from a community, it obliterates the entire idea of community. Since it pits one man against another in a never-ending competition of acquisition, it undermines the idea of a shared purpose. Contributing to a community means putting aside one's selfish interests and advancing the cause of a collective. And because contributing to a community involves moving away from one's own narrow interests and focusing on others, it is positively liberating. No prisoner is ever a success.

But more than anything else, the new definition of male success must incorporate how much love a man has in his life. If you are loved, you are successful. A paucity of love indicates failure. Period.

As a society we must begin to define male success by the ability to sustain, increase, and enhance loving relationships. Possessions are something you have. But love is something you are.

Success must also incorporate professional achievement. We all want to use our gifts in our careers and our jobs. The world needs architects, lawyers, writers, doctors, and cops. The world needs men who are professionally successful and occupationally ambitious. But even if you are a zillionaire, if your wife hates your guts and your kids don't want to speak to you, well then you, sir, are a failure. Period. Jackie Kennedy once said that if you mess up your kids, nothing else much matters. And she was talking as a first lady of the United States and arguably the most famous woman of the twentieth century. You can be famous and powerful, but if you have raised unworthy kids you have failed at life. If a guy loses all his money and ends up homeless in the street, do we consider him a success? No, because by the current definition of money making a man a success, he doesn't have any. Well, by the new definition of maintaining loving relationships, a man who is homeless is equally a failure because his family has abandoned him or he has left them.

It is high time that we declared boldly and unequivocally that the Donald Trumps of this world are not a success. They are rich and we're happy for them—let them enjoy their yachts and their champagne—but success means honoring women, inspiring your children, keeping the family intact to the best of your ability, showing noble character, being generous and philanthropic, and earning the respect of your peers through your benevolence rather than your bank account.

How can you be a success in life if the people who mean the most to you think the least of you?

The man who is a hero to the world but is not a hero to his own children is not a success. How can you be a success in life if the people who mean the most to you think the least of you?

The successful man is the man whose wife is happy and contented rather than depressed and on Prozac. The man who makes his wife feel desirable, beautiful, and special is the great man. The king is the man whose wife feels like a queen. The man who is confident enough to say he is satisfied, and comes home early to his wife and children, is the great man.

Jack Welch was one of America's greatest businessmen, building GE into a global powerhouse. NBC was only one of the many blue-chip properties that he controlled. But then one day he was interviewed by the editor of the *Harvard Business Review*. A few months later he ran off with her, leaving his wife in the process. I do not judge this man. How could I, until I have been in his shoes? But neither can I refer to him as a success. To be sure, he's a great business-man. But that is only one facet of being successful in life. And if you can't control your urges, and you run off with a woman who is not your wife, you have failed.

In the Bible, Jacob and Esau are brothers. But they couldn't be more different. Jacob is described as "a simple man who sits in tents." Jacob is studious and pious. But Esau is a hunter and a tribal chief-tain. Esau is the big businessman who has the awe of his colleagues. He is the global hunter. Everyone is jealous of him. He's the big dog, the manly man, the guy with lots of women and lots of success. No tent-sitting for him. What is he, crazy? He plays on the international stage, not in some silly tent. As for being simple like his brother, Jacob, forget it. He's incredibly complex, an international man of mystery. His business relationships are complicated, his relationships with women are complicated, his relationships with his children are com-plicated. And his very soul is tumultuous. Men of great ability are complicated.

But Jacob eschews that kind of life. He is content at home, in his tent. He seeks no complications. He is content to be content. Sure, he goes out into the world to make a buck and even prospers. In-deed, the Bible describes Jacob as an extremely astute businessman. But that's not the place where he finds himself. His principal being is found in his tent, as a husband, father, and friend. He has twelve kids.

He's intimately involved in their lives. To be sure, they're not the easiest bunch to raise, and Jacob makes plenty of mistakes, such as favoring Joseph over the others. But by and large, Jacob loves being a father and revels in raising his children. In every biblical description of him, he is surrounded by his wives and children. This is a great man, and it explains why the Jewish people are proud to call themselves "children of Israel," the new name given to Jacob after he wrestled with an angel and triumphed.

To be great men, we have no choice but to wrestle with our angels, to fight our demons. We have to fight our nature when we feel envious of someone else's success. We have to fight our inclination to bad-mouth those who have wronged us. We have to fight the unnatural feelings of failure that encroach upon us as we are overtaken in the material world by men who may be less virtuous. And we have to wrestle with the inclination to spend more time at the office and away from our children in order to prove ourselves. Jacob wrestled with these dilemmas and merited the name that reflected the greatness he acquired.

But one of the things that Jacob wrestled with most was his brother, Esau, who represented a completely different paradigm of success. Esau is a man of infinite wealth and power. And Jacob fears his retribution. So when Jacob and Esau finally meet up after an absence of twenty-two years, and Jacob is concerned that Esau, the great hunter-gatherer, wants to kill him for having legally appropriated the firstborn blessing from his elder sibling, he prepares a big present for Esau. Here is something that Esau can appreciate. Material goods, valuable property, servants and slaves. Women to pleasure him. It's too perfect. A narcissist like Esau is going to *love* his enormous present. This will calm Esau down and he'll let go of the rage against his brother. In this famous biblical meeting, Esau at first refuses the gift, saying to his brother, "I have a huge amount already." So he doesn't need the gift. But Esau lives for accumulation. He defines himself through his ever-expanding circle of possessions. He is also a primitive brute. He has money and servants but is utterly lacking in enlightenment. So he thinks he's a big deal. He's a dangerous bully, but that doesn't bother him because his definition of success does not incorporate nobility of character. He has no aspiration to be a gentleman. All he wants is *more*.

But Jacob's response is very telling. He doesn't press his brother to take the gift, because he too is wealthy and can spare the extra gifts. Rather he says, "My brother, I have enough." Wow, if that doesn't sum it up. The Esaus of this world don't seek just "enough." They want tons. They're insatiable. Enough is *never* enough. Seeking as they do an elusive success that is all about material possessions, they want to possess the whole world. And even that would not be enough. Just look at the ancient pharaohs who had to take all their wealth with them into the grave. All the gold of this world wasn't enough. They had to keep it with them in the afterlife. But simple people like Jacob, with simple values and a simple morality, are only seeking "enough." Enough to support a family. Enough to clothe their kids and send them to a good school. Enough to put away money for a rainy day and their kids' college fund. But not more than that. They're not going to spend their lives chasing more because they're empty on the inside and need constant cash to fill themselves up. And they're not going to sacrifice their families on the altar of material gain.

The successful man feels full on the inside. The successful man can come home from work at a decent hour, turn off the Blackberry and cell phone, and be fully engaged with his children because he has *enough*. When they speak, he not only listens, he actually hears them. He is completely focused. When he comes home, he *is* home. The great man sits at least five times a week for dinner with his children and is present at the table. He asks them about their day at school. He listens intently when they talk about whether they like their teachers. He comes to the table with something to inspire and entertain his children: a story from work, something he read in the newspaper, a childhood memory. He sees life through the prism of what he can bring to inspire his children and put a smile on his wife's face. He is not looking for mastery of the world. He is secure. He does not have a cavernous space inside him that he needs to fill with possession of the universe. He doesn't need to lord it over other people in order to feel good about himself. Rather, his first desire in life is to make his children feel valued and loved and to guide them to inspired heights.

Make no mistake about it. Men are a hybrid of the private and the public, the personal and the professional. They seek fulfillment in both spheres, not just the family and not just the personal. I am in no way saying that men should not seek great professional fulfillment and success. And I am not saying that men should not aspire to wealth. I am a man who wants to be a professional success. I want to write books, have you buy my books (thank you for doing so, unless of course you borrowed this book, in which case it's time to get your own copy and help me become a success), and even win awards for my books. I want to build a successful career healing marriages and families (which is really a calling rather than a career) and be acknowledged for my efforts. All that is legitimate and, if done for the right reasons, even noble. But if I fail with my family, even if I succeed in my career, it's not just that I'm half a success, that at least I've done well in one of life's important aspects. No, I'm a failure, because I have failed at the most important thing in life. That doesn't mean I haven't done great things. I may have created thousands of jobs, given millions to charity, and inspired the masses. But I am still a failure because in the area of life that is most important, I have achieved no success.

In January of 2007, right after the new year, a white man fell onto the tracks of the New York subway system and almost died. An African-American construction worker and father of two jumped on top of him as the train approached, kept his head down, and saved his life, nearly losing his own in the process. I was incredibly inspired by the story. I couldn't believe that the natural impulse of a man would be to risk his life to save that of a complete stranger. And the first thing I thought when I heard the story was "Great. Now I have an amazing story to tell the kids tonight at dinner."

The great man sits with his kids at night as they do their math homework and struggles to help them with algebra. In the course of doing so, he might feel like an ignoramus. He may not remember anything from school. He may have always been bad at math (yes, I am talking about myself here). But even while he feels dumb, he sits there knowing that for all his ignorance he is a great man. A man who will crack his head against a subject that utterly confounds him just to make his kids feel valuable. A man for the ages. And even though no one is going to make a movie of him doing the homework, and no one is going to fire a twenty-one-gun salute in his honor, and no one will erect an equestrian statue of him holding a math textbook, none of

His wife knows it. And she's the only one that matters, because he plays to a constituency of one.

that matters. It doesn't change a thing. He is a great man nonetheless. A true hero. His wife knows it. And she's the only one who matters, because he plays to a constituency of one.

I give lectures to hundreds and sometimes thousands of people. It's nice to bask in the adulation of throngs of admirers. But I have to say, honestly, that I have never once thought to myself, as I gave a speech to rapt listeners, that I was a great man. Maybe I thought that I had good speaking skills, or that I had a particularly valid insight into the subject I was discussing.

But often I will sit and play with my six-year-old son, coo with my baby of one, or speak to my teenage daughters about feminine dignity. And sometimes, as I do those things, the thought overcomes me, "Here sits a great man." For this is the stuff of true human greatness.

This is not to say that there aren't men who are legitimate successes in life, even though they were forced to forsake their families. Our soldiers in Iraq may have out-of-control kids. Their wives may be lonely. But the emergency situation of our world demands men to sacrifice, to put aside their personal responsibilities for the higher good. But this idea of being a success even if you utterly neglect your family is only true in cases of dire threats to human life and civilization. Even doctors, who rush to save lives, can still spend time with their families.

Franklin Roosevelt was not the greatest husband or father. He alienated his wife forever when he had an affair with her social secretary, Lucy Mercer. And his wife, Eleanor, further revealed in her memoirs that her children had to book time with their father through his secretary. Okay, I get it. The man was saving the world from Hitler and fascism. Fair enough. But as Doris Kearns Goodwin chronicles in her bestselling book about the FDR administration, *No Ordinary Time,* FDR also found time every day to mix cocktails for friends for about an hour. Why couldn't that time have been devoted to being a father? Yes, I know that he had to blow off steam from the pressures of his office. But do that with your kids! They're fun. They're redeeming. And spending time with them rejuvenates you because it reminds you of all the precious things you're fighting for.

The great man does not waste his life trying to gain other people's respect by flaunting how much money he has. He devotes himself first and foremost to his family. And he does it out of strength. He doesn't live to impress people. He's not motivated by insecurity. He doesn't live to impress strangers. Rather, he operates from a deep sense of personal value. He knows he has something to offer, so he

> **His first responsibility is to give the gift of himself to his wife and kids, never depriving the family of a functional head.**

contributes it. He knows he has a gift, so he gives it. And he knows that his first responsibility is to give the gift of himself to his wife and kids, never depriving the family of a functional head.

The new definition of success has to be about how greatness is determined not by what we own but by what we share, not by what we have but by what we are. We have to change how men think of themselves before they destroy themselves. A new code of honor has to be

Family, rather than money, maketh the man.

promulgated. The honorable man is the one who values his family more than money. The honorable man is the one who places his wife and children before his business associates. Family, rather than money, maketh the man.

20.

Rise, Oh Hero!

NONE OF this will happen if we don't change how we depict male success. Every time I open the *New York Times* Business section, or *The Wall Street Journal,* I read about men worth millions and billions. They are held up to me as examples of what I should be. I envy them. I want to be them. I want to have what they have. I feel bad that I am not like them.

Contrast those stories with the incredible story that I just told of Wesley Autrey, the hero who leaped on top of a collapsed man in the New York subway. As the train approached and the man had a seizure and fell, Autrey's natural instinct was to jump onto the tracks, risking near certain death, to save the life of a complete stranger. After the train passed over Autrey's head and he miraculously survived, he yelled up to people waiting on the platform, "Tell my little girls that I'm all right, that their daddy's all right." Amazing. He was even prepared to leave his children behind as he plunged to save the life of a human being in need.

Autrey has little money. He is a construction worker. He is fifty years old. Much speculation went into examining why his instincts were so selfless. At least part of the explanation was his military train-ing in the navy. The rest of the explanation came down to Autrey himself. A heroic man whose selfless instincts rendered him incapable of spending his entire life devoted to self-aggrandizement and the endless pursuit of money.

Now this is curious. We hailed the man as a hero. But in reality, society penalizes men like him. Selflessness is not praised but punished. The man who becomes a hero in our society is the one who has devoted himself to accumulating money and power. He is the guy everyone wants to know. He is the guy whose phone calls get returned. A guy like Wesley Autrey, we'll laud him for a day or two, and quickly forget him. He is, after all, a mere construction worker. Who wants to be him? And that applies to all the military men, like him, who devote their lives to protecting others. Yes, we call these men heroes. We support our troops. Blah blah blah. But our actions do not reflect our words. If we really thought of them as heroes, then we would want to be like them. Heck, we all want to have as much money as Donald Trump. We want to be like Jack Welch. But our soldiers? Of course not. Because, in the final analysis, we know that for all the talk about how much we respect and admire them, they lack money and power.

As I sat and watched Wesley Autrey's incredible act described on the evening news, I was awed. Here was a man who had no time to think and his instinct was to risk his life for another, for a stranger. This isn't a story of camaraderie, like when a man saves his fellow soldier in wartime. The victim was completely unknown to Autrey. As I went from the heights of awe and wonder, NBC transitioned immediately to another show, with other incredibly "important" news: "Justin Timberlake and Cameron Diaz Break Up." I felt immediately deflated. All the awe and wonder had disappeared before my very eyes. Who cares about this garbage? I asked myself. Is Justin Timberlake a hero? Did he risk his life for a stranger? Or is he just another friendly Hollywood celebrity who lives mostly for himself? Yes, he's talented. Yes, he has a beautiful voice. So he's a talented entertainer. But what does this have to do with heroism? What does it say about the rest of us who crave this knowledge and believe people like Justin Timberlake are heroes, whereas this construction worker from Harlem is already forgotten? The truth of the matter, of course, is quite the opposite: The man in Harlem was Superman. He lived most of his life like Clark Kent, basically in camouflage, but in that blink of an eye when his heroism was called on he ran into his metaphoric telephone booth, changed into his cape, and rescued a human life.

The damage done by the Hollywood celebrities of this world is exactly the opposite. They run around in their capes, pretending to be Superman. They love to get noticed, doing anything just to be the center of attention and living morally destitute lives because of the shock value of their actions, which never cease to amaze. And the truth is that they are the Clark Kents, unamazing and ordinary. Other than their ability to entertain, very little is special about them and they exemplify the ordinariness of human life, living entirely for themselves, money, careers, albums, or movies. And that's why it's time that society recognizes and appreciates our true heroes.

When you turn on American TV these days, the shows that dominate the airwaves are things like *American Idol, The Apprentice,* and other competitive shows. The message that men—and, increasingly, women as well—get is that to succeed is to win out against others. To succeed in life is to garner the most possible attention. The net result is that men are trained to see other men as not companions but competitors, not compatriots but adversaries. No wonder our natural instinct is not to save the life of a guy who has fallen in the subway. It's every guy for himself. But in the military it's different. Men placed in situations of life and death are trained to see their companions as brothers and are ready and willing to lay down their lives for each other.

Part of healing men has to be getting them into environments like these where other men are seen as part of a larger fraternity of brothers. It doesn't have to be the military, and I understand that not every guy is ready to ship off to Iraq. But there are other, less dramatic ways. My father gets up every morning for early prayers at the synagogue (I am lazier than he is), and hundreds of thousands of Orthodox Jewish men around the world do likewise. They say the morning prayers, which takes them about half an hour, and then they sit down to breakfast and to study for about another half an hour. So for the first hour of the day, they sit together as friends and colleagues, sharing something valuable as a way to bond and as a way of remembering that, even as they embark on the business day, it's not money that is the most important thing. G-d, community, prayer, and good deeds are far more important. And they literally come first.

I have always been impressed with doctors, not only because they save lives but also because the vast majority of them seem empathetic. I do not fool myself that all doctors care about their patients. But at the moment when they're sitting with a patient in distress, they seem genuinely concerned. And perhaps doctors have healthier outlooks about life because, although immersed in the rat race like everyone else, they are exposed daily to life and death and are therefore given constant reminders of what's really important.

The same is true of rabbis and other clerics. Most rabbis I know are genuinely not obsessed with money. To be sure, they like money as much as the next guy. Indeed, for the most part they have large families, and supporting their children can be a real struggle. But they don't love money. They won't live for it. They won't devote their life to its accumulation. And they certainly won't define themselves by it. What really matters is our proximity to G-d and what we do for other people rather than how much cash we have accumulated.

We need to expose more men to a genuine spiritual calling and immerse them in environments where they hear a different message than that of our money-obsessed culture in order for them to feel good about themselves.

Time spent with family is similar. When you spend time with your kids—when you read them a bedtime story or simply speak to them—you begin to feel heroic. You begin to feel genuinely special.

You see right before your eyes what's important in life. And when you have a genuine relationship with your kids, you actually influence them and shape and mold their characters. Then you don't need a million bucks because you feel like a million bucks. Time spent with family is one of those things that grant the greatest possible immunity to the destructive and soulless message of modern life. Indeed, I believe one of the reasons men avoid spending time with family is that they feel guilty about not spending enough time with their kids. So they avoid their kids in order to escape their feelings of shame and it becomes a vicious and destructive cycle.

We need to impress upon men that they need their families even more than their families need them, and they need to be around their kids even more than their kids need them to be around.

In the book of Ecclesiastes, Solomon, the wisest of men, explores the meaning of existence. He wants to lead a purposeful and fulfilling life. He wants his life to matter. But how? he wonders. What comes naturally is the belief that the acquisition of wealth and the pursuit of pleasure will provide the greatest possible fulfillment. In Chapter 2 he writes:

> I thought in my heart, "Come now, I will test you with pleasure to find out what is good." But that also proved to be meaningless. "Laughter," I said, "is foolish. And what does pleasure accomplish?" I tried cheering myself with wine, and embracing folly—my mind still guiding me with wisdom. I wanted to see what was worthwhile for men to do under heaven during the few days of their lives.
>
> I undertook great projects: I built houses for myself and planted vineyards. I made gardens and parks and planted all kinds of fruit trees in them. I made reservoirs to water groves of flourishing trees. I bought male and female slaves and had other slaves who were born in my house. I also owned more herds and flocks than anyone in Jerusalem before me. I amassed silver and gold for myself, and the treasure of kings and provinces. I acquired men and women singers, and a harem as well—the

delights of the heart of man. I became greater by far than anyone in Jerusalem before me. In all this my wisdom stayed with me.

I denied myself nothing my eyes desired; I refused my heart no pleasure. My heart took delight in all my work, and this was the reward for all my labor.

Yet when I surveyed all that my hands had done and what I had toiled to achieve, everything was meaningless, a chasing after the wind; nothing was gained under the sun.

So he first spends his time pursuing riches, sensual pleasure, material delights, and women, and indeed he became a fabulously wealthy king with quite a few wives (I'm using understatement). And then he wakes up one day and says to himself, "This is incredibly empty. It's all vanity. It's hot air. It's meaningless. It has not enriched me in the slightest. I'm not a success if I waste my life pursuing this hollow existence."

Modern men have to have that same epiphany and wake up. And once they do, the healing for their wives and children will begin.

21.

The Five Ingredients of Success

ACCORDING TO our new definition of success, five ingredients go into the truly successful, well-balanced, and motivated American male:

1. Professional achievement (success in the workplace)
2. Making one's wife happy (success as a husband)
3. Inspiring one's children (success as a father)
4. Service to others (involvement in a community)
5. Relationship with G-d (spiritual connection)

Professional success should never constitute more than one-fifth of a man's success. The billionaire businessman who is divorced and whose kids are alienated from him, and who has no relationship with G-d, is mostly a failure. He is rich failure, but a failure nonetheless. And what's the big deal about being a billionaire anyway? Virtually anyone who focused on making money to the exclusion of all else could probably make bucket loads of cash. But their life would be seriously out of balance.

To be sure, professional achievement is necessary. Nothing I have said in this book should be construed as implying that working hard, earning money, and climbing the professional ladder aren't important. On the contrary, they're not only important, they're G-d's work. Every time we put up houses so that people can have a roof over their heads, every time we cure a disease, we are fulfilling our biblical mandate to make the earth into a beautiful garden rather than leaving it as a place for weeds. There is, in the words of Rabbi Joseph Soloveitchik, a majestic part of our being—created in the image of G-d—that requires professional achievement in order to feel accomplished. We dare not squander that part of ourselves. We should exert ourselves totally and fully to be successful at our jobs and in our careers. And by supporting our families, giving to charity, healing hearts, and beautifying the earth with our work, we are able to transform our careers into a divine calling.

There is no dignity in poverty. It is true that not all rich people are happy, but it is probably also true that even fewer people living in poverty are happy. How can you inspire your children and love your wife when you live in constant fear of the bank foreclosing on your home? I have lived through several periods of grave financial crisis. They crushed me utterly. I know they shouldn't have, and I wish I weren't so weak. But they were absolutely soul-destroying. There are few things that destroy a man more quickly than the feeling that he can't support his family. There have probably been more male suicides over financial catastrophe than from any other cause. I have, unfortunately, witnessed it myself. When I served as a rabbi at Oxford, a male student I was close to called me up crying hysterically one night and through uncontrollable sobs told me that his father had just shot himself. I ran over to see the student. He was a complete mess. His father, to whom he was especially close, had killed himself back in Seattle when he lost most of his life's savings in a real estate deal gone bad. Ironically, although he did not leave a suicide note, he had pulled out his life insurance policy before ending his life, thereby making it clear that he committed this act so that, through his death, his family would make back all the money he had lost.

So financial security and professional prosperity are extremely important. Moreover, humans are created in the image of G-d, and in the same way that G-d is the Creator, so too are we creators. We want to improve our world by building roads, bridges, and hospitals. We want to beautify our world through art, music, and science. Those are all laudable and legitimate pursuits.

But the key to remember is balance. We humans are not oxen born to the plow. Less so are we slaves born to the shovel. We are creatures who seek the affirmation of our majesty through dignified work, yet we are also humans who crave genuine and intimate companionship.

> We are creatures who seek the affirmation of our majesty through dignified work, yet we are also humans who crave genuine and intimate companionship.

In the second creation story of Adam mentioned earlier, the Bible no longer describes Adam as having been created in the image of G-d, but rather as dust of the earth. Here, it is not Adam's majesty that is emphasized, but his vulnerability. He is made of fragile elements and is born forlorn and without a companion. He quickly grows lonely. It is then that the Bible memorably declares, "It is not good for man to be alone." So G-d famously puts Adam to sleep, and from his very own body G-d creates for him a soul mate, Eve, who forever after is bone of his bone and flesh of his flesh. In life, we seek not only the mastery of our environment and the corroboration of our splendor through work. We also seek out an intimate companion

> Sharing our lives with a soul mate is not a luxury but a necessity, and constitutes one of the most important factors in whether or not we have led a bountiful life.

and we revel in the joy and love they give us. Sharing our lives with a soul mate is not a luxury but a necessity, and constitutes one of the most important factors in whether or not we have led a bountiful life. We men have to make our wives happy. If our wives are miserable and depressed, if they are among the 33 percent of American women who are on antidepressants, then we have failed in one of the most important areas of life.

Next are our children. In life, we are all two things: individuals in our own right and links in a higher continuum of existence. As individuals we seek personal success and particularized achievement as well as an intimate companion with whom to share our lives. But as links in a higher continuum of existence, we must seek to inspire and encourage the generation that follows, those who will assume our mantle and continue our traditions. As individuals we do not live eternally. But the values for which we live and to which we dedicated our lives survive forever through our children and through our children's children. If we fail with our children there will be a break in eternity. Our children will be forced to raise themselves, to determine their own values, to find their own traditions. Failing with our children constitutes a monumental malfunction that we dare not allow.

If we fail with our children there will be a break in eternity.

Then we must seek freedom and liberation. The truly free man is he who is released from the shackles of the ego. It is the man who does not live for himself but for others who is truly free, which is why one of the five most important ingredients in success is the degree to which we are involved in a community. Do we go to synagogue or church? Do we volunteer our time for charitable work? Are we bearers of a good name communally? In the ancient Jewish books, to bear a good name is the crown of all achievement. It is said to be a higher crown than both kingship and even the high priesthood. Devotion to others is the hallmark of a purpose-driven life. The man who devotes himself entirely to his own enrichment is a failure because he has lived a life of imprisonment, caged by his own ego.

Earlier I decried the shallow and malignant interpretation of the

American dream as a purely economic one. America has many enemies in the world. They believe that this glorious country is inhabited by shallow materialists who will do anything for personal gain. Are we stupid enough to prove them right? Will we slander our beautiful heritage by defining the American dream in terms of wall-to-wall carpet and an SUV? Are such things really the stuff of dreams? Should we be proud of making material objects our highest goals in life?

> America has many enemies in the world. They believe that this glorious country is inhabited by shallow materialists who will do anything for personal gain. Are we stupid enough to prove them right?

The American dream, rather, was a dream of independence and liberty. Americans were prepared to fight for their right to self-determination. No one was going to be the master of their destiny other than themselves. Now there are two kinds of liberty: external freedom and internal freedom. External freedom comes from political liberty. It's the right to choose your own representatives and your own form of governance. Internal freedom comes from transcending genetic disposition and natural limitation in order to liberate your G-d-given potential. Internal freedom means casting off the shackles of the ego and liberating your potential to be the person you want to be as opposed to the person society wants you to be.

> Internal freedom means casting off the shackles of the ego and liberating your potential to be the person you want to be as opposed to the person society wants you to be.

Kabbalah points out that when the Israelite nation was liberated from Egypt, the Jews were not only liberated from physical bondage. Rather, in Hebrew, the word Egypt—*Mitzrayim*—connotes not only a country but also physical bounds and limitations. Freedom for the Israelites was total. In being released from the chains of slavery, they were granted physical freedom, and in being brought into G-d's covenant and a spiritual heritage, they were granted spiritual freedom as well.

My dear friend Cory Booker, the honorable mayor of Newark, New Jersey, and one of America's most electrifying politicians, often quotes Abraham Lincoln, who said that the tragedy of being human is that all of us are born G-d's original, but most die as man's copy. Inner freedom is the ability to choose your own way in life, to take all the love you have in your heart and release it. But to focus selfishly on your own interests is to live a life of total, slavish surrender. Helping others is the ultimate salve to the soul and it brings in its wake true happiness. There is no human satisfaction like seeing the face of a person whose life you have enriched.

And finally, without a relationship with G-d we cannot be said to have succeeded in life. G-d is the fountainhead: our source, our origin, our life. To be connected with G-d is to experience profound humility and blessing. To know G-d is to find wonder, awe, and enlightenment. It is to live life in the high spaces and the broad places. Without G-d our lives lack purpose, meaning, and direction. Without G-d we lack fulfillment. With G-d at our side our lives become directed and purposeful.

With G-d at our side our lives become directed and purposeful.

To attain enlightenment is to discern a cause higher than ourselves. It means finding G-d and devoting our lives to Him. The medieval Jewish philosopher Maimonides examined the reason for prayer. He concluded that the main reason we pray is to acknowledge our dependency on G-d. We pray in order to acknowledge that from G-d comes our daily bread. Although Karl Marx dismissed religious people as weaklings who turned to G-d as an opiate, it is in fact the strong man who leans on G-d. The man who is stable and sturdy inside is confident enough to acknowledge his limitations and search outside himself for meaning and

The man who is stable and sturdy inside is confident enough to acknowledge his limitations and search outside himself for meaning and purpose.

purpose. He is not so arrogant as to believe that he created himself or was created to develop only himself. On the contrary, it is the weak man, the pathetic man, who can never lean on anyone but himself, so terrified is he of ever needing another.

These are the five areas in which all men must seek to succeed. The good life is found in the development and balance of these areas.

22.

Fostering Healthy Ambition

HAVING DEFINED the five elements of success, and the five areas in which male success must be found, I turn now to ambition. Everyone wants to be a somebody and nobody wants to be a nobody. But there is one kind of ambition that is destroying American men and making them feel like failures. At the same time, there is a healthy ambition to which all should aspire.

I once recommended a bright Oxford student for a top position at a bank. The man hiring was a friend and I wanted to help him recruit the best possible candidate. Although I thought the student was highly qualified for the job, to my surprise my friend turned him down after the interview. When I called to ask why, he responded that his bank was known as a people's bank and they were proud of the team spirit that existed among their employees. "There's no way that this guy is going to work with anyone else," he told me. "He's good, but he's too hungry. So I have to sacrifice talent for teamwork." My friend obviously believed that ambition and principle could not easily coexist.

In general, we associate ambition with ruthlessness, greed, and disloyalty. Take talented investment bankers, for instance. Because they are constantly approached for hire by different banks, even their own managers don't trust their loyalty. The only way to guarantee that these highly ambitious young people—nearly all men—remain in the company is by withholding their money until the end of the calendar year, paying them in Christmas bonuses rather than salaries. The same is true of other high-paying jobs like those in the tech world. They pay their hotshots in stock options that have to vest before they can be cashed in, which is the only way they can keep these guys from jumping ship to a more lucrative opportunity.

AMBITION PROPELS US FORWARD
—

But there is a positive side to ambition as well. First and foremost, ambition is a powerful engine capable of propelling mankind forward to ever greater feats. Without it we have stasis, laziness, and mediocrity. If a doctor has no ambition, then the sick will never be cured. If a medical researcher doesn't aspire to win a Nobel Prize, chances are we will not find a cure for AIDS.

Ambition is what produces excellence, and we have yet to find a better human engine for producing such lofty results. Communism's squashing of ambition is what led to its economic and social mediocrity. Would you hire a lawyer with no ambition to represent you in court? And if your children tell you that they are content to cruise through school with Cs and Ds, would *you* be content with that? The bottom line is that ambition is necessary and good because it leads to self-awareness and improvement.

Ambition is necessary and good because it leads to self-awareness and improvement.

Nevertheless, it would appear that ambition is far more destructive than constructive. Ambition is insatiable, leaving us restless to change something in our lives, be it job, career, or relationship. Indeed, ambition and satisfaction are inversely proportional: the more of the former, the less of the latter. Ambition is therefore always accompanied by frustration. The old saying goes that there is no rest for the wicked. The truth, however, is that there is no rest for the ambitious. Those who are really ambitious are condemned to a life of endless running. They have a tiger inside them that allows them no peace. Because they are insatiable, they produce results but rarely know happiness. They cannot take satisfaction in any achievement because they are already working on the next goal. We in America are quintessential examples of this malady. We know great success, but it is accompanied by great unhappiness.

Here is the paradox of ambition: If I want to get somewhere else, that means that I'm not happy where I am. But if I'm happy where I am, then I have no ambition to be more. So contentment and ambition seem incompatible. And doesn't ambition directly contradict the Talmud's famous dictum "Who is rich? He who rejoices in his portion"? Aren't we meant to be content?

The answer depends on how we define ambition. If we see ambition as an appraisal of our G–d-given talents and then maximizing those talents, our lives have the potential to be filled with happiness. When we waste that potential, on the other hand, our lives generally are filled with discontentment and a feeling of loss. Nobody wants to waste their life.

As rabbi to the students of Oxford, I noticed something interesting about the most accomplished students. The truly bright students who performed exceptionally well on exams were also the most masochistic. They couldn't forgive themselves for being human. Once I was playing squash with Joseph, an Oxford Marshall Scholar. Joseph was in the process of having his Ph.D. dissertation—a thesis on human rights—published by one of America's leading publishing houses. But on the squash court, every time he lost an easy point he would quietly berate himself, "Come on, Joseph." When he lost a difficult point, he would scream, "That's enough, Joseph." Students like Joseph cannot give themselves a break. They constantly struggle to rescue themselves from the abyss of nothingness they feel inside.

I know this type of person well, because I am one of them. This is why I have always loved and admired those who rise above this trap, people who find an intrinsic sense of self-worth that transcends their professional accomplishments. My favorite country in all of Europe is Italy, where people seem to take it easier and still achieve a great deal. Indeed, although Italy has had few stable governments in the last fifty years, it still has one of the strongest economies in Europe. The reason is simple: it is the home of "the Mediterranean man," defined as the man who is prepared to forgive himself for being human.

Taking satisfaction from being human means putting ambition into context. It means determining what our gifts are and seeking to maximize them in order to bring purpose to our lives, rather than focusing on what the world considers successful and always aspiring to goals that may be entirely foreign to our nature.

PRODUCTIVE VERSUS POISONOUS AMBITION

—

So which is it? Is ambition a good thing or a bad thing? Does it afford us glory from achievement or pain and frustration as we inevitably fall short? The answer is that there are two kinds of ambition. Let us call them Broken Ambition and Wholesome Ambition.

Broken Ambition is based on the idea that the individual is unworthy and must seek external achievement in order to be distinguished. Wholesome Ambition, by contrast, is based on the idea that every human being is born special, with a precious gift to contribute to the world that only they can offer. And they therefore have an obligation to contribute their gift.

The difference between the two can be summed up in the personalities of Napoleon and Einstein, two of history's most fascinating men. Born to a noble family that lost its wealth, Napoleon was riddled with lifelong insecurities. He became a conqueror not because he believed himself to be superior to others but because he felt himself to be inferior. Forever ashamed of his family's situation, he constantly tried to prove that he was the better man, and he plunged Europe into incessant wars in order to feed his insatiable ambition. Napoleon was never evil, and much has been made of the fact that although he was in essence a dictator, he never became a Stalin or a Hitler. He was not brutal and he was not a despot. He preserved the rights of the people he conquered. Nevertheless, he had an insatiable desire to dominate other nations and subdue foreign peoples. He was not motivated by wickedness, but by lifelong insecurities.

Einstein, on the other hand, was motivated by lifelong innocence. Walter Isaacson points out in his magisterial biography of Einstein that the revolutionary insights of the great scientist came from a childlike curiosity that never left him. He had a child's sense of wonder, a sense we are all born with but that many adults quickly lose. Likewise, Jürgen Neffe writes in his biography of Einstein that the great man possessed "the features of a shy, almost saintly, childlike little man with the soft brown eyes, the drooping facial lines of a world-weary beagle, and hair like an aurora borealis." Einstein recognized that he was born with powers of concentration and curiosity that were equaled by few other men. He had an innate knack for theoretical physics. He could conceive entire universes in his mind. He was special, and special people have an obligation to make an outstanding contribution to the world to benefit their fellow man. Einstein was never possessed by insecurity, but powered instead by strength of purpose. This is why Einstein was never corrupted by his enormous success and lived with exemplary humility. He led a wholesome and unassuming life. I took my children to see the house he lived in for twenty years in Princeton at 112 Mercer Street. We were all astonished at its small size and simplicity. The greatest scientist since Newton, the man voted by *Time* magazine as the Person of the Century, lived in the home of an average worker. His ambition did not need external corroboration with luxuries. It was fueled by the exact opposite. He was a somebody who was born with something to contribute. Napoleon, by contrast, couldn't have enough palaces. It was the things outside of him and the giant armies he commanded that lent his otherwise lowly existence significance in his own eyes.

Broken Ambition is the most common form of ambition. Born of a profound feeling of inadequacy and unworthiness, it is predicated on the idea that doing and owning will compensate for being; that having possessions will take the place of virtue; that knowing famous people will compensate for our sense of anonymity; and that having control over others will compensate for lacking control over ourselves. Broken Ambition is human insecurity personified.

Insecurity, however, cannot be so easily dismissed. It is responsible not only for the bad things we do, but for the good as well. John F. Kennedy lived in the shadow of his brother Joe Jr., who died a hero's death on a special mission in the Second World War. Wanting to prove himself, JFK too became a hero when he rescued many of his stranded men after the destruction of his boat, *PT-109*. Richard Nixon wanted to prove his critics wrong for dismissing him as an extremist, a communism hater, so he opened the door to China. Insecurity is also what leads us into loving relationships with other human beings, since we do not feel adequate alone and crave the attention and affection of other people.

Broken Ambition is insatiable. Even though we may enjoy great professional success, we will be condemned to a life of pain and misery. One would think that the more one's insecurities fueled accomplishments, the more one's self-esteem would grow. Precisely the opposite is true. The more one who is fueled by insecurity achieves, the more insecure he feels.

There are endless examples of the rich and famous that illustrate the toxicity of this type of ambition. Nearly all the world's great screen actresses and musical performers had turbulent or difficult childhoods. Greta Garbo grew up in terrible poverty in Stockholm. Madonna lost her mother as a child. One would expect that once these women made it to the top of their fields, earning world fame and great riches, they would be satisfied. But insecurity builds and follows on the heels of their success at every turn. Garbo became a legendary recluse, as did Brigitte Bardot. Bette Davis published an autobiography entitled *The Lonely Life*. More recently, Lindsay Lohan, whom so many young girls envy as the personification of fame and success, was arrested for driving her Mercedes into a tree, drugged and drunk out of her mind. On the night she did so, she reportedly told her friends that she wished she would die. Britney Spears is the most famous twenty-something woman in the world. But she has just confessed to having hit "rock bottom." For all her money and fame, Paris Hilton seems satisfied with none of it, and her life is in the gutter as well.

SURVIVAL OF THE FITTEST

—

Broken Ambition is in part the result of living in a market economy. In such a predatory environment, where only the fittest survive—

there is a reason we call it the rat race—colleagues become competitors, comrades become contenders, and allies become antagonists. In this world a man is ambitious because he feels threatened by those whose achievements seem greater

> In such a predatory environment, where only the fittest survive—there is a reason we call it the rat race—colleagues become competitors, comrades become contenders, and allies become antagonists.

than his own. Thus, weakness and insecurity rather than strength and purpose push him up the ladder of success.

And typically he climbs that ladder alone, looking down upon those he had to step on in order to reach his heights. Like Melville's Ahab, the person motivated by Broken Ambition is often self-obsessed and tyrannical. An unyielding competitor, he is unable to form meaningful relationships because he views others only as means to his own ends. Indeed, he drives away those who are closest to him because his insatiability strips the color from his soul and the sensitivity from his spirit, making him an obnoxious bore. And although he may lead the crew to new heights in search of the great whale, he will also sink the ship rather than admit defeat, so destructive is his unquenchable ambition.

Ultimately, instead of earning the respect of his peers, he elicits enmity and jealousy. His colleagues secretly pray for his failure. And because his insularity breeds suspicion rather than admiration, he condemns himself to a life of loneliness, imprisoned within the shell of his ego.

A case in point is Kaiser Wilhelm II, the emperor of Germany at the turn of the twentieth century. The grandson of two great dynastic rulers—Kaiser Wilhelm I and Queen Victoria—young Wilhelm was born with a withered left arm that affected his balance. To suffer from a glaring physical handicap and be unable to ride a horse was certainly not easy for a boy destined to rule an empire. Wilhelm's character never recovered from the colossal insecurity that his physical disability engendered. Consequently, he exhibited an unhealthy competitive streak throughout his life.

As a boy his competitiveness manifested itself on the playing field; as a man, on the battlefield. Because he felt intimidated by the British Empire, he engaged in a meaningless arms race with the British, building huge dreadnought battleships that Germany scarcely needed. Historians concur that it was his relentless attempt to equal the strength of the British navy that eventually led to the outbreak of the First World War.

Shakespeare examined the nature of this ambitious beast in the play *Richard III*. Like Kaiser Wilhelm II, Richard III was also physically deformed, but with a hunched back instead of a withered arm. And like Wilhelm, Richard III's ambition was motivated by his feelings of insecurity and vulnerability. Indeed, Richard III was so ambitious to be king that he killed off anyone who interfered with his plan, including his own kin. But where did he end up with all of his ambition? At the end of the play, we find him isolated on the stage, desperately crying the famous line "A horse, a horse. My kingdom for a horse!"

WHOLESOME AMBITION IS HEALTHY AMBITION
—

Wholesome Ambition is predicated on the idea that all humans are born with infinite value. The rationale is that I am created in the image of G-d and am therefore born intrinsically and infinitely unique and special. And so is every other human being on this earth. And other people's specialness does not compromise my own. Each is special in his own way. Thus, while I am never more important than anyone else, I am also never less worthy. I have no need to prove myself because I am born precious and valuable. My colleagues' achievements never infringe upon my own because the world is large enough to contain all of our aspirations.

With Broken Ambition the scenario is win/lose; with Wholesome Ambition it is win/win. I look upon my fellow human beings as comrades, not competitors. I reach out to them as brothers, not belligerents. Moreover, because there is an integral plan to creation and I am central to it, as are we all, G-d endowed me with a special gift to give to the world that only I can contribute. To keep that gift locked inside me is to diminish the world in its entirety.

I do not have to establish or earn my place in society by *doing* because my essence is in my *being*. Indeed, my existence was called forth from nothingness to add to the majesty and perfection that is G-d's creation. I see myself not as an independent entity but rather as an interdependent component of the universe.

Consider how the different types of ambition play out in our role as parents. Western parents have extremely high ambitions for their children and it is all too common to compare our children to others. In addition, we typically classify development as achievement, believing that there is some merit in how fast a child walks, talks, weans, or potty trains, when all of the above will naturally occur on their own even if we don't urge the child onward. After all, these are characteristics of a biped: unless there is some physiological problem, all children eventually walk, talk, eat, and sleep through the night without diapers, no matter how gifted or average they are, and no matter how ambitious or not are their parents.

We incorrectly assume that there is some correlation between how early a child walks and how fast they will run, but there is none. Nor is there a correlation between how early a child talks and how meaningful their sentences will be. Nevertheless, you hear a proud mother describe how her daughter was walking at nine months and you wonder why your son is "lagging" at thirteen months. Or you hear a proud father tell you how little Bennett knows the alphabet while your little Betty shows no interest in letters at all. Or the day-care center tells you that Elliott must be out of diapers in order to enroll, so you rush Elliott into toilet training at two when he otherwise would not be ready until three or even later, setting up everyone involved for some degree of frustration only so that Elliott can reach the milestone earlier than is natural.

All of these feelings and actions derive from Broken Ambition. We want our kids—even as infants—to keep up and get ahead in a highly competitive world. One mother even told me that she had to buy her four-year-old daughter a computer out of fear that she would not have a competitive edge in kindergarten!

It's shocking and tragic what we fathers, persecuted and taunted by our sense of insignificance and failed ambition, do to our sons. I remember that on the occasion of my son's bar mitzvah, family came from all over the world to celebrate with us. After having prepared for twelve months, Mendy was going to read from the Torah on Saturday morning at synagogue. The night before, Friday night, the Sabbath eve, we organized a prayer service for our family and friends. Mendy put on a tie that I did not approve of, and I ended up rebuking him. This, on the most important occasion of his young life. By the time he arrived at the prayer service, his eyes were red. The last thing he wanted or needed was a reprimand from his father over not being or looking well groomed enough. He had worked an entire year for this special moment. He needed a father's assurance that his efforts had been adequate. That everything about him was good enough. But rather than allowing him to be, his father was still molding and sculpting him into a fatherly vision of perfection. With my speech and actions, I was still telling him that he wasn't good enough and thereby inadvertently making him as insecure as I was. I felt like a jerk and knew that I needed to make amends.

I turned for my sermon that evening to the concept of a bar mitzvah and how, in Judaism, a boy becomes a man when he turns thirteen. As Mendy's father, I said, I was trying to make him into a man. I wanted him to be the best he could be. I wanted him to be one of those special men who made their mark and left an impact. In short, I was passing my insecurities on to him. I was subconsciously making him into a human doing, just as I had been made into one. What was done to me I was doing to him. I was taking the American masculine dysfunction and making it into a family heirloom. Was this also meant to be a family tradition?

I told the gathered worshippers—nearly all of whom were men—that a bar mitzvah was a good time to directly address the pain that we fathers inflict upon sons as we transfer to them our insecurities and our desires and our fear that in our own lives we don't measure up. I spoke of how there is a blessing in the Jewish religion when one's son is called up to read the Torah for the very first time on the occasion of his bar mitzvah. The father recites these words: "Blessed be He who has absolved me of responsibility for this little one." The ostensible meaning of the blessing is that a father, in Jewish law, is responsible for his child's sins up until his maturity, when the child becomes responsible for his own actions. So a parent thanks G-d for absolving him of responsibility for his son's misdeeds. It no longer goes on his account, if you will. But I gave the blessing a homiletic interpretation. I said that the Hebrew can also be read, "I beseech You, O Lord, to help me stop *continually punishing* this little one." I transformed the prayer into one where we plead with the Creator to find our children good

> "I beseech You, O Lord, to help me stop *continually punishing* this little one."

enough, to stop making them feel that they have to earn love or become perfect. I was asking G-d to help us heal ourselves so that we would not continually harm our children. Then I asked Mendy publicly to forgive me for what I had done to him before his bar mitzvah and for many of the mistakes I had made as a father to that date. I told him that, unlike him, I was definitively not perfect. But my love for him was.

We are allowed to be ambitious for our children, but only so long as it is of the Wholesome Ambition variety rather than the harmful Broken Ambition. The parent motivated by Wholesome Ambition also wants his child to succeed but measures success by different standards altogether. He doesn't want to pick the fruit before it is ripe. He is willing to wait for it to fall naturally. He knows that his son is intrinsically valuable, was born a somebody, has innate G-d-given talents that will manifest by themselves if given the proper inspiration and encouragement.

Therefore, he won't force little David to take piano lessons in order to satisfy his own ambitions for his son to play in recitals and win awards. Rather, he will encourage his son to develop his G-d-given talents as a responsibility to both himself and his society to maximize his potential. If he has a talent for music, then he is born with a capacity to bring musical joy to the world, and it should not be wasted. But none of this is about impressing anyone. Similarly, such a father will be far less interested in the grades his son receives than in the substance of what he has learned. Finally, this father will be far more impressed by how his son develops his potential than by how he compares to others in the marketplace that is called a school, even though all his friends may religiously consult the charts to see how their children rank in comparison to some artificial standard.

Whereas Broken Ambition derives from a desire to prove oneself in a competitive arena, Wholesome Ambition is born of one's obligation to maximize one's potential, whatever that may be. Broken Ambition is entirely external. You live to keep up with the Joneses. Wholesome Ambition, however, is internal. You live your own life to the fullest. And your children should too.

NOT KNOWING YOUR NAME
—

Many Jewish legends tell of "the wise men of Chelm," a city filled with fools who thought they were clever. Yankel was one of these imbeciles, and one day he went to the communal bathhouse before the Sabbath. As he was about to strip down and enter the bath, it suddenly occurred to him that when he took off his clothes, he would forget who he was. Observing all the other naked men in the bath who looked just like him, he felt certain that he would lose his identity.

To prevent this from happening, he decided to tie a red string around his toe so that he would remember who he was when he came out of the bath. While he was soaping himself in the water, the string fell off and slipped onto the toe of another man. When Yankel came out of the bath, he was distraught. Because there was no string on his toe, he had forgotten who he was. He scanned the room for a clue, and soon found the red string on the foot of another bather. Yankel walked over to the man and said, "I know who you are. But pray tell me, who the heck am I?"

When our identity is dependent on some external marker for validation—like Yankel's red string or the neighborhood we live in or the car we drive—there is no guarantee that we will keep our bearings.

In fact, chances are that we will drift far off our intended path. That's why Broken Ambition leads to permanent insecurity, workaholism, and overachievement. We're always standing atop the precipice trying to keep ourselves from falling into anonymity and oblivion. Ahab's marker was Moby Dick; without the great whale, his life had no purpose. Indeed, Ahab was so ambitious that he looked for the largest creature in the sea to fill the vast nothingness he felt inside himself.

> **Ahab's marker was Moby Dick; without the great whale, his life had no purpose. Indeed, Ahab was so ambitious that he looked for the largest creature in the sea to fill the vast nothingness he felt inside himself.**

Similarly, when someone becomes wealthy and believes that their money will validate their existence, they live in paranoia and permanent insecurity. They are convinced that all who befriend them do so only for their money, because deep down inside they feel that without their money they are worthless.

Paul started his own insurance company and sold his stake of the business thirty years later for hundreds of millions of dollars. Paul's only son, Mark, dated and fell in love with Wendy. Both were puzzled about why Paul never showed Wendy any warmth and gave her only perfunctory greetings. When Mark asked him why, he replied, "She is only interested in you for your inheritance."

Although Mark and Wendy eventually broke up, Paul ended up treating all of Mark's other girlfriends the same way. I was called in to discuss the situation with Paul. "Surely you want your son to marry someone," I said, "yet you treat all your son's girlfriends with contempt. Is no one good enough for him?" Paul said, "It's just that the women he brings around have dollar signs in their eyes. All they want is his money." I responded, "It's sad that you think that, because it means that the money you worked so hard to earn has become a curse. You worked in order to give your family a better life. But here you are destroying the lives of the people you love most because money is the only thing on your mind. And because you're so obsessed with money yourself, you believe that everyone else is just as obsessed. Start believing that there is something special about you and your family that's not related to money. Once you stop seeing the dollar signs, others will too."

BLIND AMBITION
—

Broken Ambition is what we might call blind ambition. It's when you charge ahead with no identifiable destination. Your only concern is to get noticed. You are an attention-seeker, a publicity hound. You are greedy. You will do anything to acquire importance. And since you've bought the lie that without money or fame you're a nobody, you try your best to acquire both. You do not run toward any particular goal but rather away from something, the inner fear that you are worthless. You become a workaholic and berate your employees because every mistake made by someone else threatens your very existence. You are nothing without your work.

Blind ambition has gripped America in the form of reality TV shows where everyone and his uncle wants to be famous. On shows like *Fear Factor*, it seems that people are even prepared to eat their own dung just to get on TV. Countless people in America are prepared to humiliate themselves in order to make TV producers happy. Celebrity at any cost has become a sad and defining characteristic of the American celebrity culture.

Anna Nicole Smith is the martyred saint of celebrity without a cause. Here was a woman who celebrated dysfunction because it got her noticed. She made herself into a train wreck because it kept her in the tabloids and gave her a reality TV show. But for all her fame and treasure, Anna Nicole led a miserable life that was racked with heartache. Like most people, she wanted to be special, she wanted to be loved. But she mistook the amusement of the fickle public for real affection. This could only mean that she had to keep the public amused. If she had married an appropriate husband and had well-adjusted children, she would not make it onto the covers of *People* or *Us Weekly*. So instead she chose to make her life into a circus of the absurd. In a famous quote she gave when she was deposed in court and asked to comment on her fame she responded, "I like it. I love the paparazzi. They take pictures and I just smile away. I have always liked attention and I didn't get it very much growing up, and I always wanted to be, you know, noticed."

Will a woman's marriage really succeed when she is more interested in Brad and Angelina's relationship than her own?

Many other celebrities follow suit. They date, marry, and break up and in the process become slaves to the public's prurience.

I have long argued that we should wean ourselves from our obsession with celebrities for the most self-ish of reasons: if we focus less on them, we can focus more on ourselves. Will a woman's marriage really succeed when she is more interested in Brad and Angelina's relationship than her own?

But I now ask that we overcome our fixation not for selfish but for the most humanitarian of reasons: to save human life. If we continue to discuss celebrities' flimsy marriages, they will divorce to be our water-cooler chatter. If we continue to discuss their bouts in rehab, they will keep taking drugs to get on *Entertainment Tonight*. And if we continue to focus on their shattered lives, they will continue to die recklessly.

And even the most narcissistic celebrity is still a child of G-d.

And even the most narcissistic celebrity is still a child of G-d.

Like so many damaged Hollywood celebrities, those who possess Broken Ambition may end up famous in their lifetime but may be quickly forgotten in death.

Wholesome Ambition, however, forfeits narcissism in favor of altruism. It involves subordination to a cause higher than oneself. One becomes ambitious not for oneself but for the cause. One loses one's identity to something greater than oneself and begins to devote one's actions and capabilities to the furtherance of that cause. After a while, one's identity becomes indistinguishable from the cause to which one has dedicated one's life.

One can always identify those special men and women who are motivated by this higher form of ambition. It shows itself in their utter lack of fear. Whether it was George Washington crossing the Delaware with a frozen force who were about to launch themselves against a superior army, or Abraham Lincoln boldly continuing the

> The man or woman who lives for a cause has no trepidation because they have ceased living for themselves.

fight against the Confederacy after repeated defeats, or Martin Luther King Jr. declaring the night before he died, "Tonight, I am fearing no man," the man or woman who lives for a cause has no trepidation because they have ceased living for themselves.

FOSTERING AMBITION

—

In contrast to Christianity, which preaches that "it is harder for a rich man to reach the Kingdom of G-d than it is for a camel to pass through the eye of a needle," Judaism teaches that we are born to distinguish ourselves. However, although Judaism encourages ambition, it views wealth and fame not as an end in itself, but rather as a means to a more important end. In other words, we are motivated to achieve success not to further our own glory but rather to submerge ourselves in G-d's purposes.

When Jacob flees the wrath of his brother, Esau, in the Book of Genesis, he offers what seems to be a self-serving prayer: "If G-d will be with me and protect me along the path upon which I now embark and give me bread to eat and water to drink, then I will make the Lord my G-d." Sounds like a horse trade, doesn't it? And what if G-d didn't give Jacob these things? Would he start worshipping idols? The great Jewish thinker Maimonides explains that what Jacob meant was this: "If you give me the essential materials of life, O Lord, then I will have the resources with which to worship you. But if I am starving for bread and have nothing to eat myself, how will I be able to give alms to the poor and raise children? Therefore, please give me material plenty so that I can use it to serve you and do your work, Lord."

Jacob was articulating a high level of Wholesome Ambition, where one subordinates oneself and one's resources to a higher cause. He was not praying for himself. He was asking G-d to give him the tools to advance his belief system and spread the knowledge of G-d to the far corners of the earth.

Not many recognize her name, but I remember how impressed I was with Jody Williams, who won the Nobel Peace Prize in 1997 for her leadership in the worldwide campaign to discontinue the use of land mines. On the day she won she criticized the American government, President Clinton, and every other world leader who didn't sign the petition banning land mines. Had she not condemned them for failing to take the threat of land mines seriously, she would have been treated like royalty. As the winner of the Nobel Peace Prize, she would have been invited to royal receptions and state dinners. But that meant nothing to her because she lived for a higher cause.

PASSING THE TORCH

—

Many people start out believing in a cause but end up *becoming* the cause. Wicked people often subordinate the higher cause to themselves. Hitler took Germany and made it his personal fiefdom. Stalin did the same with the Soviet Union, as did Mao with China. All three indiscriminately slaughtered millions of people in the name of their own ambition.

How do we know if we are ambitious for ourselves or for a larger cause? The answer lies in our ability to subordinate our ego. If when the time comes we find it easy to pass the mantle to someone more capable than ourselves to take the cause forward, then the cause takes precedence. If, on the other hand, we cannot let go of the reins, then the cause was only the means by which we promoted our personal ambition.

Moses led the Jews through the desert for thirty years. But the moment it came time to pass the torch to Joshua, Moses did not hesitate. When G-d told him he would not enter the promised land, he had one request: please, G-d, don't leave the people leaderless, like a flock of sheep without a shepherd. And after that, he quietly retreated from the world stage without fanfare. There were no honor guards, eulogies, or twenty-one-gun salutes. He was buried alone with only G-d in attendance. The needs of the people always superseded his own.

A more contemporary example of a world leader's subordination to a cause is Nelson Mandela. Although at the age of eighty he could easily have ran for reelection as president of South Africa and won, instead he stepped down in favor of younger leadership that would better serve the purposes of his country and his cause. Mandela never made the mistake of believing, like another great champion of his people, Charles de Gaulle, that he and the country were synonymous. On the contrary, Mandela gave his life to his people and then silently retreated from power.

By contrast I offer the example of Margaret Thatcher. A great leader in her time, she possessed the courage and assertiveness to save Britain from a continuing downward economic spiral. However, when her sell-by date came she wouldn't stand down gracefully and had to be forced out. Although she saved the country and was much admired while in office, history will forever debate whether she was good for Britain or not. Indeed, there is a general feeling that while she started out serving the interests of her country, she ended up placing her own interests first. And the proof: she just couldn't let go.

In parenting, the same dilemma exists. Are we devoted to our children or merely using them to feel important by having someone dependent on us? The only way of knowing for sure is what you do when it comes time to let go and allow them to be people in their own right. Those parents who can never let go, who insist on making every decision for their children and smothering them with their guardianship, view their children's freedom as their own loss. Because of their insecurities, they treat their children like possessions. Those who are prepared to allow their child the freedom to develop their own personality, on the other hand, can be assured that all along it was the child and not themselves who was paramount.

SUBORDINATING OURSELVES TO G-D'S WILL

Judaism teaches that while we must all believe in ourselves, we must also doubt ourselves. Indeed, the Talmud makes contradictory statements about ambition and self-appraisal. It says that a person should carry two statements in his pockets. In his right-hand pocket he should carry a piece of paper that says, "The whole world was created for me." But in his left-hand pocket there should be a piece of paper repeating the pronouncement of Abraham, "I am but dust and ashes." Balance is achieved only by the eternal tension between these two postures, the belief that we are everything and the belief that we are nothing. Therefore, while we want to be ambitious, we must never allow the focus to be on us. While we should always yearn for distinction, we must do so in subordination to a higher cause.

> A person should carry two statements in his pockets. In his right-hand pocket he should carry a piece of paper that says, "The whole world was created for me." But in his left-hand pocket there should be a piece of paper repeating the pronouncement of Abraham, "I am but dust and ashes."

This subordination represents the highest form of ambition. It is where we strive to be our best with no hint of arrogance because everything we do is in the service of something higher. The highest of these higher causes is G-d. Subordinating our lives to G-d will invite both humility and purpose and is one of the strongest remedies for a life of brokenness. The Bible describes Moses as being "the most humble man who walked the earth," which is amazing given that he was also the greatest prophet of the Bible. Most people become arrogant when they achieve greatness. Moses was different. The more he achieved, the more humble he became. Because his achievements never served the purposes of ego. He had given his life to G-d. As he was absorbed into the great, infinite presence, he lost more and more of himself and was utterly liberated from the cage of the ego.

Unrestrained belief in the self is arrogance at best and dangerous psychosis at worst. Any man or woman whose ambition is unchecked by a force above them has been cut loose from the restraining force of morality and is not to be trusted. Therefore, in order to tame ambition and ensure that goodness will prevail, it is necessary to also feel subservience to G-d. Accepting that we are G-d's creatures born to execute G-d's will ensures that we never become lost in our own fantasies of divinity.

> **Any man or woman whose ambition is unchecked by a force above them has been cut loose from the restraining force of morality and is not to be trusted.**

Putting limits on the ego while retaining our ambition and upward mobility is a prerequisite to a successful and satisfying life. The arrogant man is always an ingrate. Not only is he full of himself, but he also shows no appreciation to those who have facilitated his success. Cultivating the art of gratitude is the most useful means by which to guarantee that our ambition will always be a blessing to us. But to give gratitude, you have to be strong enough to ascribe your success to a power greater than yourself.

23.

Raising Our Sons Differently

WE MUST raise our sons differently. And here, believe me, I am speaking to myself as a father as well.

The lie that a man only matters if he is professionally successful and amasses a lot of money and fame begins with the false education of our youth. Truth be told, we are much harsher on our sons than we are on our daughters. I know I am. We criticize them constantly for being imperfect. If they can't catch a football, we rebuke them for missing an end zone pass.

I know I have.

If they walk around with their shirts out of their pants, we reproach them for being untidy.

I know I have.

If they eat with their fingers, we call them slobs.

I know I have.

If they bring home bad grades from school, we admonish them for being lazy.

I know I have.

If they yell at their sisters, we reprove them for being ungentlemanly.

I know I have.

And if they fail to shower and be clean, we scold them for being slovenly.

I know I have.

All the reprimanding, reproving, censuring, reproaching, admonishing, chiding, and hauling over the coals, I did with love. I did it because I cared about them and wanted what was best for them. I did it because it was done to me, and to my father before me.

But I now know that it was all based on a lie, the lie that a boy, as opposed to a girl, has to earn love. That a boy, as opposed to a girl, must be taught to *do* before he can be allowed just to *be*. And I scarred my sons, just as I was scarred before them, as was my father before me.

And I now know that I must do things differently.

Yes, boys shouldn't pick their noses, and they should make their beds, and they should get good grades. But this has nothing to do with earning their parents' love. They should be told they are loved when boogers are dripping from their noses, their rooms are a mess, and they bring home Fs. We have to stop making men feel that they have to *do* in order to be. And it has to begin from the time they are boys.

I am the father of five daughters and three sons. For a long time I did not want to admit to myself that I was raising my sons differently, that I was harder on them and more demanding than I was with my daughters. And yet I would constantly find things wrong with my son Mendy. He is such a good boy and helps tremendously around the house. But I always found reason to criticize the things he did. Then one day, we were out working in the garden, mowing the lawn, and Mendy took the lawn mower over a large stone and broke the blade. I got really angry at him. I scolded him for being reckless. I admonished him for being careless. And as I did so, he recoiled and stood back, and I could suddenly see a river of distance opening between us. I was terrified. I feared that the river would grow into a sea, and then an ocean. I did not want to be one of those fathers who is alienated from his son, G-d forbid. My first reaction was to force the closing of that distance with sheer force. "You get back here right now. I am talking to you." He came back and submitted to my authority. But the pain in his face was unmistakable, and I was the cause of his pain.

I hated myself at that moment. I, a broken American male, was cracking my own son. To be sure, I did it for his own good. Life would not be forgiving to him as a male. Bosses would have little compassion. If he broke their equipment as he broke mine, he would be fired. If he acted recklessly at college, he would be expelled. And if he behaved carelessly around a woman, she would not be interested in being with him. I was breaking him in for his own good.

Or was I? Was there not a better way? Could I not speak to him in a manner that would inspire rather than cripple? Was I incapable of speaking to him tenderly and from the heart, pointing out to him that he was a special boy and therefore had an obligation to do good things with his life, which entailed first and foremost learning to handle responsibility?

Rather than speaking to my son in a manner that made him feel fundamentally unworthy, was there not a way of speaking to him that made him feel adequate and good enough?

By constantly criticizing our sons, we instill within them Broken Ambition rather than Wholesome Ambition. They feel flawed and blemished and spend their lives trying to prove their critics wrong. I have a friend in England who is a prominent attorney. He has celebrity clients and is a minor celebrity himself. Once when we were speaking about his success, he told me that he owes everything to a fifth-grade teacher who told him constantly that he wouldn't amount to anything. Well, that's one way to succeed, but what a harsh way. To spend an entire lifetime trying to prove your critics wrong. To be haunted by the spirit of inadequacy and to rely on that as a spur to achievement. When overcoming a feeling of worthlessness is your motivation, can you enjoy your success even if you achieve it?

In practical terms this means that we should admonish our boys for their mistakes, by all means. But the rebuke-to-praise ratio must be one to four *at least* in favor of praise. They must be made to feel special and loved even when they are imperfect.

Fathers must learn to tell their sons that they are loved just the way they are. They need to get their sons to open up to them about the pressures they are feeling to do well in sports, in school, and to be popular among girls. They have to make sure their sons understand that none of that is really important and what is important is that they be able to identify their true gifts and make the most of them.

We have to cultivate our sons' natural interests rather than force them to conform to what society considers important. I have a friend from Toronto who is a successful publisher. From humble origins, he worked his whole life to make it to the big leagues. He loves the upwardly mobile circles in which he revolves. He has two sons and a daughter. It's amazing to watch. With his daughter he is tender and loving and doesn't push her very hard. All his little girl has to do is look pretty and Daddy lights up. But with his two young sons he is ruthless. One of the boys liked playing soccer. "Soccer," the father said to his son, "nobody in America plays soccer once they grow up." So he got them a tennis coach and pressured them to keep up with their lessons and excel at tennis. After all, this is the sport that Dad plays with his rich friends. So the kids have to prepare from a young age to do the same. Then he got them horseback-riding lessons. Both kids hated horses. But here they were, model equestrians, jumping over fences and flying around paddocks—and screaming in horror while they rode. Their real interests were completely ignored.

This does not mean that we can't push our sons to do things that are beneficial to their education and development. It just means that even as we push them, we have to cultivate an interest in them rather than make them feel that they are undertaking this activity in order to measure up.

A famous Talmudic expression says, "Words that emanate from the heart penetrate the heart." If we are able to connect with our sons and speak to them sincerely about the special men we want them to grow up to be, then we will not invite the kind of rebellion that is so often seen with strong-willed children. All kids want is to be loved, valued, and special. It is our job as parents to make our boys feel that way so that they won't spend the rest of their lives trying to prove themselves.

I had a debate with a friend of mine who is a successful attorney. He was listening to one of my radio shows where I said that children require lavish praise. I then asked the question of my listeners, "Let's say your child makes an ugly picture and brings it to show to you. Should you lie and say that the picture is beautiful, or should you tell the truth and say that the picture is substandard and they could do better?" I answered my question by saying that the first response was correct. Not because we should lie. We should always avoid untruths. But rather we should say the picture is beautiful because *the truth is* that there is beauty in the picture even if we can't see it. The very fact that it was produced by a precious little child makes it beautiful. And if we miss its beauty, it's because of our cynical adult eyes, which are not innocent enough to pick up on the child's artistic thought.

My friend was livid. "Shmuley, you're being ridiculous. You're just fostering mediocrity! Will my son really benefit by my telling him that he played a great game in Little League when the truth is that he was awful? *No,* you have to be honest with him. You have to tell him that he was terrible but if he tries more and works harder, he'll do a lot better next time."

I disagreed with my friend vociferously. "All that will do is blight his confidence and destroy his ego. And yes, you might get the desired result. He might work harder next time. Not to master the game, but to prove you wrong. He will not be doing it for himself, but for you. And now you and all his other critics are his lifelong masters. And he'll spend the rest of his life trying to impress his tormentors."

We must speak to our sons about the two kinds of ambition we listed earlier, Broken Ambition and Wholesome Ambition, the former fostering lifelong insecurities, the latter ensuring that the individual makes a solid contribution to his society based on his unique talents and gifts. We should inspire our sons with the words of Abraham Lincoln: "I am not bound to win, but I am bound to be true. I am not bound to succeed, but I am bound to live by the light that I have."

Most of all we must raise our sons not to compare themselves to others and to remove themselves from the rat race before the competition even begins. We must get them to live with core convictions that are impervious to society's standards of success.

All this will come via the twin means of example and persuasion. First and foremost, we fathers must serve as an example to our sons of real gentlemanly behavior. We have to model for them extreme courtesy in the treatment of women. The Talmud obligates a husband to honor his wife more than himself. The husband who speaks to his wife courteously and politely and acts chivalrously by never allowing his wife to lift heavy packages and certainly never yelling at her, is giving his son an example of how a true gentleman behaves. By complimenting his wife constantly around his son, he teaches the boy that women are to be honored and respected, especially if they are your wife or mother. The husband who comes home at a decent hour, and certainly no later than 6 P.M., shows his son that money is subordinate to family. And the father who takes his son to church, synagogue, or charity functions, and performs volunteer work, exemplifies for his child how selflessness is a key ingredient in the successful life. Volunteering your time is liberating and makes you successful, precisely because you're *not* making money at that moment.

And then there is persuasion, especially through the power of conversation. We have to talk to our sons to inspire greatness in them. A father and mother must sit their son down and speak to him about not succumbing to peer pressure. They must tell him that there is no need for him to prove himself at school or on the sports field, that they are not interested in A's but in intellectual curiosity. They must say that all they want to know is that *he* wants to learn, so he should focus on enjoying the journey of study rather than on the goal of getting great grades. Next we have to sit our teenage sons down and talk to them about respect for women. They are at an age where they are beginning to date. Will they be the kind of boys who pressure girls to do things they're uncomfortable doing, or will they respect women and treat them as equals? Will they use coarse language about women? Will they be like those superficial men who judge a woman by her packaging? We have to consciously strive to raise sons who are different by inspiring them to be different with the right words.

This is how we will raise a new generation of American boys who grow into wholesome rather than broken men, boys who look ahead toward their own special destiny rather than at all those who will overtake them in the race to material success in life.

Finally, there is no substitute for real, intimate interaction between you and your son. My own sons are in completely different age groups. One is a teenager of fourteen, the next is six, and the youngest is a baby of one. I try every night to study with my teenage son. I don't always succeed, but on most nights we read the Bible together (the portion of the day) or study other central Jewish texts. By doing so I expose him to the understanding that his central grooming as a man is a relationship with G-d, becoming knowledgeable and wise, and loving his family. Notice that I don't read *The Wall Street Journal* with him.

With my six-year-old I try to say the daily prayers when he hasn't already said them in school. I also go bike riding with him in the beautiful outdoors in the spring and summer months nearly every day and read him a bedtime story on most nights. That way I teach him to love nature rather than man-made material objects and to love books rather than shopping.

And finally, my one-year-old, well, I just try to hold and hug him as much as possible in the full knowledge that even at that tender age he is learning that he is the most adorable person in the whole world. Even though he doesn't have a single cent to his name.

24.

Purposefulness and Direction

LIKE MANY men I know, I often find myself feeling depressed for no apparent reason. When I explore why I'm feeling down, however, it is invariably linked with being a broken American male. Low self-esteem and feeling like a loser who hasn't done much with his life are usually the sources of my unhappiness. These feelings can hit me out of the blue but are often caused by professional setbacks, however minor.

One day I was feeling this way. A prestigious lecture that I was to deliver was suddenly canceled. Loser thoughts ran through my brain. No one wants to hear you, you're washed up, etc. And since these things usually come in groups, anything else that happened that day, like hearing that sales on my latest book were down, just reinforced that feeling of failure. Boy, I thought, when it rains it pours. But such is the lot of a loser.

I was in full BAMM (broken American male mode) when an acquaintance of mine called to tell me that his sister, Joan, who had lost her five-year-old son to leukemia three weeks earlier, was deteriorating rapidly. Would I be able to go that night to visit her?

Now it's one of the truisms of feeling like a failure that the accompanying mild depression saps your energy and you don't feel capable of much. Depression, as I have often said, is not an emotion but an absence of emotion. When you're depressed you don't feel down. Rather, you don't feel at all. You're numb. You're energyless. You just want to be left alone. But I knew one thing: however big a failure I was, I could offer sincere comfort to those who had suffered terrible tragedy and given up hope. I told my acquaintance that I would drive over to see his sister after I had put my kids to bed.

> **Depression, as I have often said, is not an emotion but an absence of emotion. When you're depressed you don't feel down. Rather, you don't feel at all.**

I took my wife with me. When we arrived the house was dimly lit. The husband greeted me at the door and led me in to his wife, who was lying in a fetal position on the couch. After a polite hello and my expression of sorrow for her loss, she told me there was no need to comfort her. It was too late. She was already dead. "When G-d took away my little boy, He got two for the price of one. Only my son is dead in heaven, and I am dead on earth. And it would be good if I died physically as well, so that at least I would be reunited with him." I asked her if any other rabbis or clerics had come to see her. "Yes," she said, "they infuriated me. They told me my son was in a better place. That he was in heaven. But I don't care if he's in a better place. His place is here with me. His place is with his parents and his siblings. I didn't want to listen to them anymore."

The situation was really bad. The mother cried throughout our meeting. She had not showered or left the house since the boy died. She slept with his pajamas at night. She wailed and yelled at her husband in the morning.

I looked at her and I said, "On the last day of his life, after leading the Israelites through the desert for forty years, Moses gave a speech. He said to the Jewish people, 'I call heaven and earth to witness this day against you that I have set before you life and death, the blessings and the curses; therefore choose life, that you and your descendants may live' [Deut. 30:19]. Choose life. That's what he said. Every single day we are faced with a choice of life or death. Sometimes it's a subtle choice. We get into a fight with a friend. Will we choose the death of the relationship and not apologize? Or will we choose life and say we're sorry for any hurt we caused, so that the relationship will continue to live? And sometimes it's a lot more serious and the decision is much more weighty, like when a tragic and unexpected death is visited upon a family. In the aftermath of that tragedy, will we choose death or will it be life?

"We human beings are never meant to choose death. Often death chooses us, against our wishes, against our plans. Death barges in, the most uninvited guest, and snatches away our greatest treasure, the people we love most, our children. But after that monster, that thing that Moses calls a curse, bursts into our lives, leaving devastation in his wake, he must be shown the door. He has to be forced out. He invited himself in. We dare never ask him to stay. He is an unwelcome visitor, an unwanted guest. But what you're doing, Joan, is making him feel welcome. Death burst into your home, but then you gave him succor. You gave him refuge. You told him by your actions that he was invited to stay. He came as an invader, but was then granted sanctuary. And it's time to give him the boot and expel him. Kick him out permanently and eternally, never to return.

"You have to mourn your son, Joan. He was your baby. But you cannot choose death. You cannot die along with him. You have to choose life. If you choose death, you're sinning not just against yourself but against your husband and your other children who need you as much as you need your lost child. You're also sinning against the memory of your beloved son. Because what you're saying in effect is that all he ever did was die. He never lived. He never played. He never smiled. There is no life here to commemorate. There is only death, and that's all he represents.

"The rabbis who told you that he's in a better place, they were well intentioned. But they were wrong. You have every right to be angry at G-d. G-d gave you this beautiful soul and you were an out-standing caretaker. You loved your boy, dressed him warmly, showered him with love, and fought his illness like a lioness. G-d is the one who broke the deal and seemingly negotiated in bad faith. So take it out on G-d. He's a big boy. He can take it. When G-d does loving things for us, we reciprocate His affection and offer Him our thanks. But when He allows unspeakable tragedies, like the death of a child, we don't have to offer Him thanks and say meaningless, trite things like 'Thanks for taking my child to a better place.' We deserve an honest relation-ship with G-d. We give Him homage for all His bounty, just as we rail and thunder against the seeming miscarriages of justice. So take it out on G-d. But why are you taking it out on yourself? What did you ever do to this boy that you deserve to die along with him?'"

Joan listened attentively while I spoke. She stopped crying, and sat in silence. We spoke for about an hour, and then I left. The next morning her husband called me to say that while my words could never compensate for the loss of her son, they had comforted her.

I retell this story here not to share with you a long soliloquy about death and bereavement but to stay true to our theme of heal-ing the broken American male. A strange thing happened to me as I delivered that monologue. I was no longer depressed. I was no longer unhappy. I was no longer broken. I walked out of that tragic home whole. By seeking to mend the spirit of a fellow human being, I had mended myself, however temporarily. I knew my purpose. I was no longer a failure in my own eyes. I did not have to question why G-d had put me on this earth. It wasn't that in successfully comforting a bereaved mother I had suddenly be-come a winner. Rather, in the process of comforting a mother who had lost so much, I no longer thought in terms of being either a win-ner or a loser. And that's because I wasn't thinking about myself. It wasn't about me, it was about her. I was a winner because I was mo-mentarily liberated from the demeaning crush of the rat race. I was a

By seeking to mend the spirit of a fellow human being, I had mended myself.

winner because I had lifted from myself the burden of a weighty ego and the need to feed the beast at all times.

For those few moments, I no longer compared myself to other men. I no longer worried about whether my net worth was as great as theirs. I no longer focused on whether my TV show was as influential as Dr. Phil's. I did not think about how well my last book sold in comparison to Oprah's latest book choice. No. At that moment I was fully involved in my particular gift as a human being, which was no better or worse than any other person's gift. It was simply *my* gift, my ability to comfort, my ability to use words to bring healing. It was simply a gift that suited the needs of the moment. I was one who could bring healing. Other people had other gifts. And I was thrilled for them. G-d bless them. But this was my gift, and I was using it to brighten a darkened planet. When a man is able to focus on his gifts, when he is able to look inside himself and focus on the fulfillment of his own unique destiny, then he is liberated from the pain of an external existence. He does not compare himself with others. They are not the criteria by which he determines his value. Purposefulness becomes the key that liberates him from an identity that is determined by comparing himself with others.

For that one evening, my life was not about me and how successful or how big a failure I was. It was about this lost boy. It was about his distraught mother. It was about the human family and how we all have to care for each other, love one another, and occasionally grieve together.

A life devoted to others is the ultimate cure for the broken American male. We simply think too much about ourselves, our wants, our needs, our desire to be a somebody. When you put that much weight on your own needs, your own concerns, you're bound to break under it. The fragile shell of the human psyche can't handle that much pressure. No wonder

> We simply think too much about ourselves, our wants, our needs, our desire to be a somebody. When you put that much weight on your own needs, your own concerns, you're bound to break under it.

there are so many broken men in America. It's time to liberate your-self from the burden of obsessive focus on yourself.

What if we become a somebody specifically by focusing on the needs of somebody else? The great Hasidic master Rabbi Israel Baal ShemTov wrote that if you seek to heal yourself of something, heal someone else of the same thing. And in the process, you yourself will be healed.

Strange and antithetical as it may sound, broken American men can ultimately heal themselves by ceasing to focus on themselves.

Strange and antithetical as it may sound, broken American men can ulti-mately heal themselves by ceasing to fo-cus on themselves.

When they learn to give instead of to take, when they take the focus off themselves and place it on another, they will find all those things that have previously eluded them.

There are some illnesses in life that require you to take a particu-lar medicine. If you have a bacterial infection you need antibiotics. If you have a headache you need aspirin. But if you're afraid of the dark? Is there a medicine for that, or should you just walk out into the dark and see that you have nothing to fear?

There is no medicine for male brokenness. You can't be cured by taking some sort of drug. Rather, the whole illness consists of inten-sive self-focus. The reason you're broken is that you sit around the whole day wondering whether *you're* a success, whether *you're* appre-ciated, whether *you* were shown ingratitude, whether *you* were disre-spected, and so on. Well, you know what? If you stop thinking about yourself so much, you'll automatically be cured.

Intense focus on self is the very definition of doing as opposed to being. When you help someone in crisis, you use your G-d-given tal-ents and they just pour out of you like a river emerging from a spring. It is part and parcel of the being mode. I felt it that night when I comforted that poor mother whose son had died. The words

just flowed from my lips. I was not trying to impress. I was just seeking to comfort. My heart did the rest. And that's why it was so healing. Conversely, when you focus on your career, social standing, and
rate of accumulation, you're stuck in the doing mode, which is what
causes all the problems in the first place.

In the previous story, you may ask why it was that I took my wife
along with me. Sure, we love spending time together. But it was late
at night and it was hardly going to be a pleasant evening.

If I want to be honest about it, I took her along to impress her, to
win her respect. I always want my wife to know that I am a good
man. She is the one I most want to impress. And I wanted her to see
me making my life more purposeful.

My wife knows that I sometimes feel down. She tries to inflate
my punctured ego. She is not always successful. But I want her to
know that the man she married is not some petty narcissist who is always narrowly focused on how successful he is and where his career
is going. I don't always talk about myself or obsess about myself. I
want her to see that I don't just mope around feeling like a victim,
nursing a shattered ego, and muttering to myself that I am a loser.

I want my wife to know that I get it. That life is not just about
me. It's about G-d. It's about her. It's about our children. It's about
our families. It's about other people. And the reason that her opinion is so important to me is that I as her husband cater to a constituency of one.

We men must learn to find purpose in our devotion to causes
greater than ourselves. The apogee of human wisdom is to discern a
cause higher than ourselves and devote our lives to it. And once it is
found, we are free. We are liberated from the incarceration and
tyranny of the human ego.

Think about it. If all of us have, as Hegel said, the thymotic urge,
the desire for recognition, then go ahead and be recognized. But be
recognized for your enlightenment. As Abraham Lincoln said, "Don't

worry when you are not recognized, but strive to be worthy of recognition." Be one of those rare men, those special people, who finally get it. Who finally understand that the secret of life is that we find purpose, meaning, and ultimately success through a life lived in devotion to others.

25.

From Career to Calling

THE BROKEN American male will be healed through a life devoted to others rather than focused on the small arena of his own selfish interests. When focused on self, the ego becomes an albatross so weighty that it is crushing in its effect. Soon the self wilts under the immense burden of the oversized ego. We have to lighten the load. We have to raise men who are more outwardly directed than inwardly focused.

In pursuit of that all-important transformation, we have to move away from career and on to calling. The pursuit of career is what is destroying the American male. He thinks constantly of where he is on the professional ladder of life. Is he stagnating in a middle-management position, or is he vice president in charge of national sales? But this obsessive focus on career is what makes most men feel like failures. It puts them in a never-ending rat race, a constant competition. After a while, the repetitive bruising of the ego becomes permanent and scarring sets in.

Historians and social anthropologists make much of how the Industrial Revolution created the opportunity for careers. Prior to the Industrial Revolution most men were laborers. There was no real hope for any kind of advancement. Life was about a job, and you were usually lucky to have one. The idea of upward mobility had not been invented. The aristocracy were the products of noble birth, not hard work. But with the Industrial Revolution and the creation of enormous pools of capital, men with skills were needed for the mighty new machines of the time. They could use those skills to advance through the ranks of growing corporations in which skilled labor was so essential. And as companies grew, management was necessary. People could start at the bottom and slowly climb the corporate ladder. And so the career was born. Likewise, because capital was becoming so readily available, entrepreneurial men, armed with ambition and ingenuity, could borrow money at acceptable interest rates and start their own companies and make even more of themselves, become their own bosses. All of this is rightly looked at as an incredibly positive development, freeing people from lifelong serfdom and servitude.

What is overlooked is the price that would be paid in terms of psychological well-being. When men just accepted their station in life, they did not beat themselves up for being a great big nothing or not making much of themselves. How could they? There were no real opportunities. So they accepted their humble place and tried to find joy and meaning in other pursuits, such as religion, family, and friendship. If they couldn't master the outer world, well, maybe they could master the inner. It was in these wholesome pursuits that

Once men began to find satisfaction and prestige in amassing wealth, the traditional avenues of fulfillment—family, community, and religion—moved to the back burner. Career became the principal activity that brought stimulation and compensation.

men found purpose in their lives. The pursuit of money, for most, was simply not a possibility. But once the door of opportunity opened and the transformation of occupation to career began, the sky was the limit. Anyone could become a someone. The race was on and men began to compete against each other for the right to be noticed. Money became the arbiter of success. Once men began to find satisfaction and prestige in amassing wealth, the traditional avenues of fulfillment—family, community, and religion—moved to the back burner. Career became the principal activity that brought stimulation and compensation.

Once the traditional vehicles that sustained male ego were neutralized, however, what took their place? Now that men were spending so much less time with their wives and indeed were getting a far bigger rush from making money than from reading stories to their children, the question became, What would now nurture men and ensure that they remained wholesome and soulful? Detached as they were from family, alienated as they were from G-d, what would nurture these men's spirits and sustain their humanity? And the answer was: nothing. Nothing whatsoever. So their humanity was compromised as they slowly became machines, and deep insecurity set it. Men began to feel that nothing about them was intrinsically unique. It was the money they made that let them feel important. And this just fueled a ferocious and vicious cycle. The more emphasis men placed on factors outside themselves, like the accumulation of capital, to feel important, the more insecure they became. And the more insecure they became, the harder they had to work to prove themselves and the more time they devoted to the accumulation of wealth. And the more time they devoted to the acquisition of material things, the more they ignored their families, thereby losing a connection with something that could make them feel intrinsically valuable, the more insecure they felt.

Now, no one wants to go back to a time when most men were serfs or indentured servants. What we love about America is the vast opportunity it offers and how it rewards hard work with a high standard of living. No one would suggest that we encourage men to be satisfied with a dead-end job, and turn to family and community as an alternative to professional fulfillment. Rather, what I am suggesting is that men be encouraged to go beyond a career and find a calling.

The differences are vast. Whereas a career is all about you and your needs for professional fulfillment, a calling is all about the contribution you can make to the lives of others. A career is all about your potential rewards. A calling is all about your gifts and your ability to give. A career breeds insecurity and makes you constantly question whether you are a success or a failure. A calling breeds a sense of purpose and makes you feel that this is the reason for which you were created.

> A career is all about your potential rewards. A calling is all about your gifts and your ability to give. A career breeds insecurity and makes you constantly question whether you are a success or a failure. A calling breeds a sense of purpose and makes you feel that this is the reason for which you were created.

A good example of the difference between the two was provided recently by Oprah Winfrey. In January 2007 Oprah opened the Oprah Winfrey Leadership Academy, fulfilling a pledge she had made to Nelson Mandela six years earlier. Every year, the academy offers about 150 girls from impoverished backgrounds the chance to receive an outstanding education and develop their potential. When she opened the academy Oprah declared, "This is what I was born to do." Now think about this quote. Oprah is arguably the most successful woman in the history of American media and the world's most influential woman. She has had an astonishing career. But here she suddenly says that all that is nice but it's not what she was born to do. What she was born to do was use her vast success to build academies like these and give African girls an opportunity for a life of dignity and prosperity. What she was really saying was that she had ascended from a career to a calling.

In her career she had to worry constantly about whether she had good ratings, whether there were competitors or imitators who were gaining on her heels, and whether her fans were still loyal. But once she transformed her career into a calling, she discovered the reason for her existence. There was something she could do that no one else could do. There was a corner of the world that only she could redeem. How many people could really build a leadership academy for African girls in South Africa? It would take an incredible array of ingredients. It would have to be someone with great influence, considerable resources, an understanding of the vast contribution that black women from impoverished backgrounds could make, a passion for charity, with enough celebrity to highlight her efforts so that others would emulate her drive. How many people on earth could match those criteria? How many could pull it off? As it turned out, only one: Oprah Winfrey. And through the establishment of her academy, Oprah was able to raise her pursuits from career to calling.

Many have pondered the success of Oprah Winfrey. Why is she so trusted by America's women? What makes her so unique? There are other gifted TV hosts. There are other empathetic interviewers with a spiritual bent. I am convinced that the principal reason that Oprah enjoys such unparalleled credibility is that she is a woman with a calling rather than a career, and that especially resonates with women. Everything about her—from her desire to promote spirituality to her passion for getting people to read—speaks of the higher calling to which she has devoted her life. People see that although she is a famous celebrity, her life is not just about her but also about something more. And they buy into that vision.

It was a calling rather than a career that kept George Washington focused on winning the War of Independence through the worst setbacks and retreats of 1776 and the cruel Valley Forge winter of 1777–78. Had Washington treated his generalship as a career rather than a calling, he would have thought himself a failure, sunk into a deep depression, and lost the war. He would have compared himself to all the other winning generals who preceded him and declared himself a

> **Had Washington treated his generalship as a career rather than a calling, he would have thought himself a failure, sunk into a deep depression, and lost the war.**

loser. But he never despaired, because he never thought in terms of whether or not he was successful. It was never about him. It was about human liberty and the freedom of the colonies.

It was a calling rather than a career that made Lincoln determined to keep the Union together through the worst Northern calamities of the Civil War. Defeat after defeat, hapless general after hapless general never broke Lincoln's spirit. And let's remember that Lincoln was a man who battled melancholy throughout his life. He wanted to make a name for himself and often felt like a failure. He suffered electoral defeat after electoral defeat. He confided to his friend Joshua Speed that if he died no one would know because he had barely left an imprint on the earth, and he longed to do so. He was the quintessential broken American male, always fretting over what a loser he was.

And then Lincoln became president and he was changed. And what changed him was not that he was suddenly a success. Remember, the broken American male, even when he achieves great professional success, still feels like a loser. Besides, Lincoln was despised for most of his presidency and dismissed as an incompetent "orangutan." Rather, it was the fact that Lincoln found a calling. The Southern states seceded and the principle of "government of the people, for the people, and by the people" was challenged. The very future of democratic government and human freedom hinged on whether Lincoln could keep the Union together. And once he found his calling, he was unbreakable and unassailable, so much so that even an assassin's bullet could not squelch his vision and he remains our greatest president till this very day. It was this calling that gave him a moral certainty, born of faith, that sustained him in the war against disunion and slavery, even after two years of epic defeats. In his Second Inaugural Address, Lincoln famously said as much: " . . . with firmness in the right as God gives us to see the right, let us strive on to finish the work we are in. . . ." He likewise wrote, "I have been driven many times upon my knees by the overwhelming conviction that I had nowhere else to go." The career man does not drop to his knees. He thinks that his prosperity and ingenuity can get him out of every scrape. And when that doesn't work, he falls into a morbid depression, numbing himself to life. But the man of calling invokes the higher power of the Creator in order to discern what his calling may be. He remembers the words of Deuteronomy: "It is not by bread alone that man lives, but by the words of the living G-d that man finds life."

> "It is not by bread alone that man lives, but by the words of the living G-d that man finds life."

It was a calling rather than a career that led Martin Luther King Jr. to surmount a tsunami of white hatred in his campaign to purge America of racial injustice. Had he thought in terms of career he would have been content to win the 1964 Nobel Peace Prize and the prestige the prize conferred on him. He would not have been found with a group of garbage collectors in Memphis on that fateful April day in 1968 when his life, but not his dream, was terminated. For King the civil rights movement was never about him. It was about the people whose dignity was stripped away by segregation and racial injustice.

Contrast those examples with that of another American president who was the most gifted politician of his generation, Bill Clinton. To be sure, Clinton is a man who intrigues us all and will intrigue historians for generations to come. The principal reason, no doubt, is that he is a volatile and potent mix of talent and shortcoming, immensely gifted and immensely flawed at the same time. We are amazed that a man who is so smart can also be so stupid, that a man of such iron discipline can also be so weak, that a man who so loves his wife and daughter can have caused them so much pain as well. In this sense, in his own person Bill Clinton serves as a metaphor for mankind itself, incorporating both its promise and its pain.

Clinton's principal flaw has always been that he was arguably the most insecure man ever to occupy the White House. He was always the broken American male personified. He has an insatiable need to be loved and an unquenchable thirst for affection. No amount of attention will ever satiate him and no amount of success will ever make him feel accomplished. To be sure, his insecurities and his need for recognition were what first fueled his ambition and ultimately pushed him to the White House. But once he got there, they also made him susceptible to the charm of a buxom intern who made him feel valuable despite his inner feelings of worthlessness. Remember, the broken American male cannot be made whole by his wife because he sees his wife as an extension of his own loser status.

The broken American male does not cheat on his wife because the other woman is superior but only because the other woman *isn't his wife*.

That's why he turns to other women to feel desirable. This explains why Bill Clinton betrayed his wife for a woman who was not as smart, not as sophisticated, and, many would say, not even as pretty (although she was, of course, younger) as his wife. The broken American male does not cheat on his wife because the other woman is superior but only because the other woman *isn't his wife*.

Women like Monica Lewinsky understand men like Bill Clinton. They know how badly these men crave flattery. They know how to get through every chink in their armor. So when Lewinsky showed Clinton that she was prepared to wait on line for ten hours in order to see him for a brief moment, he slowly became putty in her hands. Indeed, anyone who reads the Starr Report will easily see that Lewinsky pursued Clinton far more than the other way around, which is not to vindicate Clinton but rather to point out just how weak even the most powerful man in the world can be.

But insecurity undermined the presidency of Bill Clinton not just because of the Lewinsky scandal. Many other presidents who preceded Clinton in the Oval Office also had a weakness for women, most notably John F. Kennedy, who is still remembered as a great president and leader. Rather, Clinton's insecurities undermined him because he was so desperate to be liked and so anxious to be loved that it prevented him from taking bold and decisive action. While terrorists attacked the World Trade Center, American embassies in Africa, the USS *Cole,* and other targets, and Saddam Hussein slaughtered his own people and fired regularly on American war planes, Clinton hurled a couple of cruise missiles at them.

These same weaknesses make visiting the Clinton presidential library, which I drove hundreds of miles to do, a disappointment. Rather than presenting the history of an eight-year presidency, the library is primarily a mammoth Clinton propaganda hut. What this library really is, is a shrine to Clinton's insecurities and incessant need for self-promotion. Believe me, as an insecure man myself who has always wrestled with his need to be noticed, I am an expert in the subject. And I have rarely witnessed a shrine to one man that speaks of greater narcissism.

Perhaps the greatest insight into Clinton's insecurity comes from the astonishing number of letters from celebrities that are highlighted in the most prominent positions in the library, in a row across the entire second floor. Does a man who served as the president of the United States really expect us to be impressed with the fact that Whoopi Goldberg called him "the cat's pajamas" or that Dom DeLuise (anyone still remember him?) expressed his undying admiration? Didn't we all think that now that he had matured and become an elder statesman, Clinton was over his obsession with Hollywood celebrities? He doesn't seem to realize that he is actually a lot more consequential than Arsenio Hall. So having his letter prominently displayed in his library just drags him down. But the broken American male always thinks of himself as a complete loser and relies on other people to prop him up, even if they are objectively beneath him on the ladder of success.

The Clinton who is dying to be loved is again on display in the introductory video of the library tour, which prominently features the great Nelson Mandela relating how much the UN loved Bill Clinton, and the enthusiastic standing ovation offered him by the

General Assembly. It is curious that Clinton would have insisted on including this particular praise, given the low standing of the UN among the American public. Why did the UN love Bill Clinton? Well, because he didn't do anything to upset them, even when Libya became the chair of the UN Human Rights Commission, and Kofi Annan refused to take any decisive action in Rwanda when he served as head of the UN's peacekeeping operations in 1994.

Great men become hated when they take bold action, the way Lincoln did when he decided to fight to save the Union or the way that Churchill did when he decided to awaken Europe to the threat of Hitler even as everyone else preferred to turn a blind eye. But aside from his commendable achievement in providing the American people with a highly prosperous economy, Clinton will be remembered for the total absence of bold and decisive American leadership on the world stage. Bill Clinton was a consensus man who preferred not to upset, but rather to work with, the amorality of the UN. That's why Clinton's greatest failure will always be not Monica Lewinsky—that was a private affair—but the genocide in Rwanda. While he served as president in April through June of 1994, 330 Africans were killed every hour—a devastating total of 880,000 people. The United States and the rest of the world knew all about the genocide. But President Clinton refused to take any action that would halt the slaughter. Indeed, he even refused to hold a single meeting with his senior advisors about the genocide. And yet some in the African-American community still call him America's first black president!

The broken American male is so desirous of external corroboration that he dare not take a controversial step that can lose him fans.

I am no Clinton hater, and find much in the man, especially what I believe to be his sincere love for humanity, to be admired. But there is much for the rest of us to learn from Bill Clinton. First is the peril of having a career as opposed to a calling. Bill Clinton always wanted to be president. Why? To implement some great plan? Not necessarily. He was a good president. He managed the country well. But he certainly didn't implement any great plan. Rather, he wanted to be president to finally feel significant. Perhaps the Oval Office would finally silence the ever-present demons.

Second is the Jewish adage that action is what counts most. It's *not* enough to *feel* people's pain. You have do something about their pain. Clinton has an irresistible and authentic love for people. But that didn't translate into bold action to help the weak and despised, as his moral failure in Rwanda—for which he later apologized—demonstrated. Had he had a calling, he would not have allowed three genocides—Srebrenica, Rwanda, and Kosovo—to occur on his watch, a higher number than during any other presidency. Yes, President Clinton feels your pain, even though you can no longer do so yourself because you are now dead at the hands of a murderous oppressor that the most powerful man in the world chose to ignore.

The third great lesson the rest of us can learn from Bill Clinton is that if you choose not to deal with your insecurities internally, only addressing them through external success, then even when you become the head honcho of the entire world you still need other people to prop you up and make you feel as if you matter.

If you choose not to deal with your insecurities internally, only addressing them through external success, then even when you become the head honcho of the entire world you still need other people to prop you up and make you feel as if you matter.

The fourth lesson is that what most destroys otherwise great men is the inability to accept criticism. Really broken men have a tough time accepting criticism because they are not strong enough to absorb it. One word of disapproval and they are crushed, such is the flimsy structure of their already macerated ego. This is what makes Clinton's dealing with his attempted impeachment in his library so disappointing. You would think that after he apologized to the American people for the—let's use an understatement—distraction of the Monica Lewinsky affair, he would be magnanimous with his enemies and show a hint of contrition in his library. Fugedaboutit! The shocking display window dealing with the impeachment hearings is euphemistically titled "The Struggle for Power" and starts by saying that in the nineties partisan politics reached a fever pitch and the Republicans decided they would destroy Bill Clinton. It then goes on to demonize Newt Gingrich, who is quoted as saying that the problem with Republicans is that they're not nasty enough, and is then shown in a picture bathed in red light and looking like Satan. Next, it's Ken Starr's turn to be pilloried. Clinton's nemesis is portrayed as a corrupt partisan hack who would do anything to bring the great man down. Oh, Monica Lewinsky is mentioned, but only in the context of a condemnation of Kenneth Starr for expanding his independent counsel remit to investigate her relationship with Clinton. There is no mention of his unfaithfulness to either the American people or his wife. Now, it could well be that the Republicans were out to bury Clinton. I don't deny that. But that doesn't excuse the abrogation of responsibility in the display. Broken men are not strong enough or secure enough to admit error. But if you can't admit error, how can you possibly heal?

Having visited Hot Springs, Arkansas, where Bill Clinton grew up, I now see the magnitude of the achievement of his elevation to the presidency. A boy from a poor background in a tiny southern town becoming president of the United States is heady stuff. Clinton's father died before he was born, and he witnessed his mother being beaten by her new husband. Even with this adversity, this was a man who made himself an Oxford Rhodes Scholar and the youngest governor in America. But for all his incredible achievements on the outside, Clinton never healed himself on the inside. He remains a broken American male to this very day, even as he has now pursued immensely commendable goals, doing philanthropic work throughout the world.

This does not mean that he cannot contribute or lead. Indeed,

Clinton is now engaged in fantastic work to help the needy through-out the world. What it does mean, however, is that for this great man the time has finally come to heal.

Broken men need to give up career and find a calling. To be sure, this does not mean that a broken man has to find some calling on the world stage like Lincoln. By a calling we mean that he has to learn to identify his principal gift, that irreducible essence that makes him unique. Once he knows what his gift is, he finds the place where it can be contributed. What this does is remove him from the rat race. Because the rat race is all about comparison. It's not about doing what you're good at, or redeeming your very special corner of the world, but about aping other people who are considered successful and going where the action is.

Imagine that a man who is trained as an attorney decides to pursue a calling and not just a career. When he is career-focused, he worries about moving up in the firm, winning cases, making a lot of money, earning a reputation, and eventually becoming a partner. But when his career is a calling he doesn't think a lot about those things. Sure, material advancement is important, but it's not the most important thing. Rather, he identifies what he's particularly good at within the law. Perhaps it is reassuring clients who find themselves in trouble, making them feel that all will be well. They see he is caring and competent, so they rely on him as he seeks to help them out. Now he will be even more successful than if he were career-oriented because his clients will see he is caring, professional, and focused. They will see that he can extend himself and worry about their cares rather than focus narrowly on his own interests.

Or let's say a man is a gardener. He determines that his calling is a special affinity with nature and an ability to make natural things shine and glow. He devotes himself not just to landscaping, but also to encouraging his clients to appreciate their gardens and to tend to them when he is not around. Now his clients become his partners in his endeavor. They value him not only because he beautifies their gardens, but also because he has taught them to really appreciate their surroundings. He has created a deep bond between them and their homes.

Whenever you stop thinking narrowly about yourself and your interests and think about some higher cause you can serve, you have a calling. And when you do that, you begin to emerge from brokenness, because the man who has found his calling need never question whether he matters and whether he is making a difference. He knows that he has a gift to contribute to the world that only he possesses, and there is a corner of the world, however big or small, that only he can redeem.

26.

Making the Broken American Male
Feel Wanted at Home

ONE OF the episodes on *Shalom in the Home* involved a broken man who felt that no one wanted him at home. In his mind he had become a paycheck, an ATM, the man who covered the bills but who otherwise was not wanted. He would regularly tell his wife and son that he was leaving. "I'm going, and I'm not coming back," he would say, obviously with the hope that they would object and tell him they couldn't live without him. Unfortunately, after hearing him threaten to leave so often, they finally told him that if he wanted to go he should stop talking about it and just do it. Wrong response. Yes, he may have been childish and his threats were completely inappropriate, but they underscored just how desperate he was to be loved by his family, so desperate that it made him pathetic. It's pretty sad that men should be reduced to such immature behavior in an attempt to feel that their families want them around.

And what would it have taken to make him feel wanted? His son running over to him when he walked through the door and giving him a kiss? His wife simply saying, "Honey, how was your day?"

One of the most important ways to heal the broken American male is to make him feel wanted at home. All too many men share the opinion of the man in the previous story: they don't feel loved or desired by their families. When they walk through the door after work, their kids barely acknowledge them. Forget running over and warmly welcoming them, they barely even say hello.

In a typical scenario, the wife is talking on the phone and doesn't interrupt her conversation to welcome her husband. And he walks in with his tail between his legs, feeling like a victim.

It may be his own fault. The disconnect men have with their families might be due to their own lack of investment in their relationships with their wives and kids. But what does it matter? He is the husband and father. And he feels like nobody wants him. He's broken and needs affirmation. And an effort should be made to make him feel like he is more than just the guy who is paying the mortgage.

On another episode of *Shalom,* we had a really broken American male who worked his guts out every day to support his family. But as a construction worker, he felt like a failure, a man whose income barely met his considerable responsibilities. He was also certain that no one really wanted him at home. He was just a robot who made the money and paid the bills. Our surveillance cameras caught what it was like for him when he came home at night. Not one of his kids even left the TV to welcome him. His wife would continue washing up as he walked in after a twelve-hour day. It sure looked like no one wanted him or cared when he walked through the door. And to his mind this reinforced his feelings of failure. *Yeah, who would want a big nothing like me? I completely understand why they won't interrupt even something as dumb as a TV show to greet me.*

So my producers and I decided that this all had to change. We organized a party for Daddy's homecoming. It was just a regular Wednesday night, but we threw a big bash. Daddy was coming home from work. There were balloons and streamers and the kids ran over to him and threw their arms around him and gave him a big hug. Obviously, this wasn't going to happen every night. But it gave their father the sense that he was loved and appreciated for being more than a credit card. I told the family that although they didn't have to throw a big party every night, they did have to make their dad feel welcome and loved. "Stop what you're doing and give your daddy a big hug and a kiss and tell him you love him. That's all it takes." We should be doing this with every husband and father. And my, how healing it would be.

In my home I have a policy that can never be abrogated. When I come home my kids have to come over and kiss me and say hello. They have no choice in the matter. If I'm home already and they are the ones who walk in, as soon as they put down their schoolbags they have to walk over to me and kiss me on the cheek and say hello. Yes, it would be nicer if they did it without my telling them. And most of the time they do. Habit becomes second nature.

As a father and a husband, I want to feel like more than the breadwinner. I want to feel like I am coming to a place where I belong. I want home be the place that I feel most comfortable. It's bad enough that I have to travel around America to support my family. I travel to give lectures and seminars and to film TV shows that heal broken families. Many people have asked me why I would leave my own family in order to help another. Is it really virtuous to neglect your own wife and kids as you help someone else's? What these people forget is that we all need to work for a living, and beyond assisting other families, I assist my own, because my work allows me to pay the mortgage and buy them food and clothing. Still, I hate leaving my family. It sucks. And when I call home at night and speak to each of the kids individually, I am often filled with envy that they all have each other, back in our warm cozy home, while I am in a hotel room all by myself. I have never dealt well with being alone. I am forty years old. But I still get homesick. I hate traveling by myself, but my wife cannot always travel with me on business trips because our eight children need to be looked after. So at the very least when I get home I want to feel appreciated. I want to feel that my wife and kids understand that I was away for their benefit. I was away to make them happy and joyous. I was away to give them a good life and a good education. But I am not a bank manager. Less so am I a ten-dollar bill. I am a person. I get homesick. I get lonely. And I want my family to miss me as much as I miss them.

A friend of mine who was going through severe depression sent me this e-mail explaining why he was down: "At night when I, the hardworking husband, come home, it is quite normal for there to be no greeting. And then for my wife to tell me, 'Here are the kids, I've been with them all day. It's your turn,' when all I want to do is have some peace and silence after a tough day in the office. And some love. Is there a family meal? No such thing. When 'Daddy' comes home, is he greeted properly? No such thing. Ask him about his day? No such thing."

Now I had to explain to my friend that he had to lift himself up and not be a victim in his own eyes. Likewise, coming home and vegging in front of a TV rather than interacting with your kids is a telltale sign of the broken American male. But be that as it may, my friend's other points were extremely valid. A man has a right to come home after a hard day's work and be greeted enthusiastically by the family he works so hard to support.

We can't have it both ways. We can't, on the one hand, complain that men define themselves by professional criteria of success to the exclusion of their homes and their families, and, on the other hand, not welcome them at home. A man's home doesn't have to be his castle. But it should be his refuge and his place of comfort. Neither can wives complain that their husbands are cold and unemotional, yet greet their husbands with such callous indifference when they arrive home at night that the husband has no incentive to jump-start his own feelings.

Wives should train their children to welcome their fathers warmly when they arrive home. They should get the kids to run up to their dads and make them feel like they've been awaiting their arrival. In this respect, there is also no substitute for a nightly family meal where the dad gets to sit at the head of the table and feel that it is his company, rather than the food he puts on the table, that is really valued. The family meal is a necessity for all kinds of reasons. But foremost among them is the cohesiveness it brings to the family and how each person can talk about how their day went.

On another episode of *Shalom in the Home,* we met Ali Waxman, who came home every night convinced that neither his wife nor his two children had any interest in hearing how his day went. He was the provider. Nothing more. He would walk in and ask himself sarcastically, "Oh, you want to know how my day went?" And he would then spend the next five minutes humorously talking to himself, out loud, about the kind of day he had. On the show it was both funny and sad. Wives should ask their husbands how their day went and, of course, the reverse is true as well. By inspiring the American male to engage warmly and emotionally with his family, we safeguard him from becoming broken.

27.

So You Want to Be Rich?

WE HAVE established that what destroys American men more than anything else is unreasonable feelings of failure that in turn create shockingly low levels of self-esteem. What many believe is that wealth is the antidote and money is the cure.

Everyone today wants to be rich. Money is the American religion. It is credited with magical powers. Like a genie that emerges from a bottle, it promises untold pleasures. The fulfillment of your heart's desires. The respect of your peers. The envy of your rivals. Heck, it can even make you irresistible to women.

But is money really all it's cracked up to be?

Wealth is profoundly isolating and leaves a great many who have it lonely. The very essence of great wealth is to be set apart. You begin life traveling in coach. You wait in a lounge next to people like you, and you sit next to them on the plane. You get to know them, you speak to them. They become your acquaintances.

But as you grow more successful, you slowly become more isolated. Now you're traveling in business class. There are fewer people and they talk to you far less. Next you're in first class—even fewer people. Then you have your own plane. It's just you and your pilots.

The air you breathe becomes as rarified as the air through which you fly.

The same is true of your living conditions. You begin life in a tenement. You have many neighbors. They borrow sugar from you. You get to know them. Then you buy a house—now you are even more isolated. And then your own private estate. And suddenly the only people in your immediate vicinity are people on your payroll.

In Robert Frank's book *Richistan,* which chronicles the lives of the superrich, he tells the story of an eleven-year-old "aristokid" who, for her birthday, asked her parents if she could fly commercial. She wanted "to ride on a big plane with other people. I want to see what an airport looks like on the inside."

When we speak of that old chestnut that the rich aren't very happy, what we mean above all else is that their money not only did not buy them love, as the Beatles might have put it, but worse, it actually left them more isolated and lonely.

By and large, the rich can only hang out with other rich people. Who else could afford their styles and tastes? And since so many people seek wealth as a statement of status, they also choose friends who will enhance their status, thereby ensuring sterile and cold relationships.

In no area do we see these developments more than in the rise of investment banking. As a Jewish boy growing up in America, I heard constantly of the pressure to be a doctor and a lawyer. Fat chance today. Gone are the days when the top two Jewish professions were guaranteed to give Mama oodles of *nachas* (joy), winning cooing competitions over her fellow yentas with stories of "my son the doctor, my grandson the lawyer," as they sipped warm borscht and played bridge. Yes, Mama's days as a major Jewish *kveller* of pride over junior's stethoscope belong to bygone years.

No respectable educated boys are today stupid enough to settle for being plastic surgeons or even Paris Hilton's defense attorney. Today, it is banking or bust.

The proverbial Jewish accountant who, as Jackie Mason says, must be somewhat retarded since he couldn't embrace one of the more fashionable Jewish professions of doctoring or lawyering, has been moved even farther down the status ladder. No respectable educated boys are today stupid enough to settle for being plastic surgeons or even Paris Hilton's defense attorney. Today, it is banking or bust. And why do so many of our brightest young men proudly don their blue pinstripes and march off to sell bonds? Because men today know how to smell good money at the source.

A successful American doctor who has spent twenty years building up a practice can expect to earn as much as one million dollars a year. (His English counterpart working for the National Health Service can expect to earn at least as much as the illegal immigrant with a part-time gardening job on the weekends.) But bankers have money-minting machines. It is not uncommon to hear of hedge-fund managers in their midthirties making hundreds of millions of dollars a year. At that level it becomes like Monopoly money. The sums are so great that they are not even real.

The rise of investment banking as the foremost profession in our culture speaks volumes about the new attitude toward money. Even doctors who chose their profession because they wanted job security and a high income could still claim—justifiably—that they were contributing to society because they were healing the sick. Sure, they may have gone into the profession for the cash. But there were some altruistic feelings, however latent, about curing disease that figured in their ambitions. But these days, it's not the money, it's the money. With the death of all professions in favor of investment banking, I fear that we are entering a new era in which people do not put money before everything else, because there is nothing else. Money is not king. There are no subjects. Money is existence itself. It is form, it is matter, and it is substance. It is the veneer atop matter as well as the essence beneath the surface. The

> **Money is existence itself. It is form, it is matter, and it is substance. It is the veneer atop matter as well as the essence beneath the surface.**

only purpose of investment banking is to make one's clients, and in the process oneself as well, rich like Rockefeller.

When I arrived in Oxford to serve as rabbi in 1988, a great many of the students were studying law and medicine. But if they were offered jobs with the leading investment banking firms—which they prayed for every Sunday at church—they would promptly pack it all in and join the banks, discarding their training and any semblance of wanting to make the world a better place. And on the Oxford nights when Merrill Lynch, Salomon, Bear Stearns, Goldman Sachs, and the other top investment banks did their recruitment thing, there was not a student in sight. Oxford became a ghost town as students flocked to find placements with the banks.

I love reading and listening to the great political speeches of the twentieth century. What is so striking about the unforgettable speeches of yesterday's immortal leaders—Churchill, Roosevelt, Kennedy, MacArthur, Adlai Stevenson, Martin Luther King Jr.—as compared with today's instantly forgettable political speeches (in reality they are impossible to forget since they are rarely absorbed in the first place) is not the oratory of the speaker, because there are still some very compelling speakers.

So why must we go all the way back to Kennedy's *"Ich bin ein Berliner"* (which, unfortunately, translates literally as "I am a doughnut") speech, Martin Luther King Jr.'s "I Have a Dream" speech, or Jesse Jackson's "Address to the 1984 Democratic Convention" to find oratory that was truly memorable? The answer lies in the themes political leaders today choose to address. What do politicians discuss today? Inflation, the economy, and kicking out illegal immigrants who are taking our jobs. And how inspiring is that?

Money has overtaken everything, and it is a damned boring world as a result. Without fail, the great speeches I listen to are remarkable because they discuss grand, majestic themes: Churchill affirming that "we will fight them on the beaches," Kennedy calling for democracy and human freedom, King appealing for equality and an end to racism. The boredom of today's political rhetoric has to do with the simple fact that the American dream is defined almost entirely in economic terms. The result is stultifying. Once upon a time a man needed only to sell his soul in return for extraordinary wealth. Then, as wealth increased and the stakes were higher, one's humanity had to be thrown into the deal as well. You want to get ahead, we were told, well, you have to be ruthless. But today, the ultimate price is required and paid on demand, that being life itself. People work themselves to the bone, morning, noon, and night, and in the process forego the extraordinary color and diversity of human life and emotion in exchange for a single monotonous emotion, greed, and a single dull color, green.

> **People work themselves to the bone, morning, noon, and night, and in the process forego the extraordinary color and diversity of human life and emotion in exchange for a single monotonous emotion, greed, and a single dull color, green.**

I do not claim to be immune to the lust for wealth. We all work for money, we all need it, and perhaps we all love it. But it does not have the capacity to excite and fire our deepest imagination. That is why the investment banking field has one of the highest rates of corporate burnout. Because every man and woman, having been created in the image of G-d, is likewise a creator. And we desire to build far more than we desire to gather and collect. Religion, with its ultimate aim of building a just society, a compassionate social order, and a better world, has forever fired man's deepest imagination. This is also why those who earn so much money are also the ones who think of such elaborate ways to spend it. This is how they get their kicks. They have little other stimulation besides making it and spending it. They're bored. And the more consumed they become, the more boring they become as well.

An elderly multimillionaire businessman told me that the difference between today's generation of entrepreneurs and his own generation is that the new guys have no hobbies. Sure, they read a bit, play a bit of golf here and there, watch TV, and go out with friends.

But they don't enjoy this half as much as making money. There is nothing that engages them as much as talking stocks and shares and

An elderly multimillionaire businessman told me that the difference between today's generation of entrepreneurs and his own generation is that the new guys have no hobbies.

investment opportunities. The result, he contends, is that they become monolithic. You take them out for dinner and you hear about Internet start-ups. Worse, he says, since they can never disengage, they can never approach their business from an entirely new perspective and take the imaginative, long-term view that business requires. The world's all-encompassing lust for riches is leading to internal collapse and external grayness.

28.

Rediscovering the Sabbath

THE TRULY wealthy people I know tell me that, in the final analysis, the only *real* advantage to wealth is greater freedom. You go where you want, when you want, without being limited by financial constraints. Warren Buffett, a man who has never allowed money to define him, expressed it best. The sole real advantage of wealth, he said, is that it allows you to choose who you do business with.

But today money ties us down and limits our horizons. Rabbi Joseph Soloveitchik once said that there are two aspects of slavery, which need not always coincide. The first is *political*, by which a man is reduced to a chattel, a form of private property, an object belonging to an owner. The slave's body and skills belong to his master by virtue of a legal system that degrades the slave's status. He is a "thing" and is subject to the whim and caprice of his master's will, to physical coercion, exploitation, and humiliation.

There is a second type of slavery, however, which is far more serious, and it is *typological,* a mental state of servility rather than a physically imposed enslavement. This is when a man is enslaved from the inside. This second type of slavery reaches its apogee when we open our eyes at the age of forty or fifty and discover that we ended up becoming something that we never planned and perhaps even despise. As Soloveitchik says, there are people who think, feel, act, and react in a distinctively docile manner which suggests that their will has been broken, their ego effaced, and their freedom warped and constricted. This is an emotional condition, a crushing of one's initiative, a submersion of one's individuality, and a distortion of one's judgment. The slave mentality can be found even among politically emancipated people. The scouts sent by Moses to survey the Holy Land in the book of Numbers summed up their dispiritedness in the words "And we were in our own sight as grasshoppers" (Num. 13:33). Such feelings of inferiority, G-d decided, could not produce the initiative and confidence required to succeed in the conquest of the Holy Land.

There is a second type of slavery, however, which is far more serious, and it is *typological*, a mental state of servility rather than a physically imposed enslavement.

Several times a day I as a Jew read in my prayers the eternal obligation to go out of Egypt. Once, when we were political slaves, the Almighty Himself redeemed us from servitude. Today, when we are typological slaves, when we are incarcerated by the lust for wealth and prestige, it is we who must redeem ourselves from the restricting clutches of materialism and egoism. If we fail at this, then we will never have lived, but merely existed. As Jesse Jackson said, "It is far easier to take a man out of prison than it is to take the prison out of a man." But those who seek it can find help in attaining liberation. Deliverance from the poisoned air of a suffocating selfishness is the ultimate purpose of a spiritual life.

Deliverance from the poisoned air of a suffocating selfishness is the ultimate purpose of a spiritual life.

We do not work six days and rest on the seventh in order to work harder in the coming six days. This skewed view would have us believe that the purpose of a Sabbath is to service the needs of the workdays of the week. The very opposite is true. We work six days in order to have food, clothing, and security so that the Sabbath can be a meaningful day of study, reflection, fraternity, and introspection, unencumbered by financial worries. The primary purpose of religion is to teach man what to do with his *leisure,* his free time, and his success. The values imparted to us by a faith-based life do not teach us how to make money, but rather what to do with money once it is made. Religion imparts to modern man the value of leading a deep life suffused with purpose,

> The primary purpose of religion is to teach man what to do with his *leisure,* his free time, and his success.

and the opportunity to fathom the infinite essence of G-d and confront the great questions of existence. On the Sabbath we are finally afforded an opportunity to read, argue, debate, study, think, meditate, pray, ponder, connect, and ultimately stand in awe in the face of what we have found. No man who is encumbered with a daily need to feed his family will ever have the time to concern himself with the whys and wherefores of existence, and in this

> We who are the most prosperous and financially well-off generation in human history feel the heat of the Bible's eternal calling: to provide for the destitute, the orphan, the widow, and the outcast; to find G-d in all our ways.

sense it is interesting to note that the overwhelming majority of great philosophers were men of means. G-d gives us the blessing of wealth so that we can have time for spouses, children, community, and friends. We who are the most prosperous and financially well-off generation in human history feel the heat of the Bible's eternal calling: to provide for the destitute, the orphan, the widow, and the outcast; to find G-d in all our ways.

That modern-day men are utterly lost without work and something to strive for, that they are confounded by excessive moments of leisure that render them ill at ease, is best demonstrated by the obsessive nature of today's career-oriented society. Professional success today is a mania that leaves virtually no time for contemplation and enjoyment of the transcendent aspects of life. We substitute the pursuit of investment opportunities for the pursuit of knowledge, and accumulate clients instead of acts of loving kindness. A case in point: Look what we have done to the Sabbath. Sunday used to be a time for church and family. Today all the shops are open and it is like any other day of the week, a time to indulge in further consumption. The Sabbath was designed as a day when man could withdraw from his constant exertion of mastery over creation and discover humility, dependency, and a common bond with all living things. But we have forsaken G-d's day in favor of unnecessary shopping and impressing the boss with overtime. Man must return to religion because it is specifically a holy way of life that gives humans something to strive for after they have made their money and built their reputations. Ancient Rome collapsed because it had nothing left to toil for after it had built its empire. Gladiatorial combat and every immoral perversion provided distraction from the boredom that permeated a society that had no higher purpose than dominion and success.

> Ancient Rome collapsed because it had nothing left to toil for after it had built its empire. Gladiatorial combat and every immoral perversion provided distraction from the boredom that permeated a society that had no higher purpose than dominion and success.

There are only two things in this world that are really interesting: G-d and man. The reason is that they are the only two things that possess infinite depth. We tire of everything else all too quickly. We cannot watch even the most sensational film more than a few times, but we can have endless hours of conversation with the same person. Because that person is infinitely creative. On days like the Sabbath we dedicate large amounts of time toward cultivating human friendship and human company and toward enhancing our relationship with G-d. By doing so, we cultivate a deeper dimension of our personalities so that instead of being two-dimensional individuals who offer clichéd opinions lifted

> We cannot watch even the most sensational film more than a few times, but we can have endless hours of conversation with the same person.

from glossy magazines and insipid television talk shows, we have a third dimension. This deeper dimension affords us a broad inner expanse so that acquaintances and friends always find something new in us, making us exciting, unique, and fresh.

During the years I served as rabbi at Oxford I often asked the students what they planned to *be* after graduating. Inevitably, I heard the same responses: I'm going to be a banker, a doctor, a lawyer. I then pointed out to them that I never asked what they were going to *do*, but rather what they were going to *be*. One does not become a doctor. Rather, one practices medicine. Neither does one become a lawyer. Rather, one engages in the legal profession. But today we have mistaken the art of *being* for the art of *doing,* so that our entire existence is summed up by our capacity for production, rather than our innate goodness and humanity.

Incurable insecurity, Prozac, and Paxil are the rewards for a generation that has learned to define its very being through material and professional success—productivity—rather than through being G-d's children, whose value is immutable and immeasurable. No wonder then that we thirst endlessly for more money, bigger homes, faster cars—anything to obviate the inner feeling of worthlessness that haunts us at every turn. Since we have failed to develop vertically by acquiring more depth and sublimity, we compensate by increasing horizontally, through acquisition and consumption.

When I chose to become a rabbi, I accepted a life that would probably not make me rich. And if I were to be accused of writing these lines in envy of all those who have forty more zeros at the end of their paycheck than I do, my response would be: guilty as charged. I am jealous. I have always loved money and luxury. But if wealth will rob me of knowing the

> If wealth will rob me of knowing the redemptive quality of prayer, the serenity of the Sabbath, the pleasure of a great book, the mind-opening sensations of transcendent thought, the serenity and innocence of a child, the beauty of marriage, and the purity of human love, then it is best that I remain jealous.

redemptive quality of prayer, the serenity of the Sabbath, the pleasure of a great book, the mind-opening sensations of transcendent thought, the serenity and innocence of a child, the beauty of marriage, and the purity of human love, then it is best that I remain jealous.

29.

Learning to Be Happy for Another's Success

PART OF the brokenness of the American male is that he has no real friends. Soulless capitalism teaches him to see every other man—even his closest buddies—as competitors. Sure, he loves hanging out with them, but he is also jealous of their good fortune. Every time one of them makes a lot of money, he is jealous. Every time one is able to afford a bigger house than he can, he is envious. Since soulless capitalism is born of a deprivation mentality in which all are seen as competing against one another, every time one of his friends takes a bigger piece of the pie, it is his piece that is being taken. True bonds of friendship are therefore abrogated. All men are set against one another as lifelong adversaries.

This is especially true of those who operate in the higher income brackets where unbridled ambition is the mainstay of manhood. I have a friend who last year made twenty million dollars as a hedge-fund manager. Yet he feels like a failure. Why? Because he has many friends who made— I kid you not—hundreds of millions in a single year, which is not uncommon for the most successful hedge-fund managers. Compared to them he was a failure.

The solution is to focus on your own gifts rather than on another's success. Our objective in life is not to be as successful as the next guy but to maximize our unique potential. But even this solution will

Focus on your own gifts rather than on another's success.

not forge true bonds of friendship among today's men. And friendship among men is a central ingredient in healing the broken American male.

The Talmud relates a story of an elderly sage name Choni the Circle-Drawer. He was the original Rip van Winkle. One day he went to sleep and awoke seventy years later. He walked around and saw that everyone he knew—all his close friends—were no more.

"Give me friendship or give me death."

He prayed to G-d that he too would die, saying, "Give me friendship or give me death."

If we want friendship, we have no choice but to be happy for another person's success. We must push ourselves to overcome jealousy for a friend's success even if it hurts. We are capable of going beyond our natural limitations and experiencing other people's joy.

And truth be told, their success is ours as well. You can look at Bill Gates's success and be jealous. Why should he have all those billions? You can character-assassinate him in order to make his success more palatable: *Oh, he's rich because he's ruthless. Had he been ethical, then he'd be as big a failure as I am.* But what will you get from dragging someone else down? All you'll achieve is leveling the playing field to mediocrity. That's why gossip is such a serious sin in Judaism, because its essence is to ensure that no one ever advances. Every time someone takes a step forward we pull them back with our malicious tongue. And once there are no more heroes, because we have ruined the reputation of each and every one, there is no one to challenge us to become heroes anymore. And we all become mediocrities.

You can also look at Bill Gates's success as something inspiring. If he can do it, so can you. All it takes is a plan, a vision, determination, and hard work. Every time someone succeeds, it doesn't take a piece of the pie from us. Rather, it expands the pie and makes it larger. These guys are pushing the frontiers of the pie. They're forging a path for you to follow. If instead of seething in envy you actually admired what they accomplished, you might even learn something from them. You might be inspired by their example and recommit yourself with even greater fervor to your own projects. You don't have to emulate them. You are your own person. But you can emulate their determination to develop their gifts.

Seeing every other man as a competitor is a lie born of a deprivation mentality. But once we convert from a deprivation mentality to a bountiful mentality, we see other people's success as intertwined with our own. We learn from other people's success that effort is indeed rewarded. All you have to do is try. And the greatest enemy of trying is tearing someone else down so that you have an excuse not to pull yourself up.

Getting over our jealousy of others comes about through focusing on our blessings. The people we are jealous of, the people we want to be, have problems of their own. They have other shortcomings that, for all their riches and fame, we would never wish to assume. We know, deep in our hearts, that if we had the choice to trade lives with them, we would never do so. Deep down we like who we are—so long as we focus on who we *are* instead of who we aren't.

> Deep down we like who we are—so long as we focus on who we *are* instead of who we aren't.

Finally, I hope you've noticed that throughout this chapter, when I spoke about the destructive practice of desiring other people's success, I used the word *jealousy* rather than *envy*. Jealousy is the act of desiring that which belongs to another. As such, it is both unhealthy and deeply sinful, being explicitly forbidden by the tenth commandment. But envy involves the desire to protect and possess that which legitimately belongs to us. A man should not covet, or be jealous of, someone else's wife. But he should be deeply envious of his own wife. He should seek to possess and protect her and ensure that he does not lose her affection to some other man through neglect. In this sense, envy helps us focus and be attentive to our own lives, our own gifts, rather than wishing we were someone else. This is why the tenth commandment says we should not covet *someone else's* wife. We should certainly be coveting our own.

30.

Rise, Oh Circle Man!

ONCE WE redefine success for men and begin to heal them, once we give men a calling as opposed to a career, our women will start becoming healthier as well. No longer feeling like a bottomless pit of self-loathing, the man will not make the woman in his life feel inadequate. Rather, he will be satisfied with his wife and make her feel that her companionship is his foremost blessing. Men who are healthy do not harm the women they marry. Once a man has a sturdy foundation, then all the love and affection that his wife gives him will not merely go in one end and out the other, making her feel she is wholly incapable of making him feel good about himself. Once the man in her life isn't miserable, she won't have to be either. Once he starts living with a healthy mind, her mental and emotional health will be restored as well.

The Jewish religion is a vast faith with myriad details and a three-thousand-year history. But if I were asked to sum it up in a simple sentence, I would say, "Judaism is about the triumph of feminine over masculine values." Judaism says that the Sabbath—the feminine-passive day of the week, in which we refrain from exerting our mastery over the world and become instead one with creation—is holier than the masculine-aggressive days of the week. Whereas the masculine days of the week are all about our mastery over nature, the Sabbath is about respecting nature. The weekdays are about work and the office. But the Sabbath is about family and community.

In the same vein, Judaism forbids the taking of revenge and says that real greatness lies in our ability to forgive. Indeed, the Jewish vision of the future is one in which "the wolf will dwell with the lamb, and the leopard shall lie down with the kid; the calf and the young lion shall browse together, with a little child to guide them. The cow and the bear shall be neighbors, together their young shall rest; the lion shall eat hay like the ox. The baby shall play by the cobra's den, and the child lay his hand on the adder's lair. There shall be no harm or ruin on all my holy mountain; for the earth shall be filled with knowledge of the Lord, as water covers the sea" (Isaiah 11:6–9). This ancient vision of what the world will be like after thousands of years of Jewish

It was a vision of the world where the strong masculine qualities like aggression and war would gradually be subsumed by the feminine qualities of relating well with each other rather than competing and devouring each other.

values are able to transform it was articulated by Isaiah two and a half millennia ago. It was a vision of the world where the strong masculine qualities like aggression and war would gradually be subsumed by the feminine qualities of relating well with each other rather than competing and devouring each other. Christianity, the daughter religion of Judaism, embraced Judaism's passion for feminine values and Jesus continued the theme with his famous pronouncements to turn the other cheek and to love your enemies. Conflict was out. Getting along with others was in. Indeed, Jesus himself is portrayed in the New Testament as an extremely loving and compassionate man with a strongly developed feminine side.

The final healing of the American male will come about through the triumph of feminine over masculine values. The feminine is redeeming to men. The presence of a woman in a man's life is what tempers his raw masculinity, domesticates him, and gets him to focus on what is truly valuable, like family and children. And by exposure to a woman, a man comes to appreciate the transcendent quality of feminine virtue. He no longer judges himself by the harsh values of masculinity. It's not about being macho and never showing emotion and never showing vulnerability and never showing pain. He no longer fears dependency, and he starts to lean on his wife. He accepts that warring with people is for pathetic men who need to tower over others to mask their own smallness. He understands that the macho, womanizing stud is likewise a pitiable creature who feels important through conquest rather than through sharing.

Warring with people is for pathetic men who need to tower over others to mask their own smallness.

With time he learns to reject the ancient and flawed view of masculine greatness as acquisition, accumulation, and conquest. His heroes are no longer the Caesars of this world who conquer Gaul, the Hannibals who cross the Alps atop giant elephants, or the Napoleons who invade Russia. Rather, he looks to those who have been even more influential through caring for others and a devotion to a higher cause. He begins to seek service over adventure and nobility of spirit over becoming part of the nobility.

He begins to seek service over adventure and nobility of spirit over becoming part of the nobility.

Notice that the greatest heroes of the Bible are feminine men who nurture rather than conquer and who contribute rather than accumulate. Abraham is described in the Bible as a man who sits outside his tent, even when he is sick from his circumcision, in order to greet and offer hospitality to complete strangers. Moses is a great teacher who describes himself as "a nursemaid" who suckles the people. Yes, King David is a great warrior. But he is remembered today for playing the harp and lyre and composing and singing the beautiful Psalms. King Solomon is famous for his wisdom. And Jesus cuts a nurturing and feminine figure, focused on caring for and inspiring his disciples while teaching them to be forgiving, gentle, and soft.

The triumph of feminine over masculine values is the final step in the ultimate healing of the broken American male.

We will not heal America's men, and in turn America's women, until women are finally valued in our society. We have to return to a time when women were respected more than men, when they were seen as wiser, nobler, and more naturally spiritual. We have to stop the exploitation—especially the sexual exploitation—of women in our time. The cultural portrayal of women as the lecherous man's playthings is even more injurious to men than it is to women, since it precludes their ever being healed by women. Can a man really be healed by a creature he treats as both beneath him and as a means rather than an end?

The cultural portrayal of women as the lecherous man's playthings is even more injurious to men than it is to women, since it precludes their ever being healed by women.

One of the main reasons men are so messed up today is that women are no longer there to redeem and heal them. Men don't feel they get anything essential from a woman, except satisfaction of their bodily urges. But this kind of silent contempt ensures that there is no one who will bring out men's more subtle and feminine qualities.

Society has to begin not just to give women rights and equality, but to cherish them. We've made our society into a giant peep show and we have to stop it, because there is no way that men are going to value women and learn from women if they see them as mannequins designed for masturbation. It's time that we finally got rid of all the degrading beauty contests. Miss Universe be damned. Men are meant to respect and look up to women, not to sit at a table and rate their body parts with a scorecard. It's time the pop starlets put their clothes back on. Let's get our young girls to dress more modestly at school. And more than anything else, let's wean ourselves off porn.

We've made our society into a giant peep show and we have to stop it, because there is no way that men are going to value women and learn from women if they see them as mannequins designed for masturbation.

This isn't about censorship. Rather, it's about healing our culture by cultivating the feminine within men and women and respecting feminine values. Because if the feminine is exploited and degraded, then all we have left is the masculine. That means a harsh world where might makes right and where human value is determined by external qualities rather than internal conviction. And sure enough, our men will continue to be broken and our women will continue to feel inadequate.

The triumph of the feminine over the masculine means a few straightforward things. First, unlike a man's body, a woman's body is more discreet. Her genitalia are hidden, whereas a man naturally struts his stuff. And this is not an insignificant point: The male and female anatomies speak volumes about the male and female character. Women are naturally more modest than men. The feminine whispers while the masculine hollers. The feminine is open while the masculine is closed. When a woman loves a man, she opens herself to receive him. She is trusting, even with the most intimate parts of her body and her heart. But even after men fall in love with their wives, they often close their hearts and refuse to share their emotions. The triumph of the feminine therefore means that qualities that are more subtle and less pronounced should be more valued than those that aggressively stick out. One of the great insights of Judaism, as the world's first monotheistic religion, is this: It's the invisible things in life, those things that cannot be seen, that are truly valuable. G-d cannot be seen. Neither can love. But it is those things that are the

The male and female anatomies speak volumes about the male and female character.

When a woman loves a man, she opens herself to receive him. She is trusting, even with the most intimate parts of her body and her heart. But even after men fall in love with their wives, they often close their hearts and refuse to share their emotions.

It's the invisible things in life, those things that cannot be seen, that are truly valuable.

most sacred of all. Men have to learn to stop seeking those things that can be grabbed, touched, and possessed. They have to live for love, commitment, and virtue.

We have to aspire to be the man who gives charity when no one's looking rather than the Donald Trump–like figure who brags not about the money he gives but the money he has. It's the man who devotes his spare time to coaching Little League and spending time with his children who deserves our respect rather than the politicians who do everything they can to remain in the news.

RISE OF THE CIRCLE MAN

—

Remember how men are lines and women are circles? Men have a linear approach to life, goal-oriented and constantly weighing their value by things like size. The line is the scepter of rule that seeks dominion and domination, and men enjoy competing against one another and being victorious. Women have a cyclical approach to life, they are more means-oriented, more naturally focused on circles of intimacy like family and relationships, less competitive and more naturally communal.

Lines are easily broken. Their harsh rigidity is the reason they break in the first place. They lack flexibility. Their natural inelasticity—their stubbornness and obtuseness—guarantees their destruction.

But lines are easily broken. Their harsh rigidity is the reason they break in the first place. They lack flexibility. Their natural inelasticity—their stubbornness and obtuseness—guarantees their destruction. Isn't this what breaks so many American men? They don't share their emotions. They refuse to acknowledge or talk about pain. Pretty soon, they are pouring their hearts out to the bottle.

But while lines are easily broken, circles seldom are. The circle has flexibility that the line lacks. When the line is pressured at one point, it breaks in two. But when the circle is pressured, every point along the circle helps to absorb the impact. Also, lines run parallel to each other. When they intersect, they do so at only a single point, which is indicative of how little interaction there is among men. If they do interact, they do so only on predictable subjects like money, politics, sports, women, cars, and BlackBerrys. But circles interconnect. They fasten hard onto one another. Women do talk about their problems. They are unashamed to lean on each other.

When a man marries a woman, he is meant to learn from her communicativeness and emotional openness. The reason the Bible says, "A man who has found a woman has found goodness," is that a woman teaches a man how to be human. She converts him from a human doing, what he is at the office, to a human being, what he becomes at home. In essence, she brings out his latent feminine qualities. This

> The reason the Bible says, "A man who has found a woman has found goodness," is that a woman teaches a man how to be human. She converts him from a human doing, what he is at the office, to a human being, what he becomes at home.

gives birth to what I call "circle man," the man who is fully masculine but who has also cultivated his more feminine traits without regret or shame. He is not embarrassed to be seen changing diapers. He is not ashamed to be found in a department store choosing clothing—including intimate apparel—with his wife. When he feels beaten up at the office, he comes home and opens up to his wife. If he feels like a failure, he is not ashamed to admit to such feelings of low self-esteem to the wife who enjoys comforting him and propping him up.

Circle man does the right thing because it is right. He is not always goal-oriented, trying to advance himself or make an impression on his peers. He does not concern himself with always being noticed. He is not a braggart and less so is he a show-off. He is not so insecure as to be a shallow attention-seeker. He lives like Moses, who ascends a mountain at the end of his life, after having led the people faithfully for forty years, to his final resting place. The Bible relates,

> *The Lord said to him, "This is the land of which I swore to Abraham, to Isaac, and to Jacob, saying, 'I will give it to your descendants'; I have let you see it with your eyes, but you shall not cross over there." Then Moses, the servant of the Lord, died there in the land of Moab . . . but no one knows his burial place to this day. (Deut. 34:4–6)*

Incredible. The great prophet accepts that he will never enter the promised land, because he never led the people for promise of material or even spiritual reward. Rather, he led the people out of his love for them. At his death, there were no people to mourn him and none to eulogize him. There was no funeral, and no twenty-one-gun salute. He had done his duty, he had lived his calling, he had done the right thing simply because it was right, and then, like silent footsteps in the night, he was gone. His work was never about him, it was never about his status, it was never about his ultimate reward.

Likewise, Abraham Lincoln was a circle man. He loved playing with children and would often interrupt cabinet meetings during the Civil War to accommodate the precociousness of his youngest sons, Tad and Willie. He did not live by a false sense of honor. Even as president, Lincoln never hid away his children, even when their behavior was at its worst. He was a father first. In her book *Lincoln's Sons,* Ruth Painter Randall relates a story told by a young woman who lived across the street from the Lincolns:

> *One evening Mr. and Mrs. Lincoln were to attend a reception at the home of Mr. Dubois, the State Auditor, a couple of blocks down on Eighth Street. My mother was helping Mrs. Lincoln dress for the party. Willie and Tad came home from a candy-pull. They were smeared with molasses candy from head to foot. When they heard of the party they*

wanted to go, too. Robert, who at that time was planning to enter Harvard, was to stay at home with the little boys. Mrs. Lincoln said firmly that they could not go, whereupon the two boys set up a cry. Their mother was steadfast, and the boys were determined. They were kicking and screaming when Mr. Lincoln entered.

"This will never do," he said. "Mary, if you will let the boys go, I will take care of them."

"Why, Father, you know that is no place for boys to be. When people give a party like that it is no place for children." By this time the boys began to listen.

"But," said Mr. Lincoln, "I will take them around the back way, and they can stay in the kitchen." He then talked to the boys about being good and making no promises that were not to be kept, and it was arranged that the boys should go if Robert and my mother should get them dressed. They were cleaned up, and in the haste Tad found his short trousers on hind side before. At this he set up another storm, because he "couldn't walk good," which his father quieted by a wave of his hand and saying, "Remember, now, remember." When the little boys were ready, they went ahead with their father, not to the kitchen but to the full reception. With Robert Mrs. Lincoln followed in a beautiful canary-colored satin dress, low neck and short sleeves, and large hoop-skirts, after the manner of the time.

This is circle man in all his glory, a man for whom family always came first, even in affairs of state. A man who reveled in being a father even when his children's behavior would have made other men bristle. Lincoln was gunned down by an assassin just days before the end of the Civil War. He too did not enter the promised land. He had given every ounce of himself in the struggle to preserve the Union and abolish slavery. And then he was gone.

Martin Luther King Jr. was similar, preaching on April 3, 1968, the night before he died, about how his people—black Americans—would make it to the promised land, even as he himself would never enter it with them.

LEARNING TO HONOR WOMEN
—

The circle man is likewise distinguished by honoring women. He does not use women, he does not merely bed women, and he does not degrade women. Rather, he respects them as his intellectual and emotional equals in every regard. The triumph of the feminine over the masculine means that we have to instill within men a desire not to conquer but to love women. We have to inculcate within men a desire to respect rather than have dominion over women. It seems that any guy who is successful in America wants to translate that success into bedding as many women as possible and refraining from committing to one. Okay, so George Clooney is the sexiest man alive. Good for him. But he can't commit to a single woman? He can't get married even at forty-six years old? Is he too busy playing the field? Where is his feminine side? Where is the domesticity? Where is the obsession with one woman? And where is his fatherhood? And since he can't find commitment and devotion to a woman as something redeeming, he should be seen for what he is: a fine actor, but not yet a role model. Without the ability to love and cherish a woman, a man's life is somewhat broken.

And lest you say that I'm taking it too far and implying that if you're not married you're messed up, that is in no way my point. What I am saying is that if you're so full of yourself that not a single woman is good enough for you, then you are pretty darn insecure. Your insecurity is the source of your arrogance. You can't love anyone because you don't love yourself. You can't be devoted to anyone because the only cause that lights your fire is yourself.

Finally, the triumph of the feminine over the masculine means being a facilitator. Notice that women are more naturally selfless than men. Just look at how many deadbeat dads there are compared to deadbeat moms. I barely know any moms who have abandoned their kids. But I know way too many dads who have done so. Women have no real problem devoting their lives to others. Indeed, in many cases, it defines them. They don't mind facilitating the success of others. And the man who has developed a more feminine side can also put time into mentoring, advising, and guiding others. Part of being broken is being so focused on yourself and what you have or have not achieved that you become a burden to yourself.

Part of being broken is being so focused on yourself and what you have or have not achieved that you become a burden to yourself. You begin weighing yourself down with the load of your own ego.

You begin weighing yourself down with the load of your own ego. And one of the main solutions to this is to devote your life partially to others. When it's no longer only about you, then you're not wondering day and night whether you're a winner or a loser.

Making women feel complete rather than inadequate will also depend on major changes in our culture. It will involve men learning to see women, and women learning to see themselves, as more book and less cover. The substance of a woman will have to be appreciated. Women can no longer be judged by their youth and beauty. Far more important factors will have to be considered, such as wisdom, kindness, sincerity, intelligence, and selflessness. In the book of Proverbs, in its final chapter, here is how King Solomon describes "a woman of valor":

> Her husband has full confidence in her
> and lacks nothing of value.
> She brings him good, not harm,
> all the days of her life.
> She selects wool and flax
> and works with eager hands.
> She is like the merchant ships,
> bringing her food from afar.

She gets up while it is still dark;
she provides food for her family
and portions for her servant girls.
She considers a field and buys it;
out of her earnings she plants a vineyard.
She sets about her work vigorously;
her arms are strong for her tasks.
She sees that her trading is profitable,
and her lamp does not go out at night.
In her hand she holds the distaff
and grasps the spindle with her fingers.
She opens her arms to the poor
and extends her hands to the needy.
When it snows, she has no fear for her household;
for all of them are clothed in scarlet.
She makes coverings for her bed;
she is clothed in fine linen and purple.
Her husband is respected at the city gate,
where he takes his seat among the elders of the land.
She makes linen garments and sells them,
and supplies the merchants with sashes.
She is clothed with strength and dignity;
she can laugh at the days to come.
She speaks with wisdom,
and faithful instruction is on her tongue.
She watches over the affairs of her household
and does not eat the bread of idleness.
Her children arise and call her blessed;
her husband also, and he praises her:
"Many women do noble things,
but you surpass them all."
Charm is deceptive, and beauty is fleeting;
but a woman who fears the Lord is to be praised.

Give her the reward she has earned,
and let her works bring her praise at the city gate.

This is an amazing passage because we so often think that the Bible is filled with misogyny toward women and simply wants them locked up in the kitchen, producing dinner and babies. But here is an ancient biblical vision of a professional businesswoman. She does not feel inadequate because her husband is whole and satisfied with himself. She is an entrepreneur, filled with ingenuity and drive. She is kind and compassionate. But she is no fool. She is an expert merchant. She is clothed modestly and with dignity. Her body is not a billboard with which she advertises erotic opportunities. And she is beautiful in the most holistic sense of the word, both inside and outside. It is not her long legs but her big heart that stands out. Not a big bust but a big brain.

Her body is not a billboard with which she advertises erotic opportunities.

Let's make this biblical vision of a woman of valor a reality and the standard by which women are judged. When men learn to cherish this kind of woman, our women will finally feel adequate. And their light will illuminate the darkness of the broken American male, making him feel whole and healed.

31.

Inspiring Our Children

ONCE WE fix the broken American male and remove the sense of inadequacy from modern women, we will finally be able to inspire our children.

Our children don't listen to what we say so much as copy what we do. Their disinterest in the family reflects our own. We wonder why our teenagers walk around today like zombies. But if we looked into a mirror we would see why. Husbands come home from work looking careworn and broken. They just want to sink down into a couch and watch TV. Small wonder that our kids have nothing to say to us. We have nothing to say to them either.

But if we were to repair the broken American male, he'd come home with a bounce in his step. No longer would he expend every last ounce of energy in the office. No longer would he come home at ridiculous hours. No longer would his family feel that they were the very least of his priorities. He would come home early so that he could play and do activities with his kids. And his kids would be more alive because there would be so much more invested in them.

Repairing our men would also mean that they would be more patient with their children. Broken men have little reserves of patience.

They are hard on themselves and, by extension, on all those around them as well. They allow themselves to get provoked over the smallest trifles. Soon their constant browbeating of their kids snuffs some of the light out of the children and they become sullen and withdrawn.

If there is one thing I positively hate about myself as a parent it is this lack of patience. I wish I never allowed myself to get upset, even if my children have done something for which they deserve a reprimand. By all means, rebuke bad behavior. But there is no excuse for losing your patience. But then, broken men like me find pressure very difficult to deal with. The pressure breaks us even further and we allow ourselves to take out our frustration on those who are closest to us. There is no excuse for this, and we know it. We have to heal ourselves so that we never inflict pain on those we love the most.

> **By all means, rebuke bad behavior. But there is no excuse for losing your patience.**

I've said that a father is the sun and the mother is the moon. It follows, as in the famous dream that Joseph has in the Bible about his brothers, that the kids are the stars, stars that burn brightly when they are immersed in a passionate environment.

There is no greater priority today than inspiring our children, lifting them up, and making them feel alive. If kids are to feel alive, then the home has to be alive. It cannot come back to life if its head is the walking dead.

> **If kids are to feel alive, then the home has to be alive. It cannot come back to life if its head is the walking dead.**

An acquaintance of mine, Jack, was having major problems in his five-year-old marriage. What made the fighting even more tragic was that it was alienating Jack's only child, an eight-year-old girl named Rebecca. It got so bad that Jack sent me an e-mail with the subject line "I CAN'T TAKE IT ANYMORE!!!!" He and his wife came to see me and I noticed right away that his was a classic case of a broken American male. Jack worked as a programmer for computer games and did well. But then his firm laid him off. His self-esteem plummeted. He fought constantly with his wife. He numbed himself with five hours of nightly TV. I told him that self-esteem has to be independent of what's happening in our lives. It has to swell from deep within us and be immune to the vicissitudes of career. We are not what we do. There is a human essence that underlies all that we do. And that can never be eroded.

He responded with the following e-mail, with "Easy for you to say, MAANNN!!!" as the subject line:

I was able to repeat what you said about husbands with low self-esteem because it hit me very hard when I heard it the first two times. BUT— and I mean this as an intellectual argument, not personally—that's easy for you to say as you are a very accomplished person. You sold over a million books, have your own TV show, etc. Men have ambition programmed into them, I think, and yes, success and disappointments do play into one's self-esteem in a big way.

I responded with the following:

Firstly, my TV show can be canceled at any minute and I am entirely in the hands of a fickle public. Second, my books. Some sell, and some sink. So to say I'm accomplished is a misnomer. The man who thinks he is accomplished one day blinks his eyes and he has become a has-been the next.

As for your point that men have ambition programmed into them, I absolutely agree. We all want to be a somebody and everybody hates being a nobody. But, it all comes down to what constitutes success. If you continued to be supersuccessful, but your wife hates your guts, are you a success? If your daughter doesn't want to talk to you, are you a success? Are you really a somebody when the people who mean the most to you think the least of you? That's why success has to first and foremost be measured by our personal relationships and commitments and that's where we have to strive to be successful before anything else.

How successful are we if we raise messed-up kids? Does money really have meaning once our kids are lost to us?

A wealthy family came to me for counseling about their fifteen-year-old son who had already become a pothead. The father, who owned his own industrial electronics firm, traveled constantly. Every week he was in South America or the Middle East. He had become wealthy and was even able to afford his own plane. Meanwhile, his kid's life went down the toilet. His father gave him objects rather than love. I counseled the teenager. He had huge anger against his father. He thought him cold and cruel. I tried to help the teenager and I did succeed in calming a lot of his anger. I spoke to the father about radically changing his life and traveling no more than ten days a month at an absolute maximum. He told me that was impossible and that his son's problem was drugs, not a lack of love. I asked the father why a teenager would be in so much pain that he would have to numb his emotions with drugs. I was not equipped to help the boy when his addiction spiraled into hard drugs, and I lost touch with the family. I heard from them suddenly a few months later by e-mail. They wrote telling me that their son had deteriorated to such a degree that they were sending him to a residential community in Nevada to save his life. It was so strict that he was not to have contact with his family in the slightest degree. And still his father continued to travel.

Amazing. Your son's life is going down the drain. Still, you continue to jet around the world on the plane that is so impressive to your friends. You're a big man. Everyone envies you. You wear expensive suits. You smoke big cigars. You're the man—to everyone except your own child, to whom you're a big loser. But why should that matter? Forget him. Everyone else thinks you're amazing. But you can't forget him. You wish his opinion of you didn't sting. But it does. You wish it didn't hurt, but you can't mask the pain because he's your flesh and blood and deep down you love him more than anything else in the world. It stings because you know he's right. You know that he alone has seen the emperor in an authentic light, and the emperor has no clothes. You can't get away from the simple fact that he knows you better than all your fans do. He lives with you. He knows that for all the hoopla, underneath the PR you're a small man with a small heart. Very insecure. Devoting your life to impressing complete strangers while your family falls apart.

Yes, we have to inspire our kids, and that will happen once men start loving themselves again and find a new definition of success.

I started this book by relating a story of how a friend of mine built an Internet start-up that was valued at six hundred million dollars. I was honest in relating the sense of failure I felt when I compared myself to him, not because I love money, because I have never been motivated by money. If anything, my personal vice is a lust for recognition even if it comes with no money. Rather, his success made my self-esteem plummet because it said to me that someone with whom I was close had overtaken me on the ladder of life. He was a success, and compared to such gargantuan success I was a failure.

The humiliation I felt in feeling envy toward a friend and down on myself for no good reason led to a lot of self-reflection. I tried to understand myself. Then one day, as I looked at the eight children with which G-d has blessed me, and especially at our baby, who at the time was just one year old, I asked myself if I would exchange any of them for six hundred million dollars. If I had been given a choice between one of my babies or hundreds of millions of dollars, what would I choose? The same question could be asked about great fame and renown. Would I choose it over being a father? The answer, of course, was a categorical no. In fact, the very question was absurd. My children are my life. I love them with every particle of my being. When they are not around me I grow sad. When they are not happy I am devastated. They are my soul and my spirit, my happiness and my joy.

And as I thought about my family, it suddenly struck me that if I would never trade fatherhood for any sum on earth, then it was logically stupid and ridiculous to be jealous of anyone's material success even if it was far greater than my own. Since I would not trade my loved ones for all the treasure in the world, it followed logically that they were a far greater treasure.

I know it sounds trite, but it's true. Our children are our greatest treasures. They are of priceless value and grant us a richness that is beyond any diamond, nobler than any crown, and more precious than one thousand Microsofts and Googles combined.

It is time we started seeing them at their true value.

Part of this process involves being so close to our children that they do not have to find a significant other—a boyfriend or girlfriend—so early in life that it pulls them away from the family. I have witnessed many parents losing their teenage kids, especially their daughters, to a boyfriend or girlfriend with whom the child spends nearly every waking moment. I disagree profoundly with those who see no harm in teen sexuality. Indeed, research suggests that there is even a direct link between teen sexuality and teen depression. A study by the Heritage Foundation, "Sexually Active Teenagers Are More Likely to Be Depressed and to Attempt Suicide" (www.heritage.org, posted on June 3, 2003), based on the government-funded National Longitudinal Survey of Adolescent Health, found that about 25 percent of sexually active girls say they are depressed all, most, or a lot of the time, while only 8 percent of girls who are not sexually active feel the same. While 14 percent of girls who have had intercourse have attempted suicide, only 5 percent of sexually inactive girls have. And whereas 6 percent of sexually active boys have tried suicide, less than 1 percent of sexually inactive boys have. The report challenges the previously held notion that teens become sexually active in order to self-medicate their own depression. "Findings from the study show depression came after substance abuse and sexual activity, not the other way around," said researcher Denise Dion Hallfors of the Pacific

> **Our children are our greatest treasures. They are of priceless value and grant us a richness that is beyond any diamond, nobler than any crown, and more precious than one thousand Microsofts and Googles combined.**

Institute for Research and Evaluation. The study, published in the *American Journal of Preventive Medicine,* analyzed data from a national survey of more than 13,000 teenagers in grades seven to eleven.

It's pretty tragic that it takes children slashing their wrists or sinking into morbidly dark depression to awaken parents to the dangers of children engaging in activities that should be reserved exclusively for adults, and married ones at that.

Sex is the most powerful impulse known to man. It is as overpowering as it is pleasurable. Do you really think that those in a rickety boat should be exposed to this storm? How could we ever have believed that allowing big children to detonate such powerful emotions, in empty relationships where neither party is sufficiently developed to assimilate such strong emotions, would do anything but eviscerate their emotional landscape? Heck, we don't even let teenagers play with fireworks for fear of them blowing their own heads off. But we've given them the emotional equivalent of a nuclear blast. And this in turn results from broken parents—but fathers especially—who shirk their responsibility to inspire and protect their children.

> Sex is the most powerful impulse known to man. It is as overpowering as it is pleasurable. Do you really think that those in a rickety boat should be exposed to this storm?

Many parents mistakenly believe that the first job of a parent is to love their child, when really the primary responsibility of a parent is to protect their child from harm. You can't love that which no longer exists. An object of love that is destroyed will forever remain unloved.

Before loving your child, before teaching your child, even before feeding your child, your first objective is to protect your child. Your role as guardian comes before any other. A parent who allows harm to come to their child is a parent who has been delinquent in the very fundamentals of child-rearing.

Most parents believe that protection involves guarding children from physical harm. You lock the door at night so that your kids won't be injured by robbers. You drop them off at school so that they won't be abducted by kidnappers. You teach them how to cross the street safely so that they won't be hit by cars.

But protecting your children from external dangers is miniscule compared to the task of safeguarding them from influences that will corrupt them from the inside, and it is much easier to recover from physical scars than from their emotional equivalents.

Look around and you'll see parents who take little kids to R-rated movies, who allow their kids to listen to and sing misogynistic and sexual lyrics, and who let their kids play video games where the most graphic violence is the main selling point. I know otherwise responsible parents who smoke marijuana with their teenage kids, and I know parents who have no problem with their kids watching MTV and VH1 music video junk for hours a day. Indeed, parents today seem to have little compunction about the tremendous amounts of garbage from the popular culture being pumped directly into their children's cerebral cortex. Will we pretend that daily loads of toxic smut will not permanently coarsen our children, robbing them of their innocence and making them grow up unnaturally? By treating our teenage children as young adults rather than big kids, we are allowing them to skip the childhood stage of life, which is essential to building a strong foundation for their later years.

Healthy parenting involves the dual role of nurturer, on the one hand, and protector, on the other. A child is like a plant that requires water and nutrients but also protection from weeds and pests. The unconditional love we give our children instills in them a sense of security and internalizes a feeling of value. If they are shortchanged of love, they will later grow to believe that things like money are currencies by which they may purchase an otherwise lacking self-esteem.

But unconditional love is just one side of the coin. All the watering in the world won't shelter a vulnerable plant that has been uprooted by a fierce wind. We have to shield our children from the increasingly malign influences of a culture that is telling them, subtly but constantly, to skip the essential stages of childhood and become adults while they are really still kids. Exposure to gratuitous violence, sex, and other uniquely adult subjects overwhelms children with emotions and experiences they cannot digest, sowing confusion and anxiety. It also imparts to them an inauthentic desire to prematurely discard the wonders of their youth and join an adult world where they trade awe for cynicism and conviction for compromises.

Our kids may not look like it, but they're crying out for protectors. It may seem that they just want to be left alone, that they crave unrestricted freedom and unbridled indulgence. But deep inside they want to be protected. They want someone to stop them from harming themselves. They want someone who says no. And if not you, the parent, then who?

32.

Reaching Out to Our Broken Men

Every day I receive e-mails from people about their personal problems. They write of their broken marriages, children who won't speak to them, and parents who have never shown them affection. The tone of anguish in these communications is excruciating and unmistakable. You can feel the pain pouring through the words. They write to me to figure out how to make the situation right so that the pain will go away.

For many years I tried to respond to the majority of these e-mails. But when the volume greatly increased, especially after *Shalom in the Home* began airing, I stopped responding to all but a very few. But still they would come, in great number, and I would peruse them quickly and decide which two or three I would answer. I noticed something happening as I quickly glanced at these anguished pleas for help. I was no longer feeling the pain of the writers. The personal nature of the e-mails was being lost to me. Indeed, many began to feel like a nuisance, since they got in the way of the many responsibilities I carry.

Then one day I had a fight with my wife. My wife and I love each other very deeply and, thank G-d, rarely argue. Indeed, when we do argue it is easy to make peace quickly because my wife is so sweet and gentle that the argument is nearly always my fault. But this was a notable exception and we wounded each other intensely, neither party being prepared to retreat from cutting and hurtful words.

I walked away from the fight numb with pain. I did not feel bad. Rather, I did not feel at all. My heart was in so much pain that it went into shock from the trauma and lost its ability to feel any emotion. It had become stone.

It was the loneliest feeling of my life. Here I was, racked with grief, desperate for someone, anyone, to pity me, desperate for someone to know the depth of my wound. But since fighting with the principal comfort and love in my life, my wife, was the actual source of my pain, I had no one to turn to for comfort.

I am blessed with many acquaintances but not a lot of friends. To be sure, I agree with the proclamation of the Talmud that without friendship, death is better than life. But with eight kids, many religious responsibilities, and a career that is a demanding calling, something's got to give, and it is mostly friendship and socializing that I have been forced to cut out. This only magnified the depth of my despair, as I felt dreadfully alone with no one to talk to. Indeed, the only thing that comforted me was wallowing in wretched self-pity, a counterfeit and toxic substitute for genuine human warmth.

It was at that moment that my mind turned back to all the e-mails I receive. All those desperate people who in their pain had turned to me because they had nowhere else to turn. They could not bear any more hurt, and neither could I. I tried to picture their faces. Did they have the same stony look that my own countenance now bore, the look of surrender, betraying an individual no longer afraid of further pain because in his catatonic state he is anesthetized against any feeling?

I thought of these innocent people and how I had closed my heart to them. Each was G-d's child, but I had not found the time to take away even a granule of their pain. And yet the knowledge that they were out there, and that they, and they alone, understood the depth of my despair, was the only comfort I could find. Their existence was what sustained me. I vowed that when I came out of the all-enveloping gloom that consumed me, I would fight with my nature and try always to have an understanding and feeling heart and devote myself even more to those in crisis.

Even as I write these words, I cannot guarantee that I will fulfill my pledge. It is a poor excuse, I know, but I lack the discipline to necessarily carry it through. But of this I am certain: the memory of the pain I felt that day will never leave me and I will tap into its scar tissue to remind myself of my obligation to my suffering fellow man.

Every day of our lives we come across acquaintances, family members, and friends who are in unspeakable emotional pain from domestic strife. But it's a pain that often does not register with us, since it does not involve the death of a spouse or extreme bodily injury. We trivialize their suffering even as they lose their sanity because they have no shalom in their homes.

And this is especially true of men, so many of whom find it utterly distasteful to betray weakness or turn to others for help. We still live in a culture where it can be seen as unmanly to lean on others. Women and girls cry; men and boys don't cry. And yet thousands and thousands of men have approached me, asking for help. What came to me as I contemplated the people who wrote to me of their pain was the disproportionately large number of men, men who were in as much pain as I was and with just as few places to turn. Men don't talk about their pain, aren't supposed to acknowledge it. And we wonder why they are so broken?

After that argument with my wife, I thought of how there were many acquaintances I could talk to about career issues, but almost none with whom I would feel comfortable discussing an argument with my wife. How many other men were there who felt the same way? They were writing to me, a complete stranger, because anonymity was the principal appeal.

Women in pain naturally elicit people's sympathy. People rush to assist a damsel in distress. But there is no such thing as a knight in distress. Knights wear shining armor with no chinks.

> **Women in pain naturally elicit people's sympathy. People rush to assist a damsel in distress. But there is no such thing as a knight in distress. Knights wear shining armor with no chinks.**

Not wanting to be a nuisance to us, the broken American male waits for us to inquire about his dejected state. We indulge him with a light sprinkling of interest by asking a perfunctory question or two, because we do care, just not enough to truly invest ourselves in helping him. And yet alleviating his pain would be as simple as lending a sympathetic ear and an empathetic heart. The most passive effort, like simply nodding in acquiescence as he shares his trauma, would often be enough to validate his pain and offer a horizon of hope. He is not necessarily looking for answers. In many cases, the broken American men who surround us already know what they must do to make the situation better. They know they have to feel better about themselves and find a more wholesome definition of success. They know they have to stop judging themselves in comparison with others. And they know they have to reconnect with their families in order to find inspiration and comfort. Rather, they are simply looking to jump-start their heart, and for that they need to know that the world is not all pain. That there are people who care and strangers who see the depth of their anguish.

When I lived in Israel as a yeshiva student, I loved and was close to an uncle named David. He nurtured me like a father and loved me like a son. After my two years of study there were over, he lit up like a fireworks display whenever I came to Israel to visit. But then a financial problem began to affect his life, and he turned to me for support on my regular visits. After a while the exposure to a problem I felt I could not help with became a terrible burden.

Whenever he brought up the issue I changed the subject. I came to Israel for inspiration, not depression. So I pretended not to see his distress and I let him down. He was a beautiful human being with a golden heart. But he was broken, and I pretended not to see the cracks.

A few years later, my beloved uncle passed away. He died without my comfort. When our son was born last year, I named him David in my uncle's loving memory. But it was second-tier compensation for one of the monumental omissions of my life. And all I had to do was listen.

> In this current state of human development it remains unclear whether we will correct one of life's greatest tragedies, namely, the inability to appreciate a blessing until it is lost.

In this current state of human development it remains unclear whether we will correct one of life's greatest tragedies, namely, the inability to appreciate a blessing until it is lost. Part of that tragedy is the inability to reach out to a broken man until he is so lost that he cannot be recovered.

A new era has dawned upon us in which we have no choice but to reach out to our broken men. They are our husbands and fathers. They are our brothers, uncles, and friends. And we must rescue them from an irreversible downward spiral.

But all too many men feel that because they're men they'll never get any sympathy. And the truth is that if a man fights with his wife, nine times out of ten people will take his wife's side. He can't win because the man is always wrong. There are a growing number of organizations that represent fathers in custody battles and claim that men have no chance before a judge. The judge, feeling that his job is to protect the weaker party, nearly always sides with the woman. And the same is true with the man's kids. When children see their parents fighting their natural sympathy goes to their mom, whom they perceive as the more emotional and the more easily hurt. I can write of this confidently because I have been guilty of it on countless occasions as well. It started when I was a little boy. I loved my father but sympathized with my mother. I didn't believe that my father could hurt, he seemed so tough and rugged. And whereas my mother cried regularly, my father never cried. It wasn't until years later that I came to know just how much pain he was in from the breakup of his marriage and the loss of his wife and children. And it didn't matter who was at fault. I was focused on the wrong thing. What mattered was that my father was in excruciating pain, made all the worse by the fact that he could not show it without, in his mind, compromising his masculinity.

Later in life I made the further mistake of gravitating to the wife's side when couples came to me for counseling. To be sure, very often the husband really was at fault. After all, I have just written an entire book explaining how the brokenness of today's men is depressing their wives and ruining their families. But it didn't matter if the husband was the guilty party. He may have been responsible for much of the marital dysfunction. But this did not mean that he wasn't in pain. I now know that if we are to heal men, we have to give them a fair and sympathetic hearing. They need to feel that being a man is not something that is going to be used against them. They need to know we understand that they can be fragile and they can be broken. And there is no shame in that. We are with them in their pain.

When my wife and I argued, I always assumed that I was wrong because she is a much better person than I am in every respect. But as our married life together progressed, I saw that sometimes my wife also made errors. Yes, she is a much kinder and nobler person than I am, but to err is human, and she isn't perfect. And by assuming her natural perfection, I was not aggrandizing her but belittling myself, convinced as I was that I couldn't do anything right. I am now more fair to myself and no longer hate myself for being a man. I understand that being male requires a certain redemption, like the love and guidance of a good woman. But that doesn't mean that I don't have my own intrinsic goodness. I believe that as a result of this conclusion I have much more to offer my wife as well.

REACHING OUT TO OUR BROKEN MEN

Let us go forth as one human family to comfort and support one another through the painful times. Let us open our hearts to today's men and not immediately assume that because they are tall and strong, they don't need our outstretched hand. It is not only bereaved parents who suffer. It is also your buddy who seems so confident holding that beer. If you have a friend who is recently divorced, go and comfort them. If you know a woman whose marriage ended and who is raising her kids alone, give her support and reassurance. And if you know a man who senselessly argues with his wife or she with him, endeavor to make peace between them. You will make the world a brighter place and G-d will smile upon you.

33.

The Wholesome American Male:
A Day in the Life

WHEN I was a boy I loved watching *The Six Million Dollar Man,* starring Lee Majors as bionic astronaut, Steve Austin. The show started every week with the terrible crash that tore Austin's body apart. The voice-over would say, "Steve Austin. A man barely alive. We can rebuild him. We have the technology."

We are capable of rebuilding the American male, healing him, and making him whole. We have the knowledge. We have the technology. The agents that are most necessary are:

1. A new definition of success, which will come from society

2. The support and comfort of a good woman, which will come from his wife

3. A new, more loving education for American boys, which will come from their parents

4. The transformation from having a career to finding a calling, which will come from a deeper spiritual bent

5. The recognition that the American father's sacrifice is heroic, which will come from his children

6. An inward focus on one's gifts rather than an outward focus on another's success, which will come from reflection and contemplation

7. An assessment of oneself as a child of G-d rather than the product of one's professional exertions, which will come with a religious awakening

8. Seeing other men as compatriots rather than as competitors and finding an honest sense of joy in another's success, which will come from a strong inner foundation and identity

9. An ability to open up and share pain and discuss emotions, which will come from cultivating the feminine within the masculine

10. And making the American home into a warm place of welcome for every American dad returning nightly from the daily grind of work, which will come from a reconstituted and healthy American family

All these ingredients are absolutely vital in healing the American male. But they will not cohere until the American male finally resolves to heal himself. To cure himself of his irrationally low self-esteem. To repair his unreasonable feelings of failure. To rid himself of the false belief that he has nothing to contribute and that no one is interested in who he is but rather in what he has and what he does. To restore his belief in the fact that he is a human being rather than a human doing.

So here is a vision of the wholesome American male, who will rise like a Phoenix from the ashes of his own brokenness.

The wholesome American male wakes up in the morning and helps get his kids ready for school. He knows his kids are tired and groggy. He walks into their room with a smile. He tells them it's time to go to school. Even when they have trouble getting out of bed, he doesn't get frustrated, because he knows his job is to be the light. He works on always increasing his store of patience, especially when it comes to his children. They're tired. He's tired. But he is the one responsible for injecting vitality into the home. He has breakfast with his kids and wishes them a great day.

He kisses his wife as he leaves for work and tells her he's going to miss her. She'll be on his mind throughout the day. She is his joy and happiness.

At work he is not motivated by malice or jealousy. He is courteous to everyone in the office. He sees his coworkers as colleagues rather than competitors, and he is a team player. He is not threatened by other people's success and struggles with himself to be happy when others progress. He judges himself not in relation to others' achievements but by the maximization of his own gifts. He treats his job as a calling rather than a career. He works hard to control his moods. He purges his heart of rancor. He doesn't allow insidious emotions to build within. If he has a problem with someone in the office, he speaks to them gently but honestly and seeks to be reconciled with them. He doesn't hold in his disappointment, but neither does he allow it to explode on the outside. Rather, he speaks forthrightly but respectfully to those with whom he has disagreements. He always talks through problems and never allows negative emotions to fester inside. He wants to feel comfortable around anyone he meets. If he has hurt someone, he musters the courage to ask forgiveness—every time. When he apologizes he never uses the word *but*. He apologizes fully and unconditionally and takes responsibility for his actions.

> He is not a suck-up in the office. Brownnosing is outside his nature. He states his opinion with humility but with conviction.

He is not a suck-up in the office. Brownnosing is outside his nature. He states his opinion with humility but with conviction. As long as he is doing the right thing, he is not concerned with what people think of him. His only concern is not to veer from the righteous path he has set for himself. He focuses on being a good person rather than a popular person.

He doesn't brag, and he doesn't drop names. That's beneath him. He knows that such weakness is inconsistent with his potential for greatness.

He does not spend time gossiping. He is not so empty that he requires other people to fill him up. Nor is he so depressed that he requires other people's travails to make him happy. He certainly doesn't talk about other people's money or how much people are worth. He doesn't brag, and he doesn't drop names. That's beneath him. He knows that such weakness is inconsistent with his potential for greatness.

He views what he does through the day in a heroic light. It might be that he does something as simple as working in a hardware store. He is a hero nonetheless. He does not view his profession as lowly or unexciting. Rather, he assesses his value by the impact he makes on other people's lives and his usefulness to the community rather than by comparison with those on the *Forbes* 400. He helps people with courteousness and professionalism. He views his job as being no less consequential than that of the president of the United States. The president fills one important role, and he fills another. He judges himself by his work ethic and professional purpose rather than by the social circle in which he is invited to participate. He is proud of what he does and he does it well. He is proud of who he is because he is not focused on who he isn't.

At work, he has a professional relationship with women. He does not flirt with them but respects them. He is always conscious that he is a married man and that his wife is with him mentally even when she's not with him physically. There is nothing of him that can be shared with another woman because it is all taken up by his marriage.

Indeed, he calls his wife several times during the day just to tell her he's thinking of her. He purposely avoids tacking on some functional request like picking up the laundry because then his wife would think that he's only calling because he needs her, when really he is calling because he loves her. He understands that his marital commitment comes before everything else and that his first priority is

He purposely avoids tacking on some functional request like picking up the laundry because then his wife would think that he's only calling because he needs her, when really he is calling because he loves her.

his wife. By calling from the office to tell her that he loves her, he lets her understand that he's at work not for himself but for her sake and the children's.

He tries to mentor younger people in the office and doesn't mind if he isn't always given credit for his ideas. He has as healthy an ego as everyone else, but understands that he is also part of a team and that means leaving plenty of room for others to shine as well.

He is completely absorbed in what he is doing and doesn't get distracted. When he undertakes something, he immerses himself in it completely and fully. Distraction is for people who get bored, and boredom is for people who feel empty. He is not empty, since he views his life as being suffused with purpose. He is not

He does not send his body home, leaving his mind at the office.

out to succeed so much as to contribute. He is therefore engrossed in whatever he is doing. When he works, he works. But when it's time to come home, he comes home. He does not send his body home, leaving his mind at the office. All of him comes home to the family and he leaves the office at a decent hour, rarely later than 6 P.M.

When he comes home, he is both mentally and physically present. He walks in with a smile and jokes with and teases his wife and kids. He is careful always to be affectionate and respectful to his wife, especially in front of his children. He sits down to dinner with his family and asks everyone about their day. He comes well prepared with a story—something humorous or entertaining—to share with the family and provoke an interesting discussion. He makes his kids feel that he is genuinely interested in their opinions and through that they acquire value. When they speak, he listens. He is curious about their experiences and school. The most trivial story from his children engages his complete and total interest. When they speak to him, he stops eating and looks them right in the eye.

After dinner he sits with his kids to do homework. He may hate every moment of it. He hated it when he had to do it himself, and he may hate

There is greatness in doing something you hate for the sake of someone you love.

it now even more since he is out of practice. But he does it because he knows there is greatness in it. There is greatness in sitting with your children and inspiring them to love knowledge. There is greatness in doing something you hate for the sake of someone you love. His friends might be out having a drink or going to a game. They might be out filling themselves up with experiences that will ultimately leave them empty. But he is content to be at home. He is not jealous of their freedom. He knows that real freedom comes from unlocking one's potential and liberating all the love in one's heart. He isn't missing anything. He knows that every second he spends with his children, both he and they grow stronger.

When homework is done, if there's time he'll play with his kids. In my home, I read a chapter of the Bible with my kids, and discuss it,

There are few things more comforting to children than having a parent tuck them in at night and say their prayers with them before they retire.

nearly every night before bedtime. Then it's time to put the kids to sleep. He reads his kids a story in bed. He knows there are few things more comforting to children than having a parent tuck them in at night and say their prayers with them before they retire. He tries never to miss that pre-

cious opportunity to sit at his children's side at night, when they feel most vulnerable, left alone in the dark. He makes them feel secure. And he says his children's prayers with them and showers them with kisses and hugs. He tucks them in as a symbol of how they are secure in their father's love.

Then it's time for him to be a husband. He goes to his wife and they sit together, in the bedroom or living room. After 9 P.M., every night, he and his wife observe a function-free zone. They don't talk about anything that has to be done. That can wait until tomorrow. Discussions about the children's after-school activities can wait until the next day. For now, he and his wife forego being partners and become lovers. They are not husband and wife but man and woman.

He doesn't put on the TV. Indeed, he tries to keep TV watching down to a half hour or an hour a night. Instead, he talks to his wife. He makes her laugh. He shares with her humorous anecdotes about what happened to him that day. He shares with her also his pain and his self-doubt. He invites his wife into the innermost recesses of his heart. He speaks to her intimately, lovingly, and with total trust. He pushes himself to go beyond his comfort zone, conquers his fear, and is unafraid to lean on, and depend on, the woman who is his bone and flesh. In so doing, he makes her feel not just loved, but necessary. Not just a housewife, but an intimate soul mate.

> **He lusts after his wife and wants to drink in every aspect of her body—indeed, every aspect of her being.**

And when it's time to go to bed, he recognizes how important lovemaking is to his marriage and seeks to pleasure and bond physically with his wife. He is not an impatient or selfish lover. His purpose is not to use his wife's body as a means by which to gratify himself by having an orgasm and falling asleep. Rather, he lusts after his wife and wants to drink in every aspect of her body—indeed, every aspect of her being. He talks to her during sex, he expresses the depth of his desire for her, and arouses her with his lust. He tells her how much he loves her and how she is the source of his happiness. He makes sure that she has as much enjoyment from the experience as he does. And when he goes to sleep, he sleeps with his wife happy in his arms.

Conclusion

My Own Healing

THE GENESIS of this book was an article I wrote for my weekly
syndicated column in *The Jerusalem Post* just days before my
thirty-ninth birthday in November 2005. Its title was "The Broken
American Male." I wrote the article from the heart. I was entering
my fortieth year, midlife, and I was thinking deeply about the effect
of American culture upon me as a man. The article generated a deluge of comment that startled and overwhelmed me. Men and
women wrote from all over the world to tell me how much the ideas
expressed in that one-thousand-word article resonated with them.
Hundreds of men told me I had described their life to a T. They
wrote of how my words helped them to understand a process that
had been slowly killing them but that they were unable to properly
identify. Likewise, thousands more women wrote that they had always understood that there was something fractured in their husbands, but only now did they understand exactly what it was. More
important, they now understood its causes and how it might be
cured.

The insight captured in that article had nothing to do with any
claims at prophecy on my part and everything to do with intense

self-examination. I was able to write an article that so deeply touched my readership because, in essence, I was writing about myself.

It followed, therefore, that in deciding to dedicate a full-length work to the subject, I would have to delve deeply into my own state of brokenness. Would I emerge more whole at its conclusion? Did I heal? Or am I still broken? Because if I can't fix myself while writing a whole book on the subject, then surely there's no hope for the rest of you out there, right?

Please indulge me as I attempt to answer this important question with a story.

In the summer of 2007 I was on a camping trip with my family. We own an RV and love spending time by rivers and lakes. At the time I was completing the final draft of the manuscript for this book. I was reading sections of the book aloud to my wife and children to garner their feedback. I purposely chose the chapter about how we fathers have to raise our children differently, especially our sons. I turned to my eldest son, fourteen-year-old Mendy, and read to him my deep confession of the mistakes I had already made in his up-bringing. I read to him how I had sculpted and carved him into a person trained to do rather than to be. I further read to him how I vowed to change and be a father who nurtured him rather than *man-*handled him.

Mendy has an incredible sense of humor. He looked at me and said in a low voice, "So when does this all start?" We all laughed, but as with so many jokes, there was much truth embedded in what he said.

> I seek to judge my success and failure less in relation to other people and more in relation to my potential and my ability to contribute.

My son is correct. I have not yet completely implemented my own suggestions of being less harsh with our sons and teaching them how to be instead of just do. Less so have I healed myself fully of my own brokenness. *But I have started the process,* even as I still have a long way to go.

CONCLUSION

In writing this book I have made great strides toward healing. Now I seek to judge my success and failure less in relation to other people and more in relation to my potential and my ability to contribute. Moreover, I have learned to share much more with my wife, especially about my struggles with self-esteem and my fear of failure and insignificance.

The principal reward of writing this book lies not in having mended myself but in understanding the real degree of my brokenness.

But have I healed completely? Far from it. In fact, if I want to be honest with myself, the principal reward of writing this book lies not in having mended myself but in understanding the real degree of my brokenness.

Legend has it that when Socrates was told that the oracle at Delphi had identified him as the wisest man in the world, he replied while chuckling that if that were true it was only because he was the only man who knew just how much he didn't know. The Zohar (the principal work of kabbalah, Jewish mysticism) reflects a similar sentiment in its statement that the only ones who really know G-d are those who know just how much they can never know.

I take solace, therefore, in knowing that amid my continued state of brokenness I am one of those rare enlightened men who know just how distant from wholesomeness they really are.

Healing, like growing, is a lifelong pursuit. It has no culmination and no real end.

And to some extent, that itself is part of the healing.

But more important, healing, like growing, is a lifelong pursuit. It has no culmination and no real end. If it can be said that to lead a wholesome life is to find meaning and purpose in one's existence, then such meaning and purpose evolve with our own development. What might have seemed purposeful to us a few years ago may suddenly seem wholly inadequate as we progress through life's cycles. For example, when my children were younger I thought that the most important part of being a good father was being around my kids, playing with them and interacting. Now that both I and my children are older, I understand that simple interaction is not enough and I have to talk to my kids and get them to talk back. I need them to open up to me or our relationship will remain underdeveloped.

No American male can simply be healed. You will not wake up one day and suddenly feel immune to the pressures of status and the rat race. What you can and will do is engage permanently in the process of healing.

Healing involves constant struggle. It involves the daily wrestling with our nature to be more secure and more at peace. It demands a constant inner struggle to be a deeper and more inwardly focused human being rather than someone who is wholly influenced by his environment.

Aren't all things that are precious worth fighting for, and isn't the truest mark of our value as human beings the fact that we are prepared to wage a constant battle for our very soul?

How could it be otherwise? Aren't all things that are precious worth fighting for, and isn't the truest mark of our value as human beings the fact that we are prepared to wage a constant battle for our very soul?

Who would prefer that it be otherwise?

I make no apologies for not having healed myself fully and completely. Even if it were possible to be wholly relieved of life's pressures, I am not sure that I would choose the option. For in my daily struggle, in my daily exertion to try to be better and free myself of the lies with which we have been raised, I find meaning and purpose and take pride in the tiny little victories I have had, even as I awake to a fresh new battle every day.

If I didn't fight with my nature to focus less on professional success and more on my family, then that would mean that my wife and children were not worth fighting for.

It has taken some time, but I have come to realize that righteousness in life is not defined by perfection but by struggle. The truly special man is not he who has no inclination to ego and pride but he who, despite that inclination, wrestles with his nature to be selfless and humble.

Writing this book has not healed me, but it has given me a greater impetus to struggle toward being whole. These days when I sit down for dinner with my children and I feel broken by some professional setback that transpired that day, my kids still say to me, "Tatty, you're not listening to us. It's like you're not here." But whereas before it would take me ten minutes to come back, now it takes but a moment. I immediately tell myself that my children are healthy, my wife loves me, and I must remember that I am a winner, even if my heart doesn't immediately agree.

Likewise, when I read of some astronomical sum made by an investment banker in a single deal, or when I see that Dr. Phil's TV ratings are pummeling my own, I no longer seethe with jealousy at their accomplishments and wish they were my own. These days, a mild grudge is more like it. And even then, I force myself to say, "I am happy for them," and try to order my heart to follow along.

Most of all, I am beginning to accept that G-d has a plan for me. It may not be the plan that I originally envisaged. It may not land me in the Oval Office, and it may not earn me the moniker "*Time*'s Person of the Year." It may also not have me in a white tie and tails accepting a Nobel Peace Prize in Oslo. But whatever that plan is, it is uniquely tailored for me. There is no other plan like it. And while it may not seem as glamorous as a plan that will one day be made into a Hollywood epic, inspire an equestrian statue, or garner a twenty-one-gun salute, it is *my* plan. It reflects my uniqueness. And I wouldn't trade it for any other in the world.

> For it is not in our success that we find specialness, but rather in our specialness that we find success.

For it is not in our success that we find specialness, but rather in our specialness that we find success.

Acknowledgments

Elizabeth Beier, my editor, brought the best out of this work with her insightful and brilliant comments. Likewise, George Witte, the editor in chief at St. Martin's, and Sally Richardson, the publisher, both of whom are dear friends, supported me and this book throughout the publishing process. Sally is a woman not only of rare refinement but also of outstanding humility amid a most distinguished career. I am less broken due to my friendship with these unique people at St. Martin's.

My mother and father, while not together, independently offer me constant love and support. My mother is one of the most secure people I know and has found lifelong purpose in performing constant acts of kindness on behalf of others. My father has always been an example to me of the ability to achieve great things and make great professional and personal progress despite a fractured male nature. More than anything else he has taught me the value of struggle.

My brothers and sisters are my closest friends and most loving confidants. They have a broken baby brother, but love him nonetheless.

My children are the light of my life and my deepest happiness. In their love and acceptance I find healing. Their very existence is my highest inspiration, and looking upon them is like looking upon the face of the divine.

The Lubavitcher Rebbe, Rabbi Menachem Schneerson, remains the inspiration behind my books, my outlook on life, my devotion to Judaism, and my reletionship with G-d. It has been thirteen years since his passing, but he remains a living and blessed presence in my life.

My wife, Debbie, is my wise mentor and she who guards me from error. She has endeavored throughout her life to give me comfort and make me believe in myself. Her love is therapeutic and medicinal. Nearly every day I wish I were a more whole male for her sake. Her very presence in my life is itself the greatest comfort.

G-d Almighty has showered incessant blessings upon me from the time I was a child. Now I am a man, and by His light I hope to one day grow to be a *worthy* man, both in His eyes and in the eyes of His children.

—RABBI SHMULEY BOTEACH
Englewood, New Jersey
June 2007